ENGINEERS AND THE LAW
An Overview

ENGINEERS AND THE LAW
An Overview

Bruce Schoumacher
McDermott, Will & Emery
Chicago, Illinois

VNR VAN NOSTRAND REINHOLD COMPANY
———————————————————————————— New York

Copyright © 1986 by Van Nostrand Reinhold Company Inc.

Library of Congress Catalog Card Number: 85–26632
ISBN 0–442–28113–7

Manufactured in the United States of America

Published by Van Nostrand Reinhold Company Inc.
115 Fifth Avenue
New York, New York 10003

Van Nostrand Reinhold Company Limited
Molly Millars Lane
Wokingham, Berkshire RG11 2PY, England

Van Nostrand Reinhold
480 Latrobe Street
Melbourne, Victoria 3000, Australia

Macmillan of Canada
Division of Gage Publishing Limited
164 Commander Boulevard
Agincourt, Ontario MIS 3C7, Canada

15 14 13 12 11 10 9 8 7 6 5 4 3 2 1

Library of Congress Cataloging-in-Publication Data
  Schoumacher, Bruce.
  Engineers and the law.

  Bibliography: p.
  Includes index.
  1. Engineers—Legal status, laws, etc.—United
States. I. Title.
KF2928.S36 1986   344.73′01762   85–26632
ISBN 0–442–28113–7   347.3041762

Preface

In this book, I cover the legal principles related to the practice of engineering. This involves discussions of the law which applies to two separate groups of engineers. The first group consists of those engineers, including architects, who work in construction and who design buildings and other structures. The second group consists of those engineers who work for companies which manufacture and sell consumer and industrial products.

Most legal publications and books upon engineering law do not cover the law related to both groups. I believe this is the first book to do so.

This book also discusses certain legal topics with which an engineer may have to be familiar in order to practice.

The book consists of four parts. The first part presents a historical introduction and considers some basic principles of the law. The second part discusses the law of negligence which applies to engineers working in both construction and industry. The third part covers contract law. The fourth part deals with legal topics which may be of interest to either group of engineers.

This book is primarily a survey of specific legal topics and is not intended to be exhaustive. My aim is to provide an introduction to various areas of the law with which an engineer should be familiar. Because the law in certain areas may differ among the states, I have not pointed out all the differences among the legal rules adopted in each state. Instead, I deal with the general rules adopted by the legislatures and courts of the majority of states.

This book has been written for the engineer. It is intended to guide both the engineering student and the recently graduated engineer, as well as the experienced one. As a result, I have attempted to cover many basic concepts with which all engineers should be familiar. Sophisticated engineers, many of whom have already been involved in lawsuits or have otherwise worked with lawyers, undoubtedly are familiar with many of the basic concepts discussed in this book.

Because of the general, nonexhaustive nature of this book and the possibility that the law governing a particular question may vary among the states, no one should rely upon this book for legal advice in a specific situation. It should not be used as a substitute for consultation with a competent lawyer. However, it is hoped that this book will give the engineer the background needed to make his discussions with his lawyer more fruitful.

In preparing this book, I have been assisted by a number of persons, but I alone am responsible for any errors it may contain. Among those who have been particularly helpful to me have been my partners, Frank M. Covey, Jr., Fred I. Feinstein, and Robert J. Schneider, and former partner C. Emmet Lucey who read various chapters and whose comments have greatly aided me. In addition, I appreciate the help of McDermott, Will & Emery's librarian, Louis Covotsos, and Gerald E. Ziebell of our library staff. I would also like to express my thanks to David Coplen, a paralegal at McDermott, Will & Emery, for checking the citations and footnotes. Further, I acknowledge the assistance of my secretary, Gretchen Brisolara, for her efforts in coordinating much of the work that was necessary to complete this project. I also thank the following persons from the word processing and proofreading staff of McDermott, Will & Emery for their efforts in making this book possible: Pennyellen Oszak, Joy Hamilton, Patti Ward, Gerri Landrey, Yolanda Glenn, Vickie Jackson, DeLisa Buffington, Sharon Winters, Faith Attaguile, Carolyn Lewis, Pam Carl, Katie Strzyzewski, Donald LaPetina, Patrick Finnegan, John Maher, Donna Kitzing, Annette Ortiz, Mary McDonald, and Christian Jenkins.

Finally, I express my gratitude to my wife Alicia and our children Liana and Janina without whose love and understanding this book would not have been possible.

BRUCE SCHOUMACHER

Contents

ENGINEERS AND THE LAW
An Overview

Part I
FOUNDATIONS
OF THE LAW

1
Fundamentals

In order to understand the law as it applies to engineers, we will first consider some basic legal concepts and how our systems of courts work.

SOURCES OF THE LAW

To determine what the law is on any particular subject, we must first determine the sources of our law. Basically, we can classify the sources of the law as follows:

1. Our constitutions, both federal and state.
2. Statutes and ordinances.
3. Orders, decisions, and regulations of administrative agencies.
4. Case law.

Constitutional Law

In most countries, the foundation of the legal system is a constitution, which can be either written or unwritten. A constitution sets the framework for the political structure of the government. Constitutions ordinarily determine how the government is organized and what the powers of its various branches are. In addition, constitutions usually define the relationship between the government and its citizens.

The constitution of the United Kingdom is unwritten. The British courts determine basic constitutional principles based upon statutes, judicial decisions, and custom and practice. The constitution may be amended by Parliament, the legislative body of the government.

The United States has a written constitution. In addition, the citizens of each of the fifty states are governed by the written constitutions of their respective states.

3

Although an engineer rarely becomes involved professionally in legal questions centering on constitutional issues, state and federal constitutions still affect his daily work. For example, the United States and the fifty states have the right to enact regulatory laws to promote the safety, health, welfare, and moral well-being of their citizens. The federal government and the states have the inherent power to control activities in their respective spheres which may be detrimental to public welfare. This inherent power is referred to as "police power." Thus, the federal and state governments have used the police power to enact statutes governing the engineering professions. They have also used it to enact laws setting forth environmental standards and establishing agencies to protect the environment.

The concept of "due process" is another constitutional principle which may affect the engineer in his daily work. Due process requires that legal proceedings be conducted according to established rules aimed at safeguarding the rights of the individual. Historically, due process was important in old English law and was incorporated in the Magna Carta in 1215. The concept of trial by jury was foreshadowed in the Magna Carta. The concept of due process is contained in the Fifth Amendment to the U.S. Constitution and applies to state action by the Fourteenth Amendment. In addition, the states through their constitutions have also provided for the right of due process.

Under due process, fundamental procedural rights must be granted when a state government acts to revoke the license of an engineer. The professional licensing statutes are usually applied by an administrative board or agency whose members are selected by the governor of the state. In the event that a board takes disciplinary action against a licensed engineer, it must follow certain steps so that the proceedings meet the constitutional requirement of due process. For example, the engineer normally must be given a written copy of the charges, an opportunity to be heard before an impartial judge or hearing examiner, and the right to appeal the order of the board sanctioning him to a civil court.

Therefore, although the engineer may not be aware that his practice is affected by constitutional law, the courses he took in American government or political science in college may be just as helpful to him in his career as the courses he took in calculus and physics.

Statutory Law

The U.S. Congress and the state legislatures pass statutes which become law. Also, local governmental bodies enact legal ordinances. An engineer's work is affected by numerous statutes. For example, states have enacted provisions requiring that certain type of engineering work be done by a professional engineer licensed by the state. All states have passed statutes of limitations prescribing the rules for determining the last date upon which a negligence or malpractice suit can be filed against an engineer or a product liability suit can be filed against a manufacturer of a product.

Statutes are interpreted by the courts. Thus, one person may raise a question about the applicability of a statute or the meaning or interpretation of one of its provisions, which under certain circumstances could become the subject of a lawsuit. The court's interpretation of the statute would be binding in the future, not only upon the parties to the litigation but also upon other persons.

In interpreting statutes, courts frequently consider their legislative history. Thus, courts may look at later amendments to the statutes, legislative hearings on them, reports of legislative committees or subcommittees written during the drafting process, and arguments in the legislative assemblies.

Administrative Law

The federal and state governments, and to a lesser extent local governments, have established administrative agencies to apply and interpret laws enacted under police power. On the federal level, examples of administrative agencies are the Occupational Health and Safety Administration, the National Labor Relations Board, the Securities and Exchange Commission, and the Federal Communications Commission. On the state level, examples of administrative agencies are licensing boards, agencies which control state construction, and environmental agencies. These agencies are established in accordance with legislation frequently referred to as "enabling acts." The legislation normally states the purpose of the act, and then the administrative agency is given broad powers in setting rules and regulations to apply it.

The administrative agencies play two basic roles: legislative and enforcement. In their legislative role, they enact rules and regulations, which become part of the law. In their enforcement role, they take steps to enforce their rules and regulations, resulting in hearings and decisions. The decisions, which frequently interpret the agencies' rules and regulations as well as the statute, also become a source of administrative law.

Case Law

Case law or court decisions constitute the body of law whose rules have been laid down by opinions of judges. The decisions interpreting statutes are not considered part of case law. In the United States, case law is an important source of law. Thus, when a new lawsuit is filed which embodies principles discussed in prior cases, the judge and the lawyer look to those prior decisions for the principles which govern the suit before them.

Under case law, prior decisions upon the same legal point raised in a lawsuit are binding upon the court. This often is referred to as the doctrine of *stare decisis. (let the decision stand)* The primary benefit of *stare decisis* is that the binding nature of prior cases makes the law predictable.

In the American legal system, the trial courts, under the doctrine of *stare decisis,* follow the rulings upon points of law made by the appellate courts that have jurisdiction over them. Similarly, the appellate courts follow their own prior rulings upon points of law. However, a court may overcome the binding effect intended by *stare decisis* by distinguishing the case before it from the case where the legal rule was developed or, occasionally, simply by overruling the rule of law established in the earlier case and adopting a new one.

Case law is often referred to as "common law," which may be a misnomer. All of our states, except Louisiana, have adopted the English law that was in effect at the time when they became states or territories. This body of English law is known as the "common law" and includes not only decisions of English courts, but also statutes passed by Parliament.

Other Sources of Law

In addition to the four primary sources of law discussed above, there are others. As an example, executive orders of the President of the United States and U.S. treaties with foreign countries can have the force of law. Industry codes and trade practice and custom may also be sources of law.

LAW VERSUS EQUITY

Equity is a distinct body of law with origins, as with our common law, in England. Historically, the principles of equity were enforced by individuals and later by courts separate from the courts of law. By 1400 in England, there were three courts enforcing the common law, which consisted of both statutory and case law. These courts were the Court of Common Pleas, which handled real estate cases; the Exchequer, which handled cases involving fiscal matters; and the King's Bench, which handled other forms of litigation. However, the English king always retained power to decide cases himself. Thus, parties who thought that they had not been treated fairly in one of the three courts could appeal to the king, who would refer the matter to the chancery, which was headed by his chancellor. The chancellor was also a member of the king's counsel and was referred to as the "keeper of the King's Conscience."

In addition, the common law did not provide for certain types of relief which would effectively bar a plaintiff from receiving relief in certain cases. For instance, none of the three law courts would issue injunctions or orders restraining someone from doing something, such as trespassing upon another person's land. Thus, persons seeking relief which they could not obtain in the law courts would go directly to the king and his counsel, who later delegated the handling of petitions for extraordinary relief to the chancellor. Gradually, the entire system of equity became a separate body of law with a court of chancery, whose judges were referred to as "chancellors." In fact, even today judges who exercise equity power are often called chancellors.

The various U.S. states, since they have largely adopted the English law, also had separate courts of law and chancery, later called "courts of equity." However, starting in 1846 in New York, the courts of equity were gradually abolished by most states, and one unified court system for hearing both legal and equitable matters was established. Only a few states, such as Delaware, still have separate courts of law and equity. Further, the separate English court of chancery was abolished in 1873 with its merger with the common law courts.

Although separate equity courts no longer exist in most states, our courts still recognize a separate body of "equity law" based upon the historical evolution of equity. Thus, since the equity courts did not provide for trial by jury, today this is not a right in a case where a party seeks any form of equitable relief, such as an injunction or even a divorce.

The remedy in a suit based upon common law is money damages. Under equity law, a person can seek other forms as relief, such as an injunction either requiring or forbidding another person to do or refrain from doing something. For example, an employee may enter into an agreement providing that if he leaves the company he will not compete with his former employer. If the ex-employee violates this agreement, the employer can try to enforce it in court, usually seeking, as an equitable remedy, an injunction barring him from engaging in competitive employment.

CIVIL LAW VERSUS COMMON LAW

Another fundamental distinction in jurisprudence is between common law and civil law. As seen above, common law most often refers to the body of English and American law with its roots in England and its primary reliance upon law made by court decision, based upon the precedent of prior decisions of courts and, in some cases, statutes.

Civil law generally refers to the legal systems of Western Europe, which are based in part upon Roman law. Civil law systems are based upon codes which cover large areas of the law. In addition, there is very little reliance upon the doctrine of *stare decisis*.

One of the most famous civil law codes was the Napoleonic Code of France, which was the basis of many civil codes adopted during the nineteenth century. Although the original Napoleonic Code is no longer the law of France, it is still the basis of the civil law of Quebec and Louisiana. Incidentally, Louisiana is our only state which has a civil law system.

ENFORCING THE LAW

Besides the public's general adherence to the law and the use of private negotiation to resolve disputes, laws are enforced through the courts, administrative agencies, and arbitration. In the United States, there are two primary court systems, federal and state.

Federal Courts

A separate system of federal courts was created by Article III of the U.S. Constitution. This article provides for federal courts to hear cases involving the interpretation of the Constitution and federal statutes and suits arising from "causes and controversies" between citizens of different states. In addition, the federal courts have jurisdiction over admiralty and maritime cases, controversies in which the United States is a party, controversies between two or more states, and controversies between a state or its citizens and foreign countries or their citizens.

For cases involving causes and controversies between citizens of different states, commonly referred to as "diversity cases," the amount of money involved, according to federal statute, must be at least $10,000. Further, only one of the parties may be a citizen of the state where the lawsuit is filed for the federal courts to exercise diversity jurisdiction. As an example, the plaintiff in a federal diversity case filed in Montana may be a citizen of Montana, but the defendant must be a citizen of another state, such as Idaho.

If a case in which a federal court has jurisdiction is originally filed in a state court, under certain circumstances the defendant or defendants may remove the case to the federal court. If a question about the U.S. Constitution or a federal statute is involved, the defendant can remove the case within thirty days after he has been served with process in the state court action. "Service of process" is the service of the paper upon the defendant informing him that he is being sued. Most often the document is a summons.

If the case involves more than $10,000 and the plaintiff and defendant are citizens of different states, the defendant, if he is the nonresident party, can remove the case to the federal court. Again, this must be done within thirty days of service of process upon the defendant.

Judges of all federal courts are selected by the President, subject to confirmation by the Senate. In addition, to relieve them of undue pressure, all federal judges serve for "good behavior," which essentially means a lifetime appointment.

All federal court cases commence in district courts, except for cases of appeal from the decision of an administrative agency or a limited number of special cases that must originate in the U.S. Supreme Court, such as a suit between states. The U.S. district courts hear both civil and criminal cases.

Congress has divided the United States into districts. Each state has at least one district court. In addition, the District of Columbia, Puerto Rico, the U.S. Virgin Islands, Guam, and the Northern Mariana Islands each have a district court. Some states have more than one district court. For example, Nebraska has one district court with judges sitting at Omaha and Lincoln, whereas Indiana has two district courts, one for the Northern District and the other for the Southern District. Moreover, district courts may be divided into divisions for administrative purposes. Accordingly, the Northern District of Illinois has an Eastern Division sitting at Chicago and a Western Division sitting at Rockford.

Most districts have more than one judge, and cases are usually assigned to the judge based upon a random selection process.

The judges of each district court may also appoint magistrates who have power to hear and rule upon certain matters, such as discovery motions arising prior to trial. Further, magistrates may try civil cases with the consent of the parties.

Each U.S. district court has a clerk of the court who handles administrative matters. The clerk's office maintains the court files and docket sheets, which are a chronological history of each document filed in a lawsuit. Moreover, each district has a U.S. Marshall with deputy marshalls who, under certain circumstances, serve court papers, such as summonses, complaints, and subpoenas for witnesses to testify at trial or deposition. Moreover, the U.S. Marshalls carry out judicial sales and execute judgments.

If a litigant is dissatisfied with the judgment of a district court, he can appeal to one of the courts of appeals. Again, Congress has divided the United States into appellate districts, called "circuits." Each district has a court of appeals. There are eleven judicial circuits and a separate one for the District of Columbia. Moreover, there is another court of appeals sitting in the District of Columbia called the "United States Court of Appeals for the Federal Circuit," which hears appeals from the Claims Court, the Court of International Trade, copyright, trademark, and patent appeals, and certain appeals from decisions of U.S. agencies. In addition, a Temporary Emergency Court of Appeals was created by Congress to hear appeals under the Economic Stabilization Act of 1970. Its judges are appointed by the Chief Justice of the U.S. Supreme Court from among the judges of the district courts and other courts of appeals.

The courts of appeals normally can review only final decisions of the district courts and federal administrative agencies. However, orders refusing or granting injunctions can be reviewed by the court of appeals prior to a final decision. In addition, certain interlocutory orders concerning receivers, as well as admiralty matters and patent cases, may be appealed to the court of appeals prior to a final decision. Moreover, the district judge in a civil action may certify a question for interlocutory appeal to the court of appeals, which has the discretion to accept.

In reviewing the decision of the district court, the court of appeals is generally limited to the record before it. The attorneys representing the parties tell the clerk of the district court which documents and which portions of the trial proceedings should be transmitted to the appellate court. Then, pursuant to the rules of the appellate court, the attorneys submit briefs discussing the basis for the appeal. After reviewing the briefs, and frequently after hearing the oral arguments of counsel, the court of appeals issues its decision. This is usually a written opinion, stating not only the result but the reasons for it. The opinion then becomes part of the body of case law.

In reviewing the decision of the district court, the court of appeals is usually limited to reviewing errors in the law or in its application by the district judge. Thus, one of the parties may argue that the district judge erred in admitting certain evidence which resulted in an improper jury verdict or court judgment. In addition, in a jury trial, parties frequently argue in the appellate court that the district judge gave the jury an erroneous instruction about the law applicable to the case.

The appellate court circuits have anywhere from four to twenty-three judges. However, decisions of the district courts are normally reviewed by panels of three judges. If a party is not satisfied with the decision of the three-judge panel, he can either seek a "writ of certiorari" (literally, "let the result be certified") to the U.S. Supreme Court, a rehearing by the three-judge panel, or a hearing by all the judges sitting in the circuit. When the full circuit court panel hears or reviews a decision of a three-judge circuit court panel, the circuit court is referred to as sitting *en banc*.

Only a very few cases are appealable by right to the U.S. Supreme Court. Most appeals are taken by the Court as a matter of discretion, and the parties seek leave to appeal by a writ of certiorari.

The U.S. Supreme Court sits at Washington, D.C., and consists of nine justices. The Court has original and exclusive jurisdiction in controversies between two or more states. In addition, it has original, but not exclusive, jurisdiction of controversies involving ambassadors and certain other representatives of foreign countries, all controversies between the United States and a state, and all actions or proceedings by a state against citizens of another state or against aliens. Any party may appeal to the Supreme Court any decision of a lower federal court holding an act of Congress unconstitutional. Further, any party may appeal directly to the Supreme Court from an order admitting or denying an injunction issued by a three-judge panel of a district court. Such panels are created to hear cases involving interpretations of the Constitution.

The Supreme Court may also review decisions of the highest court of any state which interpret the validity of any treaty or statute of the United States, the validity of any state statute as being contrary to the U.S. Constitution, and treaties or laws of the United States whose constitutionality has been upheld. The Court may also, in its discretion, hear decisions of the highest court of any state raising questions of interpretation of any U.S. treaty or statute or the Constitution.

Other Federal Courts

There are also other courts, some with which the engineer may become involved. There is the Claims Court, the Tax Court, the Court of International Trade, and the Court of Military Appeals. For example, an engineer may participate in a patent lawsuit which may be appealed to the Court of Customs and Patent Appeals. Or he may become involved in a case pending before the Claims Court, most frequently when a suit over a federal government contract arises. The Claims Court hears claims against the United States.

State Courts

All states have courts of original jurisdiction in which most cases are commenced. Courts of original jurisdiction have different names in different states. In Nebraska they are referred to as "district courts." In Indiana and Illinois they are referred to as "circuit courts.'' In New York they are referred to as the ''supreme court.'' In addition, some states have justice of the peace, police, and municipal courts which hear cases involving minor sums of money and minor crimes. The decisions of courts of inferior jurisdiction are usually appealable to the court of original jurisdiction.

Most states now have intermediate courts of appeal from which decisions of the trial court are taken. In addition, each state has a highest court of appeal, often referred to as a ''supreme court.''

In some states, judges are elected. In others, they are appointed on the basis of merit by a panel selected pursuant to state law. In addition, in some states, judges who are elected run for reelection on their record unopposed.

Administrative Agencies

Administrative agencies are established by the federal government and the states to administer specific laws. The President appoints the members of the various boards of federal administrative agencies, subject to the approval of the U.S. Senate. The first administrative agency established by the federal government was the Interstate Commerce Commission in 1887 to regulate railroad rates and facilities. Many states have also established administrative agencies such as those handling workers' compensation claims.

Administrative agencies are usually created to establish an expert body to administer technically complex laws. Generally, the administrative agencies are given broad discretionary powers in order to exercise their expertise. They are also thought to provide greater expertise in particular industries than Congress, the state legislatures, local governing bodies, or the courts. Moreover, administrative agencies remove some of the legislative burden from the U.S. Congress and the state legislatures and some of the litigation burden from the courts.

Administrative agencies usually are governed by several persons often referred to as ''commissioners,'' but they can also be headed by a single executive. The agency's staff drafts rules and regulations which are reviewed and promulgated by the commissioners. It also prosecutes persons who have violated the rules and regulations of the agency. The hearings are often conducted before an administrative law judge or hearing officer, who makes findings of fact and issues a decision. Any party is then free to appeal this decision or order to the commissioners, who make a final decision. Then the finding of the commissioners can be appealed to the courts.

In some states, administrative agency orders are appealed to the state court of original jurisdiction, such as the state district or state circuit court. In the federal system, most orders of an administrative agency are appealable to the Court of Appeals. Whatever level of the judiciary the appeal is to, it is usually based upon the record of the administrative proceeding, and normally no new evidence may be admitted.

Arbitration

Arbitration is another means of resolving disputes, but unlike courts, it does not make law. In arbitration, the parties voluntarily agree, usually in a contract, to refer any disputes between them to an impartial arbitration body for a decision. The parties also agree that the decision will be final and binding.

Thus, arbitration is similar to a court lawsuit in that it concerns a controversy between two or more parties. However, it is dissimilar because it is handled privately, usually by an industry body or a special organization such as the American Arbitration Association.

PROGRESS OF A LAWSUIT

At some point in their career, most engineers become involved in a lawsuit as either a party, an employee of a party, or a non-party witness. Hence, every engineer should have a fundamental understanding of how a lawsuit progresses through the courts.

The person who sues is called the "plaintiff." The person who is sued is the "defendant." There can be more than one plaintiff or defendant in any lawsuit. In addition, the defendant can raise a counterclaim against the plaintiff. For instance, the defendant may be an engineer who is owed fees by the plaintiff. The plaintiff, however, may think that the engineer committed malpractice resulting in damage to the plaintiff and may file a malpractice action. In such a case, the engineer who is the defendant can then file a counterclaim against the plaintiff, requesting that he be awarded his fees as damages.

In addition, a defendant may request the court to add additional parties as either plaintiffs or defendants. Also, the defendant may file a "third-party complaint" against a "third-party defendant." In a case where the defendant joins another party as a third-party defendant, the defendant usually contends that if the defendant is found liable, the third-party defendant should be liable to him for the total damages or a lesser sum. As an example, a manufacturer may be accused of producing a product that is defective in either manufacture or design by a plaintiff who sustained personal injuries while using the product. The product may have many components, and it is possible that an error in the manufacture or design of one component may have resulted in a defective product. In such circumstances, the manufacturer may decide to bring in as a third-party defendant the vendor of the component in question.

In addition, defendants in lawsuits may file counterclaims against each other. These are sometimes referred to as "cross-claims."

Although in most commercial lawsuits the plaintiff is seeking either money damages or equitable relief, occasionally a declaratory judgment may be sought. In such a suit, the plaintiff asks the court to state the rights of the parties or to give an opinion on a question of law, without an order that anything be done. There is no need for damage to have occurred to the plaintiff.

Declaratory judgment actions frequently are filed against an insured person when a dispute arises over the interpretation of an insurance policy. A claim may have been made or a lawsuit filed against a person insured by the insurance company, and the company may not think that the claim or suit is covered by its policy. In order to protect itself, the insurance company may ask the court for a declaratory judgment that it provides no coverage for the claim or suit.

Another special lawsuit is an action in interpleader. Interpleader actions usually arise when a person holds money or property to which other persons have made conflicting claims. In an interpleader action, the holder will file the lawsuit and tender the money or property to the court. The persons who are raising conflicting claims are the defendants, and after the judge orders the money or property to be delivered to the court clerk, the plaintiff normally is dismissed from the lawsuit and the court resolves the dispute.

A person may also may seek permission from the court to intervene in a lawsuit, usually as a plaintiff. An intervenor action may arise in a personal injury suit where a worker's compensation insurance company has paid benefits to the plaintiff. The plaintiff may have instituted a legal action to recover damages from the person who allegedly injured him, and the worker's compensation insurer may seek to intervene, contending that it has a statutory or common law right to a share of the proceeds of any judgment to the extent of the worker's compensation benefits it paid to the plaintiff.

A plaintiff may also file a class action suit. In such a suit, the plaintiff states that he is a member of the class and that he is suing on its behalf. For example, a person may sue as a member of a class of shareholders or taxpayers. Such suits usually require a class that is so large that it would be impractical to name all members as plaintiffs, that there are common questions of law and fact, that the claims of the plaintiffs are typical of those of the class, and that the plaintiff will fairly and adequately represent the class.

Determining Where to File the Lawsuit

The first step in any lawsuit is for the plaintiff and his attorney to determine where it should be filed. This requires several decisions. First, in what state should the lawsuit be filed? Second, should it be filed in the federal or state court for the state? Third, in which state or federal court should the suit be commenced?

If the plaintiff and the defendant reside in the same state, there is usually little difficulty in deciding to file the lawsuit there. However, if they reside in different states, the question of location arises. Usually, the plaintiff desires to file in his own state for reasons of economy. Under such circumstances, the lawyer must determine whether the courts of the plaintiff's state can exercise jurisdiction over the defendant, which determines whether these courts can enter a valid and binding judgment against him. Under the Constitution, as interpreted by the U.S. Supreme Court, the courts of one state can exercise jurisdiction over a defendant located in another state only if the transaction in which the defendant is involved has sufficient minimum contacts with the plaintiff's state. For example, if the plaintiff is a resident of Kentucky and was injured in an automobile accident in Ohio by an Ohio resident, the plaintiff probably could not obtain jurisdiction over the Ohio defendant in the Kentucky courts. Or, in a contract action, a Wyoming plaintiff may have entered into a contract with a Colorado defendant. Whether the plaintiff can sue in a court in Wyoming depends upon what contacts the Colorado defendant may have had with the State of Wyoming regarding the agreement to contract and the performance of the contract.

After the plaintiff and his lawyer have decided in what state to file the lawsuit, they must decide whether it should be filed in the state or federal court. Of course, not all lawsuits can be filed in the federal court. The plaintiff may file a lawsuit in a federal court only against a defendant who is a resident of another state, and the amount of money involved must exceed $10,000 or the interpretation of the U.S. Constitution or a federal statute must be involved.

After the plaintiff and his attorney decide in which court system to file, they must decide on the specific court. First, they must select a court which has jurisdiction over the subject of the suit. Second, they must select a court in the proper geographical location, referred to as "venue." Both Congress and the state legislatures have established venue laws. Typically, the state venue laws provide that the suit must be filed in the defendant's county of residence or in the county in which the transaction leading to the lawsuit occurred. In federal courts, venue may be in the judicial district in which either all plaintiffs or all defendants reside or in the judicial district in which the transaction occurred.

Among other questions that the plaintiff and his attorney usually discuss in deciding where to file are the quality of the judges and juries, the existence of bias and prejudice for or against the plaintiff or defendant, the location of witnesses, and the waiting period before the case is assigned for trial.

Commencing the Lawsuit

In most courts, a lawsuit normally commences when the plaintiff files a complaint or petition, naming another party or parties as the defendant or defendants. The complaint states the cause of the plaintiff's action and requests the relief sought, such as money damages. After the complaint is filed, the plaintiff must arrange for service of process upon the defendant or defendants. Service of process usually involves serving a copy of a summons and a copy of the complaint upon each defendant. The summons advises the defendant that he has been sued, and in what court, and directs him to file an answer or other response to the complaint within a specific number of days.

Traditionally, the summons and complaint are served by a judicial officer. In the state court, a sheriff or deputy sheriff will usually serve them. In the federal courts, this is usually done by a federal marshall. In many states and federal courts, however, registered or certified mail may be used. Also, where the defendant is a non-resident, the summons and complaint may be served upon a state official who in turn forwards them to the defendant by registered or certified mail. Service in these instances, however, is complete when the state official receives a copy of the summons and complaint. If the defendant cannot be located, service may consist of publication of a notice of the lawsuit in a newspaper for a specified number of days.

In the English common law system, lawsuits were initiated by a writ. The defendant was required to appear in court on a specific date to answer the charges contained in the writ. The writ was usually obtained by the plaintiff through "service of a praecipe" upon the clerk of the court, requesting the clerk to issue it. Some states still follow this practice.

Response to the Complaint

Within the time prescribed by the summons or writ, the defendant must file his answer or other responsive pleading with the court. The defendant may request that the case be dismissed upon certain grounds. For example, he may state that the court lacks personal jurisdiction over him or over the subject of the lawsuit, or that the action is barred by the statute of limitations, or that there has been an error in service of process. In addition, the defendant can request the court to strike all or certain portions of the complaint or even to dismiss the lawsuit because the complaint fails to state a cause of action by the plaintiff for which the court can grant relief or prevent the granting of relief, such as when a corporation is not licensed to do business in the state where the suit has been filed.

If the defendant does not file a motion to dismiss or strike the complaint or parts of it, or if the court denies all such motions, the defendant then files an answer. In the answer, the defendant admits or denies each allegation of the complaint. If the defendant does not know whether the allegation is true or false, he usually states that he lacks sufficient knowledge to form an opinion of its truth.

In answering, the defendant may raise affirmative defenses, such as that the complaint is barred by the statute of limitations or the plaintiff should be denied recovery because of his contributory negligence. In addition, the defendant can file a counterclaim against the plaintiff and can bring third-party defendants into the action. When a third-party complaint is filed by the defendant, he is then also referred to as the "third-party plaintiff" and the defendants in the third-party action are referred to as the "third-party defendants." When a third-party complaint is filed, the defendant must arrange for a copy of a summons and the third-party complaint to be served upon the third-party defendant.

If the defendant files a counterclaim, the plaintiff must usually reply. If the defendant files affirmative defenses or new evidence by way of defense, some states require the plaintiff to file a reply. However, under the Federal Rules of Civil Procedure, the federal courts do not require replies to new evidence raised in answers.

Discovery

Pretrial discovery is an important part of any lawsuit. Through discovery, the parties are able to gather facts to support their cases and to find the facts which may support the suit or defense of the opposing side. Discovery may require more work than the trial itself.

Discovery is a relatively recent innovation. Until the 1930s, a lawyer had no way to find out the facts which might support the opposing side or to gather the facts to support his own side other than serving a demand for a bill of particulars, requesting the other party to indicate the facts which supported his claim, or undertaking an informal investigation, usually in the form of interviews. Starting with the adoption of the Field Code in New York in 1848, a movement for more formal means of discovery was launched. The proponents of discovery said that such a procedure would allow each side to prepare adequately and not to be surprised at the trial. Prior to that time, trials often involved situations where one party would hide favorable facts and surprise its opponent at trial. To avoid such results, which sometimes resulted in unjust verdicts, formal discovery procedures were adopted in many states and in the federal courts.

Discovery had another benefit. If, prior to trial, each side understood the case of the other side, it would be possible for both parties to reach a rational settlement without the need for an expensive trial. Today, most suits do not go to trial, but are settled beforehand. Such results are often due to the opportunity for discovery.

The principal tools of discovery are:

1. Interrogatories.
2. Requests to produce documents or other things or to submit something, such as a product for inspection or a person for a medical examination.
3. Requests to admit facts or the genuineness of documents.
4. Depositions.

Interrogatories are basically written questions served by one party upon the other. The party who must answer has to furnish objections or answers to those interrogatories within a specified period of time after service. Ordinarily, interrogatories must be answered under oath, and under some circumstances, those answers may be used at trial as evidence.

A written request may direct one side to produce documents or other things (physical evidence) for examination. The recipient of the request again has a specified period of time in which to object or comply. The party serving the request then has the opportunity to examine and copy documents and to examine the physical evidence requested.

A request to admit facts or the genuineness of documents is another form of discovery. The party who receives the request must respond to it within a specified period of time by either answering it or objecting to it. If he does not respond within the time prescribed, the facts are considered admitted or the documents are considered genuine for the purposes of the trial.

Depositions are the sworn testimony of witnesses taken before a court reporter. They can be used at trial to impeach a witness. For example, if a witness makes a statement in a deposition and later makes a different statement about the same subject matter at the trial, an attorney can use the deposition to disparage his credibility. In addition, under certain conditions and in all federal court cases, depositions may be used as evidence at trial if the witness is unavailable to testify. Thus, the deposition or pertinent parts of it may be read to the jury or judge or used to impeach a witness upon cross-examination.

Pretrial Procedure

Prior to a trial, the judge frequently will hold status calls asking the attorneys to tell him how discovery is progressing. Eventually, one or more pretrial conferences are held. At a pretrial conference, the judge and the attorneys discuss how the case will be tried. The judge will attempt to have the parties agree to facts which are not in dispute and to simplify the issues which will be presented to the jury or the judge if it is a bench trial. Routine matters will be discussed and decided upon, such as the listing and marking of exhibits, agreements on which testimony will be provided by deposition, and a listing of the witnesses.

Pretrial conferences are almost always used by judges to discuss settlement. By this time, most of the discovery should be done and the parties should be aware of the strengths and weaknesses of both cases. Thus, the pretrial conference affords a judge an excellent opportunity to discuss the merits of the case with the attorneys and to encourage settlement.

If a case is to go to trial, one result of a pretrial conference is often pretrial order, especially in the federal courts. The pretrial order establishes how the case will be tried. It contains a list of the facts which are not disputed and a list of those at issue. A pretrial conference order may also list the theories of the case of each party, the witnesses to be called, and the exhibits.

Summary Judgment

Frequently, one of the parties may file a motion for a summary judgment prior to the trial. In the motion the party will argue that none of the material facts are in dispute and that in applying the applicable law, a decision should be entered in his favor. The evidence to support the motion for summary judgment is in the form of affidavits and evidence gathered during discovery, principally depositions and documents. If the judge determines that there is material fact in dispute, he will not grant the motion for summary judgment. A material fact is a fact that must be presented by the party moving for summary judgment in order to be entitled to a ruling in his favor. As an example, if a seller sues a buyer for non-payment, he must show that he delivered the goods or tendered them for delivery. If the judge determines that there are no material facts in dispute, he will reach his decision by applying the applicable law to the undisputed facts.

The Trial

If a lawsuit is not settled or dismissed, eventually it will be tried. The trial may be held before a jury or solely before the judge. In most states, twelve jurors plus alternates, and in most federal courts, six jurors plus alternates, are used. In certain cases, such as a trial for money damages, the parties have a right to a jury trial. However, they may waive that right and request a trial by the judge only. In other cases, such as cases in equity, trials are usually only before the judge, although in equity cases the judge can use an "advisory" jury.

In a trial by jury, certain things always occur. First, the jurors are selected. This may be a long process in which the attorneys and the judge question the jurors to determine whether any of them may be prejudiced. If a juror appears to be prejudiced, one of the parties may challenge him for cause. Further, each side has a certain number of "preemptory challenges." Such challenges give each party the right to exclude a certain number of jurors for whatever reason they desire.

Following their selection and swearing in, each attorney makes a presentation to the jurors called the "opening statement." In this statement, the attorney tells the jury what evidence he will present and what he intends to prove.

Following the opening statement, the evidence is presented through testimony, documents, and other exhibits. In legal terms, the plaintiff and then the defendant each present their "case-in-chief."

The plaintiff first presents his witnesses and elicits the testimony he desires. This process is called "direct examination." The defendant's attorney has the opportunity to follow up the testimony of any witness by asking that witness questions. This is called "cross-examination."

Following cross-examination, the plaintiff's attorney may again question the witness; this is called "redirect examination." Further, additional questions by the opposing side are called "recross-examination."

Ordinarily, leading questions cannot be used by the examining lawyer during either direct or redirect examination. An example of a leading question is one which starts, "Isn't it true that you. . . ." Leading questions, however, can be used during cross- and recross-examination.

Compelling people to appear as witnesses at a trial is important. Frequently, witnesses will appear voluntarily. In some states, a party and employees of a party to a lawsuit may be compelled to appear to give evidence at the trial if the attorney requests their appearance to serve a notice on counsel for the other party, requesting that the party or certain of its employees appear at the trial to be questioned. Under the Federal Rules and the law of other states, the appearance of a witness can be compelled only by "subpoena." A subpoena is a written demand served upon a potential witness ordering him to appear at a trial upon a certain date to give testimony. If the witness does not appear, the court can use its power to force an appearance, such as by requesting the sheriff to bring the person to court. A "subpoena duces tecum" is a subpoena ordering a person not only to appear but also to bring certain documents.

In the federal courts, if a witness is beyond subpoena power, his deposition may be used as evidence. Some states follow this same rule. Other states require that a specific "evidence deposition," as opposed to a "discovery deposition," be taken. When depositions are used as evidence at a trial, questions and answers which an attorney wishes to present are read to the jury. Those questions and answers then become part of the record of the trial.

Naturally, there are limitations on the types of evidence that either party may present to the jury. These limitations have been imposed by case law over the years or imposed by statute; they are called "rules of evidence" and in some jurisdictions are statutory. For example, only relevant evidence is admissible. Hearsay evidence is not admissible unless it falls within an exception that as a matter of common sense shows the statement to be true. For example, many business records could be excluded as evidence if the party seeking to present them is unable to produce as witnesses all the persons who helped to create them. Obviously, because business records generally are kept for purpose other than a later lawsuit, they are assumed to be accurate reflections of the entries or facts contained therein and common sense dictates that it should not be necessary to produce as witnesses all the persons who helped to create them, such as bookkeepers. Thus, under the rules of evidence, a person who is generally familiar with the manner in which the records are produced and kept can testify about their existence and how they were made without the need to admit any other evidence about them.

Following presentation of the evidence, one or more of the parties may present a motion for a directed verdict. In such a motion, the party argues that, based upon the evidence and the applicable law, he is entitled to a verdict in his favor.

Next, each attorney presents his "closing argument" to the jury. In the argument, the attorney presents his case, emphasizing the favorable facts and stating why, given those facts and under the law, regarding which the judge will issue instructions, a verdict should be entered for his client.

Following the closing argument, the judge gives the jurors the "instructions." These are statements on the law applicable to the case. The jurors in some courts are allowed to take the instructions into the jury room with them, along with certain evidence such as relevant documents.

The jury then returns its "verdict." This is usually a simple written document in which the jury finds one party guilty or not guilty. After the verdict, the jury is dismissed. Each party then has a certain period of time in which to present a motion to the court challenging the result. One party may ask for a new trial because certain evidence was admitted which should not have been or because erroneous instructions were given to the jury. Further, one party may request a judgment, regardless of the verdict, on the basis that the verdict was clearly not in accord with the law.

Appeal

Following the ruling upon the posttrial motions, and assuming that all of them have been denied, the judge enters a final judgment which confirms the jury verdict, or his earlier decision if the case was a bench trial. Either party may then appeal the judgment to the appellate court. If a money judgment has been entered, the party who owes the money must provide a supersedeas bond or obtain a court order to stay enforcement of the judgment. A supersedeas bond is one under which a party puts up money, other property (if allowed), or a bond of surety from which the judgment will be paid if his appeal is unsuccessful. If a bond is required but is not furnished, the party who has received the judgment may take steps to collect upon it. For example, he may garnish the bank accounts or wages of the judgment debtor. Garnishment is a proceeding in which the judgment creditor seeks to collect money owed him from money or property of the judgment debtor in the possession of third parties.

A notice of appeal must be filed within a certain number of days following the judgment, normally thirty days. Transcripts of testimony, exhibits, and court documents are then transferred from the trial court to the appellate court for review.

Essentially, the attorneys representing the parties before the appeals court argue in written memoranda, called "briefs," that the trial court made an error in ruling upon the law. This could have been an error in admitting evidence or in instructing the jury. Further, one of the parties may argue that the verdict was against the manifest weight of the evidence. After the briefs are submitted to the appellate court, the attorneys usually have the opportunity to present oral argument. The appellate court does not hear any evidence such as the testimony of witnesses, but relies instead upon the record of the trial. During the oral argument, the appellate judges may question the attorneys to clarify crucial facts or points of law.

After the briefs have been submitted and oral argument has been heard, the appellate judges often meet to discuss the case. During this discussion, they reach a decision. One of them is instructed to write an opinion stating the court's decision and the reasons for it. The appellate court may affirm the trial court's judgment or reverse it, remanding the case to the lower court for a new trial. Occasionally, the appellate court may affirm in part and reverse in part if many issues were tried.

If an appellate judge does not agree with a decision of the panel, he may write an opinion called a "dissenting opinion." Alternatively, another judge, although concurring in the result, may not like the basis for the majority opinion and may write a "concurring opinion."

Part II
LEGAL RESPONSIBILITIES
OF THE ENGINEER

2
The Engineer's Responsibility
for Negligence

As the result of performing professional services, the engineer may become liable for injuries or damages caused by his negligence. A consulting engineer working in the construction industry may make an error in a plan which could result in a building failure. Or, an engineer working for a manufacturer could make an error in design, resulting in a defective product. In either case, property may be damaged or someone may be injured, causing a claim to be made or a lawsuit to be filed against the engineer or the manufacturer.

In this chapter, we will study some basic concepts applicable to situations in which an engineer may be liable for negligence. In Chapters 3, 4, and 5 we will apply those concepts to the consulting engineer, and in Chapter 6 we will apply them to the engineer working in manufacturing. As the discussion develops, we will see that the law in recent years has drawn a clear distinction between the rules applying to the engineer working in construction or other consulting areas and the engineer working in manufacturing. The law places significantly different burdens upon a plaintiff suing an engineer working as a consultant than upon a plaintiff suing the manufacturer of a defective product.

The subject matter of the law is divided into various branches, such as constitutional law, contract law, and administrative law. A consulting engineer may be liable for negligence to his client or even to third parties. Similarly, a manufacturer may be liable for negligence to customers and subsequent users for damages caused by a defect in the design or manufacture of its products. Suits for negligence fall into the category of the law called "tort law."

There is no generally accepted definition of a "tort." Basically, a tort is "a civil wrong, other than breach of contract, for which the court will provide a remedy in the form of an action for damages."[1] A tort occurs when a person interferes with another person or his property. As an example, while driving, you may hit the car in front of you. A person in this car may have a cause of action in tort against you for damage to his automobile or for personal injuries he may have sustained in the accident. He may thus have a private right of action against you for which he may seek redress in the courts. This is an action for damages, that is, an action to recover money from you in payment for the damage or injuries he has sustained.

Torts fall into one of three broad categories: (1) negligence, (2) intentional tort, and (3) strict liability. A suit for a tort must be distinguished from a suit for breach of contract. In a breach of contract lawsuit, the plaintiff seeks to recover damages for a breach of the contract by the defendant. Tort law has created an independent concept of a duty which one person owes another person, a duty not to injure or damage him, and is unrelated to the law of contracts.

ACTIONS FOR NEGLIGENCE

English common law initially held that a person could be liable for injuries or damages he may have caused to another person, even though he was not at fault. However, by the early nineteenth century, the doctrine of negligence had become accepted. Accordingly, a person could be held liable for causing injury or damage to another person only if he was negligent. At first, this concept was applied to certain tradesmen or professionals, such as blacksmiths or surgeons. The courts reasoned that such persons represented themselves as having certain skills in which the public could place their confidence. Accordingly, the courts determined that they owed the public a certain degree of service, and that if any one of them breached this concept of expected service by being negligent, he could be held liable for damages. Negligence could take the form not only of a positive act, such as a careless surgical procedure, but also of an omission.

Eventually, courts in England and the United States developed numerous rules governing negligence suits or actions. Among those rules are the four elements which the plaintiff must show in an action in order to prove his negligence case against the defendant. These four elements are:

1. A duty which the defendant owed to the plaintiff to conform to a certain standard of conduct as established by the law. For instance, when driving an automobile, a person must drive in the proper lane.
2. A breach of a legal duty by the defendant. As an example, driving a car in the lane of oncoming traffic could be a breach of a duty which the defendant owed to the plaintiff driving an oncoming vehicle.
3. The breach of duty must have a causal connection to the injury sustained by the plaintiff. The law requires that the breach of duty (the defendant's action or failure to act) must be the "proximate cause" of the harm suffered by the plaintiff.
4. Damage suffered by the plaintiff. Obviously, if the plaintiff has not sustained any personal injury or damage to his property, he is not entitled to recover any money from the defendant.

Standard of Care

In order to apply the concept of negligence to a particular case, the courts developed the standard of the reasonable man. Under this standard, the jury determines if the defendant's act or failure to act was something which a reasonable man would or would not have done. Thus, one version of an instruction used by a Illinois judge to define negligence reads:

> When I use the word "negligence" in these instructions, I mean the failure to do something which a reasonably careful person would do or the doing of something which a reasonably careful person would not do, under circumstances similar to those shown by the evidence. The law does not say how a reasonably careful person would act under those circumstances. That is for you to decide.[2]

In giving this instruction, the judge states that the jury must determine how a reasonable person would act under the circumstances. The judge tells the jury the duty under the law which the defendant owes the plaintiff. The jury decides whether the defendant was acting reasonably or not. Thus, in an automobile accident case involving a head-on collision, the judge may instruct the jury that the defendant has a duty to drive in the proper lane of traffic. However, the jury must determine whether the defendant was negligent in driving in an oncoming lane, relying upon the standard of the reasonable man.

However, what happens in those situations outside the experience of the ordinary juror? Most, if not all, jurors have had experience driving automobiles. But how is a juror to decide whether a consulting engineer acted reasonably in rendering services or whether a manufacturer of a product acted reasonably in designing a product?

The courts resolved this dilemma by adopting two concepts. First, when the defendant was a person whose knowledge and skill were greater than those of the ordinary person, the law expected that person to conduct himself accordingly. Thus, a physician was expected to render medical treatment in accordance with the standards applied by similarly skilled and knowledgeable doctors. Second, the courts decided that since jurors lacked the knowledge to determine which standards of conduct would be expected by a defendant in such a situation, an expert witness must testify as to what standards of care apply in the specific case under consideration. Further, the courts reasoned that a professional person cannot guarantee the result of his services, but is only responsible for rendering those services with the same skill as others ordinarily practicing his profession.

The Standard Care of the Consulting Engineer

The first case in which a United States court held that an architect only owed a duty to render professional services in accordance with the skills of those ordinarily practicing architecture occurred in nineteenth-century Maine. The court stated:

> The undertaking of an architect implies that he possesses skill and ability, including taste, sufficient to enable him to perform the required services at least ordinarily and reasonably well and that he will exercise and apply in a given case his skill and ability, his judgment and taste, reasonably and without neglect. But the undertaking does not imply or warrant a satisfactory result.[3]

In a recent Minnesota case, the court noted:

Because of the inescapable possibility of error which inheres in these services, the law has traditionally required, not perfect results, but rather the exercise of that skill and judgment which can be reasonably expected from similarly situated professionals.[4]

In order to show that the consulting engineer has breached his professional duty, the plaintiff usually must have an expert testify as to the standard of care which allegedly was breached. In several cases, the courts have stressed the need for an architect or engineer to testify as to the relevant standards of professional care. As an example, in a 1979 Kansas case, the defendants were architects who allegedly committed malpractice in designing a walkway that resulted in runoff and the flooding of a newly constructed gymnasium. In holding that the plaintiffs needed expert testimony to prove their case, the court noted that the architectural design used was technical and beyond the understanding of the ordinary juror.[5]

Moreover, the relevant standards about which the expert must testify must be those standards used in the local community. For example, the standards of mechanical engineering for heating, ventilation, and air-conditioning systems design may not be the same in Alaska as in Texas.

There are times, however, when the plaintiff need not present expert testimony to show the applicable standards. These are cases in which a professional error has been made which is so obvious that the jurors can weigh the evidence without the need of expert assistance. Thus, in a Delaware case, where the architect had designed a showroom-warehouse building which suffered repeated flooding, the court held that no expert testimony was necessary, since the architect was aware of the possibility of flooding and had not considered it in his design.[6]

In most jurisdictions, the expert who testifies must practice the same profession as the defendant. Thus, in most instances, a mechanical engineer cannot testify as to the professional standards of structural engineers. However, in most states, and under the new rules of evidence adopted in the federal courts, the judge determines whether the expert is qualified prior to admitting his testimony.

Thus, there have been cases in which the trial judge has been extremely liberal in accepting the testimony of an expert, since he is skilled or knowledgeable in the field about which he is testifying. In a product liability case, one trial judge allowed a garage mechanic to testify that an automobile tire was defective in material and workmanship. The defendants had argued that this man's opinion should not be accepted, since he had previously testified that he had no experience in tire manufacturing and could not determine whether the defect was due to poor workmanship or defective material.[7]

Standard of Care of the Manufacturer

Under the law of negligence, a manufacturer has a duty to produce a product which is not negligent in manufacture or design. These concepts will be discussed in detail in Chapter 6. However, we shall briefly consider the duty of the manufacturer, who often employs engineers, not to be negligent in designing his products.

Under the law, a manufacturer must design a product in such a manner that it is reasonably safe for its intended use. In one case, a manufacturer was found liable when a crane did not have enough resistance to prevent it from overturning.[8] In another case, the manufacturer was held liable when a brake handle and drum for a crane were not protected from the weather so that rain could enter, resulting in slippage.[9]

In order for a plaintiff to prove negligence in design, he must show a standard and demonstrate how the manufacturer's design deviated from that standard. Usually, the plaintiff will use an expert witness, most often an engineer. This witness may testify that either a written or informal industry standard had established certain design criteria, which were not met by the manufacturer.

In some states, the manufacturer may rely upon industry design standards, using an argument similar to that used by the consulting engineers. In those states, the manufacturer may show that he was not negligent because his design was common to the industry and had not before produced any injury. A manufacturer cannot be held liable for negligent design where the defect is obvious.[10] In a 1982 North Carolina case, the plaintiff had been struck by a crane and filed a suit against the manufacturer, alleging that the crane was negligently designed because the operator's visibility was limited. The plaintiff, however, knew about this problem. Accordingly, the court held the manufacturer not liable for negligent design because the danger was obvious.[11]

The Doctrine of Privity

For decades, the courts wrestled with the problem of the classes of persons to whom the engineer or manufacturer owed a duty not to be negligent in rendering professional services or in designing and manufacturing a product. In a historically important 1842 English case, the court stated that a manufacturer could not be held liable in negligence for harm suffered by users who had not purchased the product directly from him.[12] This is referred to as the "doctrine of privity" and was applied not only to manufacturers, but also to design professionals. Under the doctrine of privity, only an injured person who was in privity of contract with the manufacturer or the consulting engineer could sue for damages caused by negligence. Thus, for manufacturers, only the purchaser of the product could sue for damages caused by negligent design or manufacture. For design professionals, only a client could sue for damages due to negligent design.

By 1903, there were only three limited exceptions to the doctrine of privity. First, a defendant could be held liable for injuries caused by an "imminently dangerous" product whose dangerous nature he had failed to disclose to the buyer. Second, the defendant could be held liable when he provided a defective product for use by the plaintiff on the defendant's premises. Third, the defendant could be held liable for the negligent manufacture or sale of an imminently dangerous product "intended to preserve, destroy or affect human life."[13] Such products included food, beverages, drugs, firearms, and explosives. However, the user who had not purchased the product directly from the manufacturer could not sue the manufacturer for injuries caused by the product's defective design or manufacture, unless it fell within one of those three exceptions.

In the 1916 landmark decision in *MacPherson* v. *Buick Motor Co.*,[14] the New York Court of Appeals signaled the demise of the doctrine of privity. In that case, the owner of an automobile with a defective wheel sued the manufacturer, even though he had purchased it from a dealer. The court held that the automobile was not an inherently dangerous product, but reasoned that it might become dangerous if it were negligently manufactured. Thus, the court concluded that the plaintiff, although not in privity of contract with the defendant, had the right to sue him.

The movement to abandon the privity doctrine swept the United States, so that by 1967 most states no longer required privity of contract in negligence cases. Thus, product manufacturers are now subjected to numerous law suits by users of their products, alleging that those products are defective in either design or manufacture.

Architects and engineers are also not immune to such suits. They too can be sued by persons with whom they had no contract. For instance, in a 1959 Rhode Island federal court case, the court determined that an architect was liable for injuries to the patron of a race track club house who was injured when a heating duct fell upon him. The plaintiff showed that the architect had been negligent because his design provided that the duct be attached on hangers on a ⅞-inch thick ceiling panel and not to joists.[15] However, the courts of some states have not completely abandoned the doctrine of privity. In an Illinois case, the court held that the purchasers of condominium units and the condominium association could not sue the architects and engineers who designed the building, since those professionals had contracted with the developer, not with the individuals or the association.[16] The courts of other states, however, have held that condominium purchasers can sue the architects and engineers even though no in privity of contract existed.

Breach of Duty

After being instructed by the judge on the standard of conduct established by the law, the jury retires to the jury room to determine whether the defendant breached any legal duty owed to the plaintiff. In his closing argument to the jury, the plaintiff's counsel stresses that the defendant's actions did not conform to the required standards, whereas the defendant's attorney argues that the defendant's actions did not breach the legal duty or duties owed to the plaintiff. By reaching a decision on this point, the jury determines whether the defendant is guilty or not guilty, the most important function of the jury in a negligence case.

Proximate Cause

Obviously, a defendant in a lawsuit, even though negligent, should not be held liable if his negligence did not harm the plaintiff. The courts have wrestled with this seemingly simple concept, referred to as "proximate cause," for years. They have had difficulty defining this concept and handling problems of intervening cause or cases in which more than one person has caused injury to the plaintiff. The courts have handled this problem using a two-step analysis. First, they must determine whether the defendant's action or failure to act did harm the plaintiff. Usually, this determination is made by the jury because it is a question of fact. Second, the courts must determine whether the defendant should be held responsible for the injury. This is a question of law, decided by the judge, often involving questions of public policy.

As part of the first step of the analysis, many courts have adopted a "natural and probable consequences" test. This states that a proximate cause is any cause "which in natural and continuous sequence, unbroken by any efficient intervening cause, produces the injury complained of and without which the result would not have occurred."[17] To define proximate cause more clearly, some courts have used the "but for" test, which means that in order for the action or failure to act to be the proximate cause of the injury, the injury would not have occurred "but for" the negligence of the defendant. However, this simple definition does not cover cases in which two or more causes may have resulted in the harm. Thus, some courts have adopted the "substantial factor" test, which means that the negligence of the defendant must be a substantial factor in the cause of the injury.

In cases where the independent negligence of two (or more) defendants has been the cause of the plaintiff's injury, both (or all) defendants may be held jointly liable. As an example, if a person leaves his keys in his car's ignition and another person steals the car and has an accident that injures a third party, the person who left the keys in the ignition and the car thief can both be held liable.[18]

The defendant is usually not liable if there is a "intervening cause" between his act of negligence and the harm to the plaintiff. For instance, in one case, the plaintiff sued the owner of a parking garage and the architect who designed the garage when he was injured while in a "runaway" car which crashed through a wall and landed on the street. The court held that the runaway car was an intervening cause and that the architect and garage owner could not be held liable, even though the wheel curb may not have been designed properly.[19]

Contributory Negligence

If the negligence of the plaintiff may have caused or contributed to his injury, the defendant may not be held liable even though his negligence was also a cause of injury to the plaintiff. The doctrine of "contributory negligence" implies that the plaintiff himself should have followed certain standards of care for his own protection, as any reasonable man would.

As an example, the plaintiff, a pedestrian, may not be looking when the defendant, while driving a car, backs into him. In the suit, the plaintiff would contend that the defendant was negligent, whereas the defendant could argue that the plaintiff had been negligent for not keeping a proper lookout for traffic.

In many states, contributory negligence is an affirmative defense which must be raised and proved by the defendant. In other states, the plaintiff bears the burden of showing that he was free from negligence.

Comparative Negligence

Under the doctrine of contributory negligence, even if the plaintiff is only slightly negligent, the defendant may be found not guilty. Hence, in recent years, the concept of "comparative negligence" has been developed. Using this concept, the jury weighs the negligence of the plaintiff and the defendant, and may reduce the award of damages by the degree of the plaintiff's negligence. Comparative negligence has been adopted in many states by legislation and in a few states by court decision.

Some states have adopted either the concept of "pure" or "modified" comparative negligence. Under the pure comparative negligence theory, the plaintiff's recovery is diminished by the degree of his negligence. Thus, if the plaintiff's negligence was 40% of the cause of his damages, the damages should be reduced by 40%. Under the modified form of comparative negligence, adopted in Wisconsin, Colorado, Hawaii, Idaho, Minnesota, North Dakota, Oklahoma, Utah, and Wyoming, the plaintiff may not recover anything if his negligence is equal to or greater than that of the defendant.

Nebraska and South Dakota have adopted a third form of comparative negligence referred to as "slight negligence." Under this concept, the plaintiff may recover only when his negligence is slight compared to that of the defendant.

Contribution

Many states, primarily by legislation, have adopted the doctrine of "contribution" among defendants. Prior to the acceptance of this doctrine, if two or more defendants were found negligent and the negligence of each was the proximate cause of the plaintiff's injury, the jury could not apportion the damages between or among them.

For instance, the plaintiff in a product liability case may show that his injuries were caused by a component of the product which was negligently designed or manufactured by a vendor of the manufacturer. Further, he may prove that the manufacturer negligently tested or inspected the component. Under such circumstances, the jury could find both the vendor and the manufacturer guilty. In doing so, it could only find them jointly and severally liable and could not allocate the damages between them. Thus, they would be jointly liable to the plaintiff for the full amount of his damages, as found by the jury. Moreover, each would be severally or individually liable, so that the plaintiff could collect the entire amount of his damages from one of them. Further, the party who paid the entire amount of the damages could not recover from the party who had not paid anything. Under the doctrine of contribution, the jury determines the degree of negligence of each defendant and the damages are apportioned accordingly. As a corollary, a defendant who must pay all or part of the damages may seek a contribution from other persons whose negligence may have caused the plaintiff's injuries or damages but who were not parties to the lawsuit.

ASSUMPTION OF RISK

"Assumption of risk" is another rule of law which frequently appears in negligence cases. Under this theory, the plaintiff cannot recover damages, even though the defendant may be negligent, when the plaintiff has agreed to assume the risk of injury. Assumption of risk differs from contributory or comparative negligence, since the plaintiff may not be negligent in assuming the risk. The defense of assumption of risk requires the plaintiff to be aware of the risk he is taking and to incur the risk freely. The defense of assumption of risk is often used in situations where spectators at sporting events are injured, such as by flying baseballs at baseball games or hockey pucks at hockey games.

STRICT LIABILITY

During the evolution of the doctrine of negligence, the courts still recognized a few situations in which the defendant was liable for harm to the plaintiff, even though the defendant may not have been negligent. In those situations, the law holds the defendant strictly or absolutely liable. For example, the keeper of a wild animal is absolutely liable for any injury caused by the animal to third parties, regardless of how careful he may have been in confining the animal. On the other hand, the owner of a domesticated animal is not absolutely liable for injuries caused by the animal, unless he was aware that the animal was dangerous.

The defendant may also be held strictly liable when he engages in extremely dangerous activities. In a nineteenth-century English case, the owner of a reservoir was held strictly liable for the harm caused when water broke through an abandoned mine and flowed through connecting passages into a connecting mine.[20] Thus, defendants engaged in such activities as blasting, pile driving, and storing explosives may be strictly liable for the harm caused by use or application.

The concept of strict liability has also recently been adopted in product liability cases. However, when the manufacturer or vendor of the product is sued, the plaintiff must show that there was a defect in the product's design or manufacture, which need not necessarily be proved in cases involving very hazardous activities. Strict liability in product liability cases will be discussed further in Chapter 6.

INTENTIONAL TORTS

In order for the defendant to be held liable for an intentional tort, the plaintiff must show that the defendant intended to cause the harm. The intent need not be malicious. The plaintiff must merely show that the defendant intended his actions and that his actions were voluntary.

Examples of intentional torts involving injury to the person are battery, assault, and false imprisonment. Battery involves the actual touching or striking of the plaintiff. Assault requires an action by the defendant which makes the plaintiff fearful that he may be hurt. False imprisonment occurs when the defendant, through his acts, physically restrains or, through the threat of force, inhibits the plaintiff's freedom of movement.

Intentional torts may also involve damage to the property of the plaintiff. An example is trespassing. The defendant may have cut some trees on the plaintiff's land and may thus be held liable for damages to the plaintiff. Or the defendant may take certain personal goods from the plaintiff and convert them to his own use. Under such circumstances, the plaintiff could sue the defendant for conversion.

More recently, the intentional tort of "inducing breach of contract" or "interference with contractual relations" has been adopted. In such a case, the plaintiff must show that he has a contract or other protected right with a third party, that the defendant knew of the contract or right, that the defendant intentionally induced the third party to breach it, that the defendant had no justification to do so, that the contract or right was breached by the third party, and that the defendant suffered damage.

STATUTORY LIABILITY

A consulting engineer or a product manufacturer may also be liable to third parties under special statutes. For example, an architect may be liable under certain circumstances to injured workmen under "structural work" or "scaffold" acts which have been adopted in Illinois, Missouri, and Oregon. These statutes state that if a workman is injured on the job under certain conditions, those persons in charge of the work will be liable for the injuries, even though they themselves were not negligent. Thus, if the architect is held to be a person in charge of the work, he may be liable for injuries sustained by an injured workman.

RESPONDEAT SUPERIOR

The doctrine of *respondeat superior* holds that a master is liable for the acts of his servant done within the scope of his employment. Similarly, a principal is responsible for the acts of his agent done within the scope of his authority. The reasoning behind this doctrine is that the master or principal is deriving benefit from the work of his servant or agent.

A typical example of the application of this doctrine is in an accident involving a truck and a car. If the truck driver is an employee of the truck owner and his negligence has harmed someone in the car, the truck owner can be held liable for damages to the injured third person. Moreover, since the truck driver was negligent, he too can be held liable.

In order for the courts to apply the doctrine of *respondeat superior,* there must be an employment or agency relationship, with or without compensation. If the employer has the right to control the employee or agent, the relationship of employer and employee or principal and agent is established. However, the employee or agent must be acting within the scope of his employment at the time of the occurrence. If he is engaged in a "lark," the principal or employer is not liable.

An employee may also be a "loaned servant," that is, he may be loaned by his employer to another employer. Under such circumstances, the employer who loaned him is not liable for his acts. However, the employer who is receiving the benefit of his work may be held liable, since the borrower is responsible for supervising the employee.

The doctrine of *respondeat superior* does not apply to "independent contractors." An independent contractor is a person who does a job for another, but the employer has no right to direct the method of doing the work. Frequently, construction contractors or subcontractors are independent contractors and the person who employs them is not responsible for their negligence or intentional torts. However, there are exceptions to this rule. For example, if the employer does not exercise due care in selecting the independent contractor, he may become liable for the contractor's acts.

BREACH OF WARRANTY

A plaintiff who has been injured or whose property has been damaged by the defendant may also bring an action in breach of warranty to recover damages. Such an action is for breach of contract, not for tort or negligence.

Breach of warranty actions for personal injury or property damage are brought against sellers or manufacturers of products. Such suits are based upon a breach of either an express or an implied warranty. An "express warranty" is a statement by the seller or manufacturer that the product will conform to certain requirements. An "implied warranty" is a warranty implied by the law.

Under the Uniform Commercial Code, which governs the sale of goods in all states except Louisiana, a seller of goods as a matter of law impliedly warrants that they are "merchantable." Under certain circumstances, the seller may also impliedly warrant that the goods are fit for a particular purpose. However, as discussed in Chapter 9, both of these implied warranties can be disclaimed by the seller.

To be "merchantable," the goods must meet certain standards, such as fitness for ordinary use. In addition, if the merchant or manufacturer knows how the goods will be used, he may also be liable for a breach of the implied warranty of fitness for a particular purpose if the product does not perform the function for which it was purchased.

Although ordinarily the only person who can sue for breach of contract is a party of the contract, prior to the adoption of the Uniform Commercial Code the courts generally negated the doctrine of privity in breach of warranty cases involving personal injury and property damage. Thus, in many states, a subsequent purchaser or user of a product was allowed to file a breach of warranty action directly against the seller or manufacturer. The Uniform Commercial Code, as adopted by most states, has also abandoned the requirement of privity for breach of warranty actions. We will discuss this aspect of the doctrine of privity in further detail in Chapter 9.

REMEDIES

The plaintiff's remedy for the injury he has suffered due to a tort is to recover money damages from the defendant. If the plaintiff has been personally injured, he is entitled to recover his expenses, lost income, future lost income, and money for his pain and suffering.

The plaintiff can recover the cost of medical treatment, nursing, hospital services, drugs, and other medical expenses. In most states, he can recover those sums even though they have been paid for by another person, such as his employer or a group medical insurance company. He is also entitled to recover the wages and income he lost while recuperating or receiving medical treatment. Further, if his future income is reduced due to the injuries, he is entitled to receive the present value of the lost future income. In addition, he is entitled to receive payment for any pain and suffering he sustained due to the injuries he received. Moreover, any payments the plaintiff may have received (for example, workman's compensation payments) normally are not considered to be a deduction from the amount of damages awarded to him.

The defendant is also liable to the estate or personal representative of a person whose death may have resulted from his negligence. In common law, when a person died, any action he may have had for personal injury died with him. Most states have now adopted statutes which allow an action for injuries prior to death to be prosecuted in a lawsuit by the personal representative of the deceased. These statutes are known as "survival acts."

Further, in common law, when a person was killed through the negligence of another, his family had no right to sue the defendant for the loss due to his death. All states have now enacted "wrongful death acts" which permit the personal representative of a deceased person to sue for such loss.

Under survival acts, the personal representative may usually recover damages sustained by the deceased prior to his death, such as expenses for medical treatment and lost earnings.

There are two methods of computing damages under wrongful death acts. Some acts only allow the personal representative to recover for the loss of support to the family of the deceased. Others allow recovery of the lost income of the deceased for the remainder of his life.

In property damage cases where the property has been destroyed, the plaintiff ordinarily is entitled to receive the value of the property at the time of destruction. When the property merely is damaged, the plaintiff is entitled to recover the difference between the value of the property just before and just after the occurrence. However, if the property may be repaired, the plaintiff is only entitled to recover the reasonable cost of repair, along with the difference between the value of the property before the damage and after the repair. In no event is a plaintiff entitled to recover more than the difference between the value of the property just before and just after the occurrence. Further, if the plaintiff is entitled to recover the cost of repair, he is also entitled to recover damages for loss of the use of the property while it is being repaired.

Normally, once the court finds the defendant guilty and awards the plaintiff monetary damages, the defendant must pay interest on the judgment according to a rate set by statute until the judgment is paid. In many states, the plaintiff is not entitled to receive any interest on the amount of damages before the judgment is entered, but in an increasing number of states he is allowed such prejudgment interest as a part of his damages.

The plaintiff is not entitled to recover his attorney's fees as part of his damages. The traditional American law is that neither litigant is entitled to recover the attorney's fees. Under English law, however, the winner of the case may recover reasonable attorney's fees from the loser.

Punitive damages may also be awarded in certain cases. In intentional tort cases, the plaintiff generally is entitled to receive them. In ordinary negligence cases, the plaintiff usually does not receive punitive damages, unless he is able to show that the defendant was "grossly negligent" or that his negligence was "willful and wanton."

NOTES

1. W. L. Prosser, *Handbook of the Law of Torts*, 4th ed. (St. Paul, Minn.: West, 1971), 2.
2. Illinois Supreme Court Committee on Jury Instructions, *Illinois Pattern Jury Instructions*, 2d ed. (St. Paul, Minn.: West, 1971), 53.
3. *Coombs v. Beede*, 89 Me. 187, 188, 36 A. 104, 105 (1896).
4. *City of Mounds View v. Walijarvi*, 263 N.W. 2d 420, 424 (Minn. 1978).
5. *Seaman Unified School Dist. v. Casson Constr. Co.*, 3 Kan. App. 2d 289, 594 P.2d 241 (1979).
6. *Seiler v. Levitz Furniture Co* ., 367 A.2d 999 (Del. Super. 1976).
7. *Smith v. Uniroyal, Inc.*, 420 F. 2d 438 (7th Cir. 1970).
8. *Hyatt v. Hyster Co.*, 106 F.Supp. 676 (S.D.N.Y. 1952), *rev'd by stip.*, 205 F2d 421 (2d Cir. 1953).
9. *Brook v. Allis-Chalmers Mfg. Co.*, 163 Cal.App.2d 410, 329 P.2d 575 (1958).
10. Louis R. Frumer and Melvin I. Friedman, *Products Liability*, Vol. 1A, §§7.01 and 7.02 (New York: Matthew Bender, originally published 1960, last updated 1984).
11. *McCollum v. Grove Mfg. Co.*, 58 N.C. App. 283, 293 S.E. 2d 632 (1982), *aff'd.*, 307 N.C. 695, 300 S.E.2nd 374 (1983).
12. *Winterbottom v. Wright*, 10 Meeds 109, 152 Eng. Reprint 403 (1842).
13. *Huset v. J.I. Case Threshing Machine Co.*, 120 F. 865, 870 (8th Cir. 1903).
14. 217 N.Y. 382, 111 N.E. 1050 (1916).
15. *Pastorelli v. Associated Engineers, Inc.*, 176 F.Supp. 159 (D.C. R.I. 1959).
16. *Waterford Condominium Assoc. v. Dunbar*, 104. Ill.App.3d 371, 432 N.E.2d 1009 (1982), *disagreed with, Minton v. Richards Group*, 116 Ill. App.3d 852, 452 N.E.2d 835 (1983).
17. James A. Dooley, *Modern Tort Law: Liability and Litigation*, Vol. 1, §8.02 (Wilmette, Ill: Callaghan 1982), 226–227.
18. *Ibid.*, §§8.04, 234.
19. *Minor v. Zidell Trust*, 618 P.2d 392 (Okla. 1980).
20. *Fletcher v. Rylands*, 3 H. & C. 774, 159 Eng. Rep. 737 (1865), *rev'd.*, L.R. 1 Ex. 265 (1865), *aff'd.*, L.R. 3 H.L. 330 (1868).

3
The Consulting Engineer in Construction: Legal Liability for Negligence

In Chapter 2, we briefly considered the liability for negligence of engineers working as consulting design professionals in the construction industry and of manufacturers for the defective design or manufacture of products. In this chapter, we will discuss in further detail the legal liability of the engineer working in construction for negligence in rendering, or failing to render, professional services, usually services related to design or on-site observation.

The engineer working in construction may be liable not only for his negligence, but also for damages to the plaintiff under other theories of law. Among these other bases of liability are (1) contract, (2) statutory, (3) agency, (4) warranty, (5) negligent misrepresentation, and (6) fraud. In the next chapter, these and other theories are discussed. In Chapter 5, we will consider specific situations commonly faced by the consulting construction engineer and problems pertaining to the proof of damages, statutes of limitations, and licensing of engineers. Then, in Chapter 6, we will consider theories of law under which a manufacturer may be held liable for producing and selling a defective product.

In Chapter 2 we listed the four elements which the plaintiff must prove in a legal action for negligence in order for the defendant to be found guilty or liable. Those four are:

1. A duty owed by the engineer to the plaintiff to conform to a certain standard of conduct as established by the law.
2. A breach of legal duty by the engineer.
3. A causal connection between the breach of duty and the injuries sustained by the plaintiff.
4. Damage suffered by the plaintiff.

We also pointed out in Chapter 2 that the engineer is liable only for his failure to render services in accordance with the applicable standards of his profession. He is not a guarantor of the result of his design or other work.

LIABILITY FOR NEGLIGENCE

Historically, the architect played the role of "master builder." Not only did he design a building, he also supervised its construction. Accordingly, ancient law provided severe penalties for the master builder in the event of a tragic result. For example, under the Babylonian Code of Hammurabi, the master builder could be put to death if a collapse caused the death of the householder.[1] Similarly, Roman law provided for "like-for-like" punishment.

Eventually, as the law became more humane, such severe penalties no longer were mandated. However, for a period of time, architects and engineers were held absolutely liable for failures. For instance, the Napoleonic Code provided that if a building collapsed, due in whole or in part to the poor workmanship of an architect or other workman, the architect or workman should bear the loss.[2]

As time progressed and the roles of architect and builder became more distinct, the English and American courts gradually developed a body of law which no longer held an architect absolutely liable for the results of his design. By the late nineteenth century, the courts reasoned that the professional duty owed by an architect to his client was the same as that owed by a lawyer to his client or a physician to his patient. An architect or engineer was expected to render professional services only in accordance with the skill and ability of those ordinarily skilled in his profession.

In a landmark decision, the Supreme Court of Maine in 1896 declared:

> The responsibility resting on an architect is essentially the same as that which rests on the lawyer to his client, or upon the physician to his patient, or rests on anyone to another where such person pretends to possess some skill and ability in some special employment, and offers his services to the public on account of his fitness to act in the line of business for which he may be employed. The undertaking of an architect implies that he possesses skill and ability, including taste, sufficient to

enable him to perform the required services at least ordinarily and reasonably well; and that he exercise and apply, in the given case, his skill and ability, his judgment and taste, reasonably and without neglect. But the undertaking does not imply or warrant a satisfactory result.[3]

In a more recent case, the U.S. Court of Appeals noted:

An architect is not a guarantor or an insurer but as a member of a learned and skilled profession he is under the duty to exercise the ordinary, reasonable technical skill, ability and competence that is required of an architect in a similar situation; and if by reason of a failure to use due care under the circumstances, a foreseeable injury results, liability accrues.[4]

Frequently, negligence actions against engineers for professional liability are referred to as "malpractice" suits or cases. Professional negligence or malpractice may result from a single act or omission or from a series of actions or omissions. When deciding whether an engineer has committed malpractice, the court is not concerned with his general competence or creative ability. The court is concerned with a specific situation, and in that situation it attempts to determine whether the engineer rendered his services with the same skill and care as those similarly skilled in the relevant area of engineering.

The concept of using professional standards in determining whether the engineer has breached the duty of care he owes the plaintiff in a lawsuit has been criticized. In negligence cases involving the ordinary man, such as automobile accidents, the conduct of the defendant is considered in terms of a standard of care based upon how the hypothetical "prudent man" would act in the same situation. However, the standard of care applied to an engineer in a malpractice case is the average conduct of other engineers. Moreover, the standard of care is based in part upon the conduct of the engineer's peers in the locality where the alleged malpractice occurred. Thus, some commentators have noted that the defendant in a simple automobile accident is held to a higher standard of conduct than an engineer in a complicated construction disaster case. Those commentators have been particularly critical of the use of an average standard of care in cases involving professionals when they are retained by laymen because of their expertise.[5] However, in a professional liability case, the conduct of the engineer is judged in light of the conduct of similarly skilled engineers, usually those who have many years of education and experience. Thus, this criticism of the use of an average standard of care for professionals may not be justified.

Contract versus Negligence

In the next chapter, we will discuss the legal liability of the engineer for breach of contract. However, in malpractice cases where the client has entered into a contract with the engineer, either verbally or in writing, the courts have wrestled for years with the issue of whether the party with whom the engineer has contracted, usually the owner, must sue for breach of contract or for negligence if he has been damaged because of the engineer's allegedly defective services. This question is important because the answer determines the proof the client must provide for the court to find the engineer liable and determines which defenses may be available to the engineer. Thus, the client may wish to sue for breach of contract, and not for negligence, preferring to argue that the engineer had a contract to furnish plans and specifications which were not defective and contending that the engineer warranted or guaranteed that they would not be defective. The client may then argue that the engineer had guaranteed that the plans and specifications were not defective, and that if they were, there is no need for the client to show that the engineer violated a professional standard of care. Further, the client may wish to present a breach of contract case instead of a negligence case in order to avoid the defense of contributory or comparative negligence, which would be available to the engineer in a negligence suit.

Initially, American courts permitted the owner to recover damages from the engineer for either negligence or breach of contract. However, they have now basically limited the suit to one of negligence. Of course, when the engineer by contract has broadened his traditional standard of care, resulting in a more inclusive warranty, the courts have allowed the owner to sue for breach of contract.

In many states, where the engineer has not given such a broad warranty, the owner is limited to a suit for negligence. In some states, the courts allow the owner to sue for either breach of contract or negligence, but in both situations they require the owner to show that the engineer breached a professional standard of care which was the proximate result of the damage. Thus, in a breach of contract case, the breach is the failure of the engineer to render services in accordance with the applicable standards of care.

The Oregon courts have recently considered the problem of whether a malpractice case is really a suit for breach of contract or for negligence. They have determined that in medical malpractice actions the courts must look to the "substance of the action" to determine whether the plaintiff is suing for breach of contract or for negligence. Thus, although the plaintiff seeks recovery for damages due to breach of contract in a liability suit against an engineer, the Oregon courts apply the negligence law in determining whether the engineer is guilty.[6]

Most American courts which have considered this problem are in accord with the Oregon courts and require the plaintiff, even in a breach of contract case, to show that the engineer violated an applicable standard of care, absent a broader warranty in the contract between them. In such a suit, the engineer can use the usual defenses in a negligence case.

Traditionally, the architect or engineer working in construction performs certain functions during each phase of the project. First, he provides plans and specifications. Second, he observes the progress of the construction. This involves on-site observation to determine whether the contractor is following his plans and specifications. Third, the architect or engineer frequently certifies payment requests made by the contractor. In performing each of those tasks, the architect or engineer ordinarily is liable to the owner only if he violates an applicable standard of care.

SOURCES OF STANDARD OF CARE

Throughout the discussion of professional engineers working in construction, we will refer to standards of care. The sources of those standards are (1) community practice, (2) government standards, (3) industry standards, (4) statutes and regulations, and (5) judicial decisions.

Under the law, the engineer working in construction is required to render services in accordance with the standards of professionals in the community where he practices. For example, if he is designing a roof support system for a warehouse, he is expected to use the design alternatives regularly used by other structural engineers in the community. Further, in his design, the engineer is expected to take into account local climatic and other conditions. Thus, a structural engineer practicing in many different areas of the country must be alert to the different standards of practice for each area. Moreover, he must be alert to changes in the design standards of the profession. As more knowledge is gained about materials and as new materials are produced, the engineer must keep abreast of these new developments, especially if they are being adopted in his community.

Various government agencies publish standards for construction materials and products with which the engineer should also be familiar. In addition, professional and trade organizations regularly publish standards of which the engineer should be aware. Groups that publish such standards include the American Society for Testing and Materials, the American Standards Institute, the American Concrete Institute, and the American Society of Heating, Refrigerating and Air-Conditioning Engineers.

Engineers must also be cognizant of local building codes, as well as pertinent statutes and regulations. Many communities have adopted the Uniform Building Code. In such communities, the engineer must be aware not only of the requirements of the code, but also of the local amendments to it. Moreover, the engineer must be aware of zoning ordinances, fire codes, health codes, and other codes.

Generally, the courts consider compliance with relevant codes as a minimum standard expected of the engineer. However, professional standards in many communities often require a specific design to exceed these requirements. Further, the courts usually hold that if the engineer's design has violated a specific code provision, negligence is presumed.

Finally, court decisions may also be a source of standards of practice.[7]

FORM OF BUSINESS ORGANIZATION AND LIABILITY

Engineers may form sole proprietorships, partnerships, or corporations. In addition, they may form joint ventures with architects or other engineers. The form of business adopted by the engineer determines which member(s) of the firm may be liable to the owner or other parties if professional negligence has occurred.

In a sole proprietorship, one engineer practices either under his own name or another name. He may have employees. A sole proprietor is liable not only for his own professional negligence, but also for the malpractice of his employees. Thus, not only can the plaintiff recover damages from the investment of the sole proprietor in his business, but he may also be able to recover from the personal assets of the proprietor, such as his house, car, stocks and bonds, and other property.

In a partnership, two or more engineers form a business and act as co-owners. Many states have adopted the Uniform Partnership Act, which sets forth not only the rules concerning formation and dissolution of partnerships, but also the liability of the partners. Generally, all partners are personally liable if the partnership has committed malpractice. Thus, as with a sole proprietorship, if the partnership is found guilty, the plaintiff may collect not only from the business assets, but also from the personal assets of the partners. For instance, if one partner or an employee of the partnership is working on a project with which none of the other partners are involved, and this person commits malpractice, all the partners may be held liable for any damage caused.

A corporation is a business entity formed under the laws of a specific state. The owners invest capital in a corporation and receive in return shares of stock in the corporation. Depending upon the law of the state, engineers may form a corporation either under the general business corporation law or under a special professional corporation act. In either event, the main advantage of a corporation is that it affords the owners limited liability for the debts of the corporation. Usually, if the plaintiff recovers a judgment against the corporation, he can recoup his losses only from the assets of the corporation, and not from the personal assets of any of the shareholders. Thus, if one of the shareholders or an employee commits malpractice, the owners' liability is limited to their investment in the business. However, if one of the owners himself committed the professional error, not only may the corporation but also he personally may be held liable. Thus, his personal assets could be collected in a judgment, assuming he was the defendant in the lawsuit and was found personally guilty. The assets of the other shareholders who were not found personally guilty would not be subject to collection, although they would risk losing all or part of their investment if a judgment was entered against the corporation.

Employees of either a sole proprietorship, a partnership, or a corporation may also be personally liable for their professional error. Even though a structural engineer may be an employee of a corporation, if he commits a professional error that causes damage to a client of a corporation or another person, he, along with the corporation, may be held personally liable.

A joint venture essentially is a partnership in which two or more professional firms agree to provide services to a client. However, a joint venture is usually limited to a specific project. Since a joint venture is a partnership, each co-venturer firm is liable for the malpractice of any of the other co-venturers, in addition to its own.

DEFENSES IN NEGLIGENCE ACTIONS

In a negligence action for malpractice, the owner must show that the engineer breached a relevant standard of practice which resulted in damage to the owner. In addition, third parties who sue the engineer for malpractice bear the same burden. In such a suit, some of the more common defenses of the engineer are as follows:

1. The engineer is not a guarantor of the result.
2. The engineer owes no duty to the plaintiff.
3. The plaintiff's action is barred by the plaintiff's contributory negligence, or his recovery should be reduced by the doctrine of comparative negligence.
4. The plaintiff's suit is barred because the plaintiff assumed a certain risk.
5. The engineer reasonably relied upon information furnished by others in doing his design, and this information was not accurate.
6. The engineer does not control the methods of construction.
7. Defective work done by a contractor was concealed from the engineer during on-site observation.
8. The contract deviated from the engineer's plans and specifications.
9. The alleged error or omission of the engineer was not the proximate cause of the damage.
10. The engineer's decisions made during construction are covered by "quasi-judicial immunity."
11. Certain of the engineer's decisions were made as the agent of the owner.

12. The engineer, by law, had to comply with a statute.
13. The engineer could not perform due to the illegality of the contract.
14. The engineer doing certain work in the public sector is immune to suits brought against the state.
15. The plaintiff has either waived or is stopped from bringing the suit.
16. The engineer has received a release from the plaintiff.
17. The plaintiff and the engineer have entered into an accord and are satisfied.
18. The action of the plaintiff is barred by a prior judgment.
19. The engineer cannot be responsible for what occurred because the damage was due to an "act of God."

There are other defenses frequently used in malpractice actions, which will be discussed in Chapter 5. They state that a reasonable cost of repair due to the alleged malpractice is less than the cost of repair actually incurred by the owner or third-party plaintiff, or that the owner or third-party plaintiff, in repairing the damage, is not entitled to reimbursement or costs which resulted in betterment. Still another defense is that the lawsuit is barred by the statute of limitations.

Engineer not a Guarantor

Under professional liability law, an engineer is not a guarantor of a result. His only responsibility is to render services in accordance with the applicable standards of his profession. As an example, an engineer was sued in a Louisiana court for negligent design of a foundation piling which was displaced due to latent unstable soil conditions. When the engineer first learned of the problem, he redesigned the project, relying upon a floating concrete slab foundation. The contractor advised against the redesign, stating that the slab would settle. However, prior to doing the redesign, the engineer had undertaken an investigation and had contacted other engineers for advice. Unfortunately, after the corrective work was done, the floating concrete slab did sink. All the experts who testified stated that the engineer had met the applicable standard of care in the design and that the settlement was unpredictable. Accordingly, the court found the engineer not guilty.[8]

In another design case, an architect had done the plans for a sliding roof panel, which did not work. The court concluded that the architect had not violated any professional standards, was not an insurer of a result, and was not guilty.[9]

In an earlier case, an architect failed to observe that the contractor had not driven pilings steeply enough for a bridge abutment. The architect, who was employed to observe the progress of construction, had been present when the pilings were driven and had been assured by the contractor's workmen that they were deep enough. The court held that the architect had exercised the necessary degree of professional care and found him not guilty.[10]

Thus, so long as the engineer uses the same degree of skill used by other local engineers, he is not liable for an unsatisfactory result. Of course, an engineer may become liable for an unsatisfactory result if he has made a contract guaranteeing a result or has told the owner, either in writing or verbally, that he will guarantee it.

Lack of Privity

An engineer who is a defendant in a lawsuit may argue that he owed no duty to the plaintiff. Historically, the courts have referred to this as a "privity" defense. Under this doctrine, the plaintiff can recover damages only if he can show that he was in privity with the engineer, that is, that he had a contract with him.

As discussed in Chapter 2, the courts have gradually abandoned the defense of privity, starting with product liability cases early in the twentieth century. After World War II, the courts started limiting an engineer's right to use the privity defense. New York was apparently the first state to retract the doctrine of privity as a defense for architects. In a 1957 case, the New York Court of Appeals held that it no longer applied to them.[11] Shortly thereafter, many other states abandoned the doctrine of privity as applied to architects and engineers.

Many early design cases in which the doctrine of privity was rejected involved personal injuries. As an example, a Rhode Island federal court in 1959 declared that an architect could be held liable for injuries to a race track clubhouse patron when a heating duct fell upon him. In that case, the court noted that the duct was attached by hangers to a 7/8-inch ceiling, not to joists.[12] In a subsequent case, a prospective tenant recovered for the loss of profits due to a floor settling because the architect failed to analyze subsoil conditions properly.[13] Contractors and subcontractors have also been allowed to sue architects and engineers when design errors or delays have resulted in increased construction costs or delay damages to the contractor. In other cases, courts have held that an architect or engineer may be liable to a lender for an error in certifying payment to contractors and condominium purchasers, even though the contract is with the developer.

However, the defense of privity may still be used in some states. In North Carolina, a subcontractor cannot sue an engineer for negligence because of the engineer's failure to comply with the contract documents.[14] In Louisiana, a federal trial court held that a contractor who suffered damage due to the alleged errors in plans prepared by an architect could not recover from the architect. Further, he could not recover for damages due to the architect's failure to issue change orders and to deliver timely plans.[15] And in a recent Illinois case, the court held that a condominium association and purchaser of a condominium could not sue the architects and engineers for alleged errors in the building design since neither of them had contracts with the professionals. The professionals' contracts had been with the developer.[16]

In general, however, the doctrine of privity has been abandoned, or nearly abandoned, in most, if not all states. Occupants, workmen, contractors, and other third parties who are injured due to negligent design or the negligent rendering of other services by an engineer may sue him for damages proximately caused by the engineer's negligence.

Contributory and Comparative Negligence

The contributory or comparative negligence of the plaintiff is another defense which may be used by an engineer defending a malpractice case. As discussed in Chapter 2, the plaintiff's contributory negligence traditionally barred his recovery for damages. Recently, many states have adopted the doctrine of comparative negligence. Under this doctrine, the plaintiff's recovery is not entirely barred, but his damages are reduced in proportion to his degree of negligence.

Although contributory negligence of the plaintiff may be used as a defense, it is rarely successful. There are only a few reported appellate cases discussing the use of this defense by either an architect or an engineer.

In a 1913 California case, the court held that an owner could not recover for construction costs which exceeded the architect's estimate when the owner went ahead with the project after he became aware that the construction costs would exceed the budget.[17]

In a 1969 Louisiana case, the contractor had cross-claimed against an architect after being sued by an owner for the failure of a roofing system. The architect had specified the system, but only after being asked to do so by the contractor, who assured the architect that the system would be adequate. The court refused to allow the contractor to recover from the architect.[18]

Assumption of Risk

Assumption of risk, also discussed in Chapter 2, is another defense which may be used by the architect or engineer working in construction. This may happen when the owner has selected one of several design alternatives after the architect or engineer has explained the risk involved in using each of them. Frequently, an owner may choose the alternative that has the least construction cost, despite the risks involved.

This defense may also be important to the engineer when he specifies new products or construction methods. If the engineer has adequately explained to the owner the risks involved in their use, and has stated that unknown hazards may occur, he may be able to use the defense of assumption of risk by the owner if there is a subsequent problem with the product or method of construction.

A prime example of the successful use of this defense occurred in the 1965 Louisiana case discussed earlier in this chapter. The engineer who had designed the floating slab foundation explained to the owner the risks involved. The owner decided to use it in order to minimize construction costs. The court declared that the owner had assumed the risk and held that neither the contractor nor the engineer was liable.[19]

Justifiable Reliance

An engineer's defense in a negligence action may be that he reasonably relied upon information provided by another professional or other person for whom he had no responsibility. Even though the information may have been wrong, he performed his services in accordance with the standards of his profession, so that any resulting damage to the plaintiff due the other person is not his responsibility. In this defense, the engineer probably must show that he was not relying upon that information unreasonably or that he had no way of knowing that this information was incorrect. Further, even though the engineer who relied upon this information may not be responsible for the resulting damage, the party who furnished the information may be held liable.

For example, in construction projects, the owner frequently retains a soils engineer to furnish him and the architect with a report on existing soil conditions. Or the owner may retain other engineers for a building project, such as structural and mechanical engineers. In such situations, since the soils, structural, and mechanical engineers were directly retained by the owner, the architect is not responsible for their professional errors. Of course, if the architect has retained these engineers, he then may become responsible for their malpractice.

In a 1966 Louisiana case, an architect relied upon a topographical survey done by a consultant retained directly by the owner. The court concluded that the architect was not responsible for an erroneous survey.[20] Further, in a 1978 Florida case, the court noted that an architect usually had to prepare drawings that conformed to applicable zoning and building codes. However, where the architect reasonably relied upon the advice of the client's attorney, the architect was not held responsible for the failure of the plans to meet the codes.[21]

Construction Methods

Traditionally, an architect or engineer working in construction does not control the methods of construction. That is usually for the contractor to determine.

Most of the cases concerned with whether an architect or engineer controls the method of construction involve injuries to construction workers. Since the construction worker receives worker's compensation benefits from his employer, he is barred in most states from filing an action against the employer for negligence. If he has been seriously injured, the worker's compensation benefits may not make him whole. As a result, injured construction workers often attempt to sue the architect or engineer, along with other contractors or subcontractors. In such cases, the attorney for the injured worker may argue that the architect or engineer was in control of the construction, was negligent, and his negligence was the proximate cause of the worker's injury.

However, standard contracts used in the construction industry usually state that the contractor, not the architect, is responsible for the method of construction. Hence, in most situations, since the architect does not control the method of construction, he owes no duty to the injured worker and cannot be held liable in a negligence case.

In a 1978 opinion, the Maryland Supreme Court reviewed the law on this subject and concluded that unless a contract placed the burden for supervision or control of the construction method on the engineer, he could not be held liable to an injured construction worker. The court noted, however, that if the engineer disregarded the contract and voluntarily assumed either supervision of the construction or responsibility for safety, that engineer might then owe a duty and could be sued for negligence by an injured worker.[22]

However, in one unusual situation, the Iowa Supreme Court in 1972 did hold an architect responsible for the results of the construction methods used by the contractor, even though the architect had no responsibility for controlling them. The architect was employed to design a new high school. During construction, the contractor diverted storm water to an adjoining property, where it entered a house. The plaintiffs had to vacate the first floor of the house because of the flooding. They complained to both the architect and the contractor, and both continued with the project. The court stated that in preparing his design, the architect had a duty to protect the adjoining property from storm water, even though the contractor was responsible for controlling storm waters during construction.[23]

In discussing statutory liability in Chapter 4 and job site safety in Chapter 5, we will again consider the circumstances in which the architect or engineer in construction may become responsible for the methods of construction.

Concealed Work

Occasionally, problems arise during a construction project because, due to the method of construction, nonconforming work done by a contractor or subcontractor has been concealed from the architect or engineer doing on-site observation. An engineer rendering on-site services during construction cannot be everyplace at once. In small projects, the architect or engineer usually is not expected to be at the job site at all times. Further, in larger projects, where the professional may have a staff of on-site observers, they cannot be everyplace at once.

The duty of the contractor is to build the project in accordance with the construction documents, which include the plans and specifications of the architect or engineer. When the architect or engineer has on-site observation duties, his job is to determine, as best he can, whether the work performed by the contractor conforms to the construction documents. Thus, defects may occur in construction which the architect or engineer has no reasonable way of discovering.

However, during construction, the engineer may be expected to observe certain critical elements. In a New York case, the architect was retained to observe construction. The contractor shortened certain floor beams and improperly attached them to cross-beams in violation of the city building code. The beams had been floored over before the architect could observe their construction. The floor then settled, causing considerable damage to the owner. The court found the architect liable because he had contractually agreed to ensure that the construction conformed to the building code.[24]

In a Minnesota case discussed earlier, the court determined that an engineer could not be held liable for his failure to discover pilings which were improperly driven. In that suit, the engineer was employed for on-site observation of the construction. The piling design required it to carry a load of fifteen tons. After the project was completed, cracks were noticed and it was determined that the piling would support loads of only seven to thirteen tons. The court, finding the engineer not liable, stated that he had observed construction two or three times a day, but he was not present when the defective piles were driven. However, he had talked to the contractor's employees, and they had assured him that the piles had been driven properly. He had no reason to doubt their reliability.[25]

Deviation from Plans

Frequently, because the contractor did not construct the project in accordance with the plans and specifications, the engineer may use the contractor's deviation as a defense, especially where the engineer had no responsibility to ensure that the construction complied with the plans and specification. Under the law, the plaintiff must show that the plans were followed by the contractor. If he cannot, he probably cannot recover from the engineer, unless the engineer had contracted to observe the progress of construction and was negligent in doing so.

In a Michigan case, a building collapsed during construction. Apparently, the builder had omitted steel called for by the plans and had extended the length of the building without advising the architect. Accordingly, the architect was found not guilty.[26] However, in a more recent Illinois case, walls had tilted and separated. The architect argued that because of the contractor's failure to follow the plans and specifications, he should not be held liable. The court rejected this argument, noting that the architect was to provide on-site observation for at least half an hour each day and stating that while doing so, he should have discovered the nonconformity.[27]

Proximate Cause

Lack of proximate cause is another defense. The engineer contends that his negligence, if any, was not the proximate cause of the plaintiff's injury or damage. For example, if the contractor did not follow the architect's plans and specifications, any malpractice of the architect in preparing them may not be the proximate cause of the plaintiff's damage. In a 1967 Florida case, a restaurant patron was injured when a counterweight became dislodged from a ceiling fan, falling upon him. Apparently, this was due to a faulty weld by the metal fabricator. The court concluded that any reasonable observation of the fan by the architect would not have disclosed the faulty weld and that the architect's conduct was not the proximate cause of the patron's injury.[28]

Quasi-Judicial Immunity

In a typical construction situation, the architect or engineer may play as many as three roles. First, he may be a consultant to the owner in preparing plans and specifications. Second, he may act as an agent of the owner in certain aspects of administration of a construction contract. Third, he may act in a quasi-judicial capacity, arbitrating disputes between the owner and the contractor. When he acts in a quasi-judicial capacity, he is immune from certain complaints of either the owner or the contractor.[29]

Usually, the contract between the owner and the contractor provides for the architect or engineer to arbitrate disputes between them in certain situations. Such provisions frequently state that the architect shall judge the quality of the contractor's work or determine whether it conforms to the contract documents. If the owner and contractor cannot agree, the contract then provides that the architect will arbitrate the dispute, assuming a quasi-judicial role.[30]

In order for an architect or engineer to use the defense of quasi-judicial immunity successfully, he must show that he was acting in his role as arbitrator, that he did not delegate his function, and that he did arbitrate. The architect is immune from suit when he resolves disputes between the owner and the contractor as stated in the contract. He must act in good faith when making his decision, and he must be arbitrating a genuine dispute.[31]

He cannot delegate his duty to arbitrate to any other persons. In one interesting case, the federal trial court for the District of Columbia noted that an architect had delegated this responsibility to two of his staff members. The court stated that the duties of design and supervision could be delegated, but not the quasi-judicial duty of arbitration.[32]

Further, if the architect or engineer fails to act as an arbitrator or does not render a decision, he is not protected by quasi-judicial immunity, because he has not met all the elements of the defense.[33] Finally, even though an architect or engineer may be able to use the defense of quasi-judicial immunity in an action brought against him in acting as an arbitrator, he is not necessarily relieved of any liability he may have for preparing defective plans or specifications.

Acting as Agent

In certain situations, the design professional may be able to defend an action brought against him by a contractor because he had been acting as the agent of the owner. Those cases typically involve situations where the contractor has settled with the owner for extra construction costs incurred by the contractor due to a defect in the plans and specifications of the architect or engineer. The contractor, after settling with the owner, may then sue the design professional. The engineer can argue that the settlement agreement encompassed his defective design and that the contractor, in settling with the owner, released the engineer from any claim the contractor has against the owner. However, the claim which the owner may have against the design professional for the defective design may not be barred.[34]

Statutory Compliance

In some situations, an engineer may be able to use the defense of statutory compliance if he was required by statute to do his design in accordance with mandated standards. In a 1970 Kentucky case, a person was killed when his car struck a bridge abutment. At the trial, the plaintiff argued that pursuant to the applicable standard of professional care, the designer should have specified a guard rail. The designer argued that under the rules of the highway department, he could not require guard rails and those rules did not allow any alternative design. Thus, the court found the designer not liable, stating that he had to comply with the mandatory regulation under such circumstances.[35]

Illegality

A contract for engineering services is unenforceable if it is illegal. In a Pennsylvania case, the architect had agreed to prepare plans for a building to house a motion picture theater along with stores and apartments. The applicable building code stated that a building used as a motion picture theater could not be used as a dwelling house. Because the architect had entered into an illegal contract, the court refused him the right to recover his fee.[36]

In recent cases, courts have held that an architect's fee for services rendered to a municipality are limited by the amount of the governmental appropriation. In one case, the architect did not recover a sum in excess of the appropriation even though an arbitrator, under an arbitration provision of the contract between the architect and the municipality, awarded the architect a sum for fees greater than the appropriation.[37] Further, the courts have held that an engineer who had obtained a contract as the result of bribing a city official cannot recover his fees, even though he has done the work.[38]

Sovereign Immunity

The doctrine of sovereign immunity has been used as a defense in actions for negligent design brought against the state and its agencies and officials, as well as consulting engineers employed by those agencies. Originally, suits against the state and design professionals employed by it were barred by the doctrine of sovereign immunity, which simply means that a citizen could not sue the state. However, a citizen could sue the state if it consented to being sued.

The doctrine of immunity, however, has been attacked in all states. Accordingly, few, if any, states still accept this doctrine in its pure form, which would bar suits by citizens of the state under all circumstances.

The strongest attacks against the doctrine of sovereign immunity have come from cases where persons have been bodily injured due to a negligent act of a state employee. For instance, state courts have wrestled for years with the issue of whether a person who was injured in an automobile accident with a state vehicle could sue the driver and the state for his injuries. Gradually, through court decisions and legislation, various states abrogated much of the doctrine of sovereign immunity. However, the status of sovereign immunity varies according to the state and it is difficult, if not impossible, to summarize the situation for each state in a few pages.

In cases involving consulting engineers retained by state agencies, one of the primary distinctions drawn is whether the engineer is performing "discretionary" or "ministerial" functions. Under this distinction, consultants who are acting in a discretionary manner are not liable for damages resulting from an error in selecting various alternatives. These cases typically involve decisions made during the design stage. However, consultants retained by a state agency who are performing in a ministerial capacity can be held liable for negligence. Those cases involve instances in which the consultant is implementing a policy or design which has already been decided.[39]

Some states have granted, by special statute, immunity to government employees working as design professionals. In California, government employees are not responsible for approving designs for improvements in public property. In Connecticut, they cannot be held personally liable for damages they may cause when acting within the scope of their employment. In New Jersey, they are not liable for negligent inspections. In Arizona, the state and its employees are immune from suit for damages resulting from dam failures.[40] Many states, however, have rejected the doctrine of sovereign immunity in suits filed against state agencies or their consulting engineers for professional malpractice.[41]

Waiver and Estoppel

Waiver and estoppel are two other defenses which may be successfully used by an engineer in a malpractice suit. "Waiver" is an abandonment of a right. For example, one party to a contract may voluntarily decide not to enforce a provision of it. Hence, he is said to have waived the provision. "Estoppel" is similar to waiver, except that the conduct of one party has caused harm to the other party. Accordingly, the party whose action has caused the harm is "estopped" from enforcing a particular provision of a contract.

The doctrine of waiver frequently appears in change order situations. Contracts may require written change orders to be approved by the owner in order for a contract or to be paid extra money for additional work. However, the change order provision is frequently ignored. For example, in a California case, the owner had demanded that the contractor use sand for a temporary surface in road construction, but then changed his mind and insisted that temporary paving be used. The contractor sued to recover damages for the extra work, which the court allowed, stating that the owner had waived the written change order provision.[42]

In another California case, a contractor argued that he had incurred extra costs due to the architect's delay in approving the change orders. The court reasoned that since the contractor had accepted the change orders without requesting additional sums due to the alleged delay in approving them, he had waived the delay claim.[43]

A Mississippi case affords a good example of the application of the doctrine of estoppel. In that case, the owner has sued an engineering firm. The suit centered on the installation of a pipe line, and there was a dispute over the amount the contractor should be paid pursuant to the contract. The contractor eventually stated that he would stop work unless the owner paid a specific sum. The engineer suggested to the owner that a lesser sum be paid. The owner then told the engineer to certify payments at the higher figure. Next, the owner sued the engineer for issuing the payment certificates. The court stated that the owner had waived his right for damages for the increased cost and was estopped from pursuing any action against the engineer.[44]

Release

The design professional may be able to use a release from the claimant as a defense against any damages due to the alleged negligence. Usually, the release is a formal document, but it can also be a signed letter or the negotiation of a check which states that it is issued in settlement of demands and claims.

Accord and Satisfaction

An "accord and satisfaction" is similar to a release. It is simply an agreement between two parties, which need not be formalized, under which one party gives up a right against the other. In exchange, the other party agrees to do something to satisfy that right. As an example, the owner may negotiate with a contractor the final settlement of a dispute which arose during a construction project. If the contractor agrees to the sum negotiated as final payment, an accord and satisfaction has resulted. In one case, the owner went as far as sending a check to the contractor with a letter noting that the check was for final payment, which the contractor cashed. The contractor then sued the owner and the court held that acceptance of the final payment was an accord and satisfaction, barring the suit.[45]

Barred by Prior Judgment

An engineer may also defend a malpractice action using the doctrine of *res judicata*. Under this legal principle, the final judgment of a court determining the rights of the parties in a lawsuit, which can be no longer appealed, are binding and cannot be relitigated in another suit.

Collateral estoppel is a variant of this defense. It holds that matters decided in one lawsuit, under certain circumstances, may not be relitigated, even though different parties may have been involved. As an example, in a Missouri case, the owner in the first suit sued a contractor for failure to install the heating, ventilation, and air conditioning (HVAC) systems and roof and for failure to grade and drain certain property pursuant to the plans and specifications of the architect. At trial, the jury found the contractor not guilty. In the second suit, the owner sued the architect for failure to observe the alleged construction deficiencies. The court stated that the owner could not retry the issues based upon faulty construction but that he could try a negligent design case, since the contractor had apparently proved in the first trial that he had done the construction in accordance with the contract. Hence, the owner could proceed against the architect for negligent design, but not for his negligence in failing to observe the construction deficiencies.[46]

Act of God

Another defense which may be used in a malpractice action brought against a design professional is the act of God defense. This defense, however, may be a variation of a defense based upon the engineer's rendering service in accordance with the generally accepted standards of the community. Such a defense may arise in cases of roof collapses due to snow loading. Many communities have records of snowfalls for only a limited number of years. Accordingly, engineers have limited information on maximum snowfalls and generally design roof support systems based upon an interpretation of the historical data. Similarly, engineers working on dam designs also have limited information on rainfalls. Moreover, design standards may require the engineer only to design for a once in 50 or 100-year maximum rainfall.

In a recent Oregon case, the appeal court stated that the trial court erred when it refused to instruct the jury that an act of God may have caused the collapse of a church building during a wind storm.[47]

Approval of Plans

One defense which design professionals occasionally attempt to use is the approval of plans by the owner, the building department, or other authorities. Generally, approval of plans by a government authority is not conclusive proof that those plans have complied with the appropriate regulations.[48] Hence, even though the building department may have reviewed the plans and failed to notice a design error, the design professional is not relieved from his responsibility to the owner for designing the building in accordance with the appropriate building codes, as well as the applicable design standards for the community.

Similarly, approval of the plans by the owner usually cannot be used as a defense.[49] However, as mentioned earlier, if the owner insists that certain alternatives be used, over the objection of the design professional, then the design professional may be relieved of responsibility for any design error mandated by the owner.

NOTES

1. C. Edwards, *The Hammurabi Code and Sinaitic Legislation*, 2d ed. (Port Washington, N.Y.: Kennikat, 1971), 65–66.
2. *Code Napoleon: Being the French Civil Code, Literally Translated from the Original and Official Edition Published in Paris in 1804*, tr. Samuel A. Richards (London: Wiley, n.d.), 490.
3. *Coombs v. Beede*, 89 Me. 187, 36 A. 104, at 104–105 (1896).
4. *Aetna Insurance Co. v. Hellmuth, Obata & Kassabaum, Inc.*, 392 F.2d 472, 476–477 (8th Cir. 1968).
5. James Acret, *Architects and Engineers*, 2d ed. (Colorado Springs, Colorado: Shepard's/McGraw-Hill, 1984), 8–10.
6. *Bales for Food, Inc. v. Poole*, 246 Or. 253, 424 P.2d 892 (Or. 1967) and *Ashley v. Fletcher*, 275 Or. 405, 550 P.2d 1385 (Or. 1976).
7. Alexander L. Brainerd and Paul J. Sanner, *Architect-Engineer Malpractice* (Federal Publications, Inc., Washington, D.C. 1980), 63–67.

8. *Pittman Construction Co. v. New Orleans*, 178 So.2d 312 (La. App. 1965), *application denied*, 248 La. 434, 179 So.2d 274 (1965).
9. *Surf Realty Corp. v. Standing*, 195 Va. 431, 78 S.E.2d 901 (1953).
10. *Cowles v. Minneapolis*, 128 Minn. 452, 151 N.W. 184 (1915).
11. *Inman v. Binghamton Housing Authority*, 3 N.Y.2d 137, 143 N.E.2d 895 (1957), *overruled, Micallef v. Miehlef Co.*, 39 N.Y.2d 376, 348 N.E.2d 571 (1976), *according to, Roberts v. MacFarland Construction Companies*, 102 App. Div.2d 981, 477 N.Y.S.2d 786 (1984).
12. *Pastorelli v. Associated Engineers, Inc.*, 176 F.Supp. 159 (D. R.I. 1959).
13. *A.E. Investment Corp. v. Link Builders, Inc.*, 62 Wis2d 479, 214 N.W.2d 764 (1974).
14. *McKinney Drilling Co. v. Nello L. Teer Co.*, 38 N.C.App. 472, 248 S.E.2d 444 (1978).
15. *C.H. Leavell & Co. v. Glantz Contracting Corp.*, 322 F.Supp. 779 (E.D. La. 1971).
16. *Waterford Condominium Ass'n v. Dunbar*, 104 Ill. App.3d 371, 432 N.E.2d 1009 (1982), *disagreed with, Minton v. Richards Group*, 116 Ill.App.3d 852, 452 N.E.2d 835 (1983).
17. *Benenato v. McDougall*, 166 Cal. 405, 135 P. 8 (1913).
18. *New Orleans Unity Society of Practical Christianity v. Standard Roofing Co.*, 224 So.2d 60 (La. App. 1969). *application denied*, 254 La. 811, 227 So.2d 146 (1969).
19. *Pittman Construction Co. v. New Orleans*, 178 So.2d 312 (La. App. 1965). *application denied*, 248 La. 434, 179 So.2d 274 (1965).
20. *Jacka v. Ouachita Parish School Board*, 249 La. 223, 186 So.2d 571 (1966).
21. *Krestow v. Wooster*, 360 So. 2d 32 (Fla. App. 1978).
22. *Krieger v. J. E. Greiner Co.*, 282 Md. 50, 382 A.2d 1069 (1978).
23. *McCarthy v. J. P. Cullen & Son Corp.*, 199 N.W.2d 362 (Iowa 1972).
24. *Straus v. Buchman*, 96 App. Div. 270, 89 N.Y.S. 226 (1904), *aff'd.*, 184 N.Y. 545, 76 N.E. 1109 (1906).
25. *Cowles v. Minneapolis*, 128 Minn. 452, 151 N.W. 184 (1915).
26. *Bayne v. Everham*, 197 Mich. 181, 163 N.W. 1002 (1917).
27. *Corbetta Construction v. Lake County Public Building Commission*, 64 Ill. App.3d 313, 381 N.E.2d 758 (1978).
28. *Mai Kai, Inc. v. Colucci*, 205 So.2d 291 (Fa. 1967).
29. *Huber, Hunt & Nichols, Inc. v. Moore*, 67 Cal. App. 3d 278, 136 Cal. Rptr. 603 (1977).
30. David C. Little, *The Architect's Immunity or Arbiter*, 23 St. Louis U. L.J. 339 (1979).
31. *Lundgren v. Freeman*, 307 F.2d 104 (9th Cir. 1962).
32. *John W. Johnson, Inc. v. Basic Construction Co.*, 292 F.Supp. 300 (D. D. Col. 1968), *aff'd.*, 429 F.2d 764 (D.C. Cir. 1970).
33. *E. C. Ernst v. Manhattan Construction Co. of Texas*, 551 F.2d 1026 (5th Cir. 1977, *rehearing granted in part*, 559 F.2d 268 (5th Cir. 1977), *cert. denied*, 434 U.S. 1067 (1978).
34. *Transpac Construction Co. V. Clark & Groff, Engineers, Inc.*, 466 F.2d 823 (9th Cir. 1977).
35. *Rigsby v. Brighton Engineering Co.*, 464 S.W.2d 279 (Ky. 1970).
36. *Medoff v. Fisher*, 257 Pa. 126, 101 A. 471 (1917).
37. *City of Marlborough v. Cybulski, Ohnemus & Associates, Inc.*, 370 Mass. 157, 346 N.E.2d 716 (1976).
38. *Manning Engineering, Inc. v. Hudson County Park Commission*, 74 N.J. 113, 376 A.2d 1194 (1977).
39. Brainard and Sanner, *Architect-Engineer Malpractice*, 148–149.
40. *Ibid.*, 149–150.
41. *Ibid.*, 149.
42. *Weeshoff Construction Co. v. Los Angeles County Flood Control District*, 88 Cal. App.3d 579, 152 Cal. Rptr. 19 (1979).

43. *Huber, Hunt & Nichols, Inc. v. Moore,* 67 Cal.App.3d 278, 136 Cal. Rptr. 603 (1977).
44. *Newton Investment Co. v. Bernard and Burk, Inc.,* 220 So.2d 822 (Miss. 1969).
45. *Cox v. City of Freeman,* 321 F.2d 887 (8th Cir. 1963).
46. *Teachers Credit Union v. Horner,* 487 F.Supp. 246 (W.D Mo. 1980).
47. *Northwestern Mutual Insurance Co. v. Peterson,* 280 Or. 773, 572 P.2d 1023 (1977), superseded by statute, *State v. Smith,* 59 Or.App. 92, 650 P.2d 178 (1982).
48. *Johnson v. Salem Title Co.,* 246 Or. 409, 425 P.2d 519 (1967).
49. Acret, *Architects and Engineers,* 175–176.

4
The Consulting Engineer in Construction: Other Theories of Legal Liability

In Chapter 3, we discussed the legal liability of the engineer working in construction for his negligence in rendering, or failing to render, professional services. We also briefly discussed many of the defenses which the design professional can use in a negligence action brought against him. In this chapter, we will consider other legal theories under which a professional engineer working in construction may be held liable. The concepts discussed in this chapter are the engineer's liability for (1) breach of contract, (2) breach of statute, (3) breach of his duty as an agent to the principal, (4) breach of warranty, (5) breach of the warranty of habitability, (6) strict liability, (7) negligent misrepresentation, (8) fraud, (9) slander, and (10) interference with contractural relations.

BREACH OF CONTRACT

In the preceding chapter, we considered whether the courts draw a distinction between actions in negligence and actions for breach of contract against the engineer for failure to render services to the client in accordance with the applicable standards of care. We noted that even though the engineer may have a contract with the client to render professional service, many courts permit the engineer to be sued only for professional negligence or malpractice. Other courts may permit a suit for breach of contract in such circumstances, but will only apply the concepts of professional negligence arising from malpractice cases.[1] However, in contracting with the client, the engineer may undertake additional duties, increasing his responsibility beyond the traditional standards of care. The engineer may then be sued for breach of contract.

Obviously, to determine whether the engineer has breached the contract, the parties, the lawyers, and the court must examine the language of the contract. The more precise the language, the easier it is for everyone to interpret the contract. Naturally, the more contingencies covered in the contract, the easier it is to interpret.

The contract may contain promises, conditions, and warranties. A "promise" is a statement by one of the parties to a contract to do, or not to do, something. A "condition" is an event which may happen only after a promise has been kept. As an example, the engineer must perform a service before he is entitled to a fee from his client. A "warranty" is a promise that a certain result will be achieved. In a contract, an engineer may warrant that he will render services in accordance with the applicable standards of his profession. Or he may give a broader warranty and state that the building designed by him will meet certain defined requirements, such as a roof that will not leak. Such an expanded warranty could create problems for the engineer in a lawsuit if the roof leaks, since the engineer may not have been responsible for the methods of construction used in installing the roof.

Whether the courts determine that the suit by the owner or client against the design professional is for breach of contract or professional negligence can be an important distinction. Many states have different statutes of limitation for breach of contract and negligence suits. In addition, some states have separate statutes for professional malpractice actions or any action against design professionals working in construction. Thus, the plaintiff may want to have his case considered a breach of contract suit to avoid application of the shorter statute of limitations period applicable to negligence or malpractice.

The plaintiff may also want the case to be considered one for breach of contract in order to prevent the use of the defense of contributory or comparative negligence by the engineer. In addition, one of the parties to the contract may want the court to consider the suit as a breach of contract case, since the breach of a contract by one party will excuse performance by the other party. Such a defense cannot necessarily be used in a malpractice case.

The courts, however, have traditionally looked upon suits against an architect or engineer as cases of professional negligence or malpractice and have generally applied negligence theories. However, when the design professional has undertaken duties beyond those traditionally taken by engineers, the courts have been more willing to look upon these suits as cases for breach of contract.

Two areas in which a design professional may expand his traditional role by contract occur in warranties and supervision. A contract may contain a warranty specifically broadening the traditional duty owed by the engineer to the client. Such warranties will be discussed in a later section of this chapter. In addition, the architect or engineer may agree in the contract to supervise construction.

In a 1968 federal court of appeals case, an architect had agreed to supervise construction. He failed to notice that certain concrete forms were not constructed properly. He also did not observe backfill tests. Unfortunately, the wall and certain pavements were defective. The court concluded that because the architect had agreed to supervise construction, he was liable for the damages due to the faulty construction for his breach of contract.[2]

Most cases in which the appellate courts have considered the design professional's duty to supervise construction have involved suits brought by injured workmen or on behalf of workmen killed during construction. Generally, the architect or engineer will not be held liable for a workman's injuries or death, unless he has agreed by contract to assume some supervisory or safety duty or has voluntarily assumed such duties during construction.[3]

Thus, the architect or engineer may be liable to suits by his client or other parties, including injured workmen, when he undertakes supervisory duties under the contract with his client.

STATUTORY LIABILITY

The design professional may also be liable for violation of a state statute, a municipal or county ordinance, or a provision of a building code. For a violation of such a law, the appropriate government body or agency may prosecute the engineer either criminally, seeking a jail sentence or a fine, or civilly, seeking censure, revocation of the engineer's license, or other relief. Moreover, a person who was injured by the engineer's violation of the law may have the right to sue the engineer in order recover damages resulting from the violation. Such suits are actions for negligence.

Generally, the violation of a statute, ordinance, or code provision intended to protect a person who has been injured by the violation is held by the courts to be negligence in itself or negligence per se. Usually, the courts state that the statute, ordinance, or code must require the person who is charged with violation of the provision to do or not do something.

As an example, some states have adopted scaffolding or structural work acts to protect the safety of workmen at the work site. The Illinois statute requires guard rails with a minimum height of 34 inches to be used upon certain scaffolds which are more than 20 feet above the ground. In a case where this provision is not met, the Illinois courts have held that the injured workman need show no more in a suit to establish the negligence of the responsible defendants.[4]

Some states have not accepted the doctrine of negligence per se in suits for violations of statutes, but instead have adopted the doctrine of prima facie negligence. Under this doctrine, a violation of the statute is presumed to be negligence unless the defendant can show a proper excuse. In those states, the plaintiff still must show a violation of the statute, but the defendant may argue that he was not negligent. For instance, the defendant may argue that the period of time between construction of the scaffold and the accident was so short that he could not have observed the condition.[5]

A few states have adopted neither the doctrine of negligence per se or prima facie negligence in suits for damages caused by a statutory violation. In those states, however, the violation may be offered as evidence of negligence by the defendant.

In a state where negligence per se has been adopted, the plaintiff need only show the statutory violation by the defendant in order for the defendant to be found negligent. In a state where the doctrine of prima facie negligence is followed, the conclusiveness of the statutory violations may be rebutted by the defendant's demonstration that he was not negligent. And in the state which holds that the statutory violation is evidence only of negligence, the jury may draw any conclusion it wishes from this violation.

In some states, a statute may also give a person a specific right to file a lawsuit. In such a situation, the states usually follow the negligence per se doctrine in applying the statute. However, the statutory language itself may create special requirements for proving the violation. Hence, in a scaffolding act case in Illinois, the injured workmen must also show that the responsible defendant knew or should have known of the violation of the statutory provision.[6]

Here are a few examples of cases which involved statutory violations. Under the Little Rock, Arkansas, building code, the owner was required to employ an architect or engineer to inspect and supervise construction. In addition, the architect or engineer had to have the authority to stop work. Under that provision of the building code, a federal court held an architect liable for the death of workmen at the construction site.[7] In an Illinois case, an architect was held responsible for damages which resulted when a wall panel he specified did not meet the Chicago fire code.[8] In a Florida case, the appellate court reversed a trial court ruling which allowed an engineer to show that he met the applicable standard of care in designing a swimming pool. Regulations of the Florida Board of Health required that gratings be placed over the swimming pool drains which could not be easily removed. The Florida appellate court declared that a violation of the regulation could not be rebutted by testimony that the engineer had rendered services in accordance with the standard of his profession.[9] In a Washington case, the court denied an architect the right to recover his fee when the building he designed was not built due to his failure to follow the applicable building codes.[10]

Therefore, the design professional working in construction not only must be alert to building code provisions which may affect the design and construction of the project, but must also be aware of statutory provisions, municipal county ordinances, and the rules and regulations of federal and state agencies which may govern design and construction.

AGENCY

Earlier, we noted that when the design professional prepares plans and specifications, he acts as an independent contractor. During the construction phase, the architect or engineer may act as an agent of the owner. When the owner becomes liable to third parties for acts of the design professional while acting as his agent, he may have the right to seek redress from the professional for breach of his duty as an agent.

Ordinarily, when an agent acts within the authority granted to him by his principal, he does not become liable to third parties when so acting unless his actions amount to a tort. In such a situation, then, the agent could be liable to the third party for the injuries or damages caused by his negligence or other tortious conduct.

Under the law of agency, if the third party has been damaged by the acts of the agent acting within the scope of his authority, the third party usually will seek redress from the principal. However, under certain circumstances, the principal may, in turn, seek to recover the sums he must pay to the third party from the agent due to breach of a duty owed by the agent to the principal.

In the ordinary construction project, the owner is the principal and the architect may act as his agent. For example, in an early Nebraska case, the court held that the owner was responsible for extra work ordered by his architect, since the architect was acting as the owner's agent.[11] In another Nebraska case, the owner was held responsible for the acts of his architect in certifying payments. The contractor had followed the plans and specifications, but unfortunately, after construction, the building settled. The architect had certified final payment. The court concluded that the architect was acting as agent of the owner and that the certificate of final payment showed that the contractor had complied with the construction documents.[12]

When the design professional is acting as the owner's agent, the owner may be liable to third parties for damages caused by the professional's negligence.[13] In a Texas case, a hotel customer was injured as a result of certain remodeling work that was being done in the hotel. The customer sued the contractor, who alleged that the negligence was that of the hotel, since the hotel's architect was unaware of a defective condition. The court concluded that the architect was the agent of the hotel, and that therefore the hotel could be responsible for the architect's negligence.[14]

Of course, the owner is not liable for the acts of an independent contractor. Usually, in the construction process, the contractor doing the construction is an independent contractor, because the owner does not control how the project will be built. Similarly, the design professional is usually looked upon as an independent contractor when preparing plans and specifications. In a Texas case, the architect had prepared the plans and specifications for a building which collapsed after construction, damaging adjoining property. The court held that the building owner was not liable, even though the plans contained defects, since the architect was acting as an independent contractor in preparing them.[15]

Of course, when the design professional employs consultants directly to assist him in rendering services to the owner, he may become liable for their negligence. This topic will be discussed further in the next chapter.

WARRANTY LIABILITY

Under the law, there are express and implied warranties. An "express warranty" is a representation by the party that work performed by him or products manufactured or sold by him will meet certain specific standards. An "implied warranty" is created when the courts or statutes imply that the party bound by the warranty owes certain duties to the other party based upon the circumstances.

A design professional may create an express warranty when he agrees, either by contract or otherwise, that the project will meet certain standards or that his design will achieve a specific result. Some authorities state that all architects and engineers owe an implied warranty to render services in accordance with the applicable standards of their profession, which is just another way of stating the traditional duty owed by the professional to his client and other parties. The courts in a few states, however, have held that the architect, by undertaking design responsibility, owes an implied warranty that the plans will result in a structure which will meet the requirements of the owner.[16]

In a nineteenth-century Washington case, the plaintiff alleged that the architect had stated that he could design a well-lighted, first-class building. The plaintiff further alleged that the building was neither. The Washington Supreme Court held that the trial court had erred in not admitting evidence on the express warranty alleged by the plaintiff.[17]

Similar to those cases, in which plaintiffs have unsuccessfully argued that the architect owes the plaintiff an implied warranty, are others in which plaintiffs have urged that design professionals be held to strict liability. As discussed in Chapter 2, this doctrine has been adopted in product liability cases. In such suits, the plaintiff must show that there was a defect in the design or manufacture of the product, but need not show that the defendant was negligent. The doctrine of strict liability has been used successfully in some cases against mass home builders in New Jersey and California. However, most, if not all, of the attempts to apply this theory to design professionals have failed.

WARRANTY OF HABITABILITY

The doctrine of strict liability as applied to mass builders of homes apparently has led to the adoption in many states of the theory of the implied warranty of habitability. The purchaser of a new house usually buys it from a model and relies upon the builder to construct it in a workmanlike manner which will be fit for habitation. The purchaser usually has no architect and no means of verifying how the house is constructed. Gradually, the courts in many states have laid aside traditional principles of real property law and have held that the builder owes at least the first purchaser an implied warranty of habitability. However, this implied warranty has not been applied to design professionals.[18]

STRICT LIABILITY

Numerous attempts have been made to impose responsibility upon a professional engineer based upon the theory of strict liability. Under this theory, the engineer is looked upon as a guarantor of the result of his plans and specifications. The plaintiffs in such suits have argued that there is no need for the engineer to be found negligent in order to be liable for damages sustained by the plaintiff. The overwhelming majority of courts faced with arguments attempting to sue a consulting engineer under the doctrine of strict liability have rejected them. The courts generally hold that in rendering services, a professional should be judged under the concept of negligence.

With the adoption of strict liability in actions against manufacturers, plaintiffs also frequently argue that a building is a product and that strict liability standards should therefore be applied in assessing the responsibility for damages among contractors and design professionals. The overwhelming majority of courts have rejected the argument that a building is a product. Instead, they have insisted that the plaintiff show that either the contractor or the design professional was negligent and that his negligence was the proximate cause of the plaintiff's injuries.

When plaintiffs sought to apply the doctrine of strict liability to architects and engineers in California, the courts rejected their attempt, holding that they were limited to the traditional theory of professional negligence or malpractice.[19] In apparently only one case, which was an opinion of a trial court, has an engineer been held strictly liable. There, however, the engineer furnished not only the design, but also the skip bridge which allegedly was defective, causing injury to a worker.[20]

NEGLIGENT MISREPRESENTATION

Engineers may also be held liable for negligent misrepresentation. The application of this doctrine to engineers is rather recent and has been used successfully in cases against surveyors. This theory grew out of cases for fraud, but they do not require the plaintiff to show that the defendant had any fraudulent intent.

Under the doctrine of negligent misrepresentation, the plaintiff must show that a misrepresentation was made to a specific class of persons, that the defendant was aware that members of the class would rely upon the misrepresentation and could incur damage, and that the defendant was negligent in not knowing that the statement was false.

In an Illinois case, a surveyor had prepared a plat, expressly guranteeing its accuracy. The plaintiffs relied upon the survey and had a driveway and garage constructed, which encroached upon adjoining property. The plaintiffs subsequently purchased the house, and the survey had been done for the contractor who built it. However, the court said that the plaintiffs could recover for negligent misrepresentation even though they were not in privity with the surveyor. The court noted that the surveyor made the guaranty, knowing his plat would be relied upon by subsequent purchasers, and stated that the innocent plaintiff should not bear the responsibility of the surveyor's error.[21]

In another case, the California courts held a soils engineer liable when he told his client that there would be only twelve to sixteen inches of top soil on a piece of property. However, three to six feet of fill were required.[22] Architects have also been held liable for negligent misrepresentation when incorrectly certifying work for payment.[23] In a 1984 Maryland case, however, the court held that a third-party adjacent landowner could not sue for negligence a surveyor employed by the landowner where the adjacent landowner had not relied upon the survey.[24] The plaintiffs had alleged that the surveyor had negligently prepared an erroneous survey plat based upon an incorrect monument. The court found that the adjacent landowners could not sue the surveyor for negligence even though the survey allegedly resulted in a trespass on the adjacent landowner's property.

FRAUD

Our system of jurisprudence is based upon good faith, and the courts do not sanction fraud. If one person intentionally deceives another person by making a false statement or concealing facts, the person engaging in the deceit will be held accountable. However, in a fraud action, the courts require the plaintiff to show that the defendant intended to deceive him. This is referred to as "scienter," a basic element of any fraud case.

To show fraud, the plaintiff must prove that the defendant made a representation while knowing it to be false or concealed crucial facts. In addition, the plaintiff must show that the representation or concealment was done with the intent to deceive in order to induce the plaintiff to act upon it. Finally, the plaintiff must show that he relied upon the representation or concealment and was induced by it to act, sustaining damage.[25]

In a few cases, the courts have said that under certain circumstances a design professional can be held liable for fraud. As an example, in a South Dakota case, a church had retained an architect to perform supervisory duties during construction. The court noted that under such circumstances, the architect could be liable for fraudulent concealment. The church alleged that the architect knew that unsuitable fill had been used and an auditorium had been built on it. The church further alleged that the architect had concealed this information from them and had issued a final certificate for acceptance of the auditorium.[26]

In another case, the contractor filed a fraud suit alleging that certain engineers had dug trenches to investigate water conditions, had disclosed only favorable information to the contractor who had bid on the project, and had concealed unfavorable information. The court found that the allegation of fraud could defeat a motion for judgment upon the pleadings.[27]

SLANDER

Occasionally, a design professional is sued for slander. "Slander" is a spoken defamation. "Libel" is a written defamation. Basically, they require the same elements of proof.

Slander per se or libel per se consists of defamatory statement impuning the business or profession practices of the plaintiff. In such a case, the plaintiff usually may be awarded punitive damages even though he cannot show that he had actually been damaged.

Libel or slander requires the showing of injury to the plaintiff's reputation and the communication of a defamatory statement which injures, or is likely to injure, that reputation. The few cases in which the design professional has been sued for libel or slander have involved situations where the engineer has made comments about the competence or financial responsibility of a contractor or the competence of another professional. However, the courts recognize that the architect or engineer has a qualified privilege to comment on the competence or financial responsibility of a contractor and that this privilege can be rejected by the courts only if the plaintiff shows that the architect is acting with malice.

For instance, in one case, the general contractor delayed performance. The architect informed the bonding company in writing of the delay. He also accused the contractor of being negligent. The contractor then sued the architect for libel, stating that the architect's letters had caused the contractor to lose his bonding capacity and to cease business. The trial court directed a verdict for the architect, which was affirmed on appeal. The appellate court noted that the architect had a qualified privilege to make the statements he made and did not act with malice. The court also stated that the architect was acting on behalf of the owner and had the duty to protect the owner's interests.[28]

INTERFERENCE WITH CONTRACTUAL RELATIONS

Occasionally, an engineer is sued for inducing breach of contract or interfering with contractual relations. Some states only recognize an intentional tort for inducing breach of contract, whereas others recognize a broader concept of interference with contractual relations.

In a suit for inducing breach of contract, the plaintiff must show that he has a contract or other protected right with a third party, that the defendant knew of the contract or right, that the defendant intentionally induced the third party to breach it, that the defendant had no justification to do so, that the contract or right was breached by the third party, and that the defendant suffered damage. In those states which are more liberal and recognize only the tort of interference with contractual relations, it is not necessary to show that the contract was breached.

In a recent federal case, the trial court found an engineer liable for inducing breach of contract. A mechanical contractor and his supplier of sludge-dewatering equipment alleged that the engineer had patterned his specifications upon the equipment of a competitor of this vendor and insisted upon confirming to these specifications, despite federal regulations requiring free competition. Because of the engineer's insistence upon conforming, the mechanical contractor canceled his contract with the supplier. The court found for the mechanical contractor and his original vendor and awarded them damages.

On appeal, the federal court of appeals held, however, that the engineer only could be found liable if he had acted to protect his own interests rather than his principal's interests in insisting that the contractor comply with the specifications.[29]

However, where the design professional has some justification for taking the action he did, he is protected by a qualified privilege. In a Connecticut case, a municipality hired an architect to review bidding documents for a remodeling project.[30] The municipality gave the architect authority to reject subcontractors he found unacceptable. When the architect discovered that the successful bidder was to use a certain subcontractor, he requested certain information from the contractor, who did not reply. The architect then recommended to the municipality that it request the prime contractor to hire a different subcontractor. The subcontractor sued the municipality and the architect. The court held that the architect had a qualified privilege to evaluate bids and that he had not exceeded his privilege.

NOTES

1. *Navajo Circle Inc. v. Development Concepts Corp.*, 373 So.2d 689 (Fla. App. 1979).
2. *Aetna Insurance Co. v. Hellmuth, Obata & Kassabaum, Inc.*, 392 F.2d 472 (8th Cir. 1968).
3. *Krieger V. J. E. Greiner Co.*, 282 Md. 50, 382 A.2d 1069 (1978).
4. Ill. Rev. Stat. ch. 48, §60 (1984) and James A. Dooley, *Modern Tort Law: Liability and Litigation*, Vol. § 22.86 (Wilmette, Ill: Callaghan, 1982), 608.
5. *Gannon v. Chicago, Minneapolis-St. Paul & Pacific Railway Co.*, 26 Ill. App.2d 272, 167 N.E.2d 5 (1960), *rev'd on other grounds*, 22 Ill. 2d 305, 175 N.E.2d 785 (1961) and Dooley, *Modern Tort Law: Liability and Litigation*, Vol. 1, § 22.88, 609.
6. *Gundich v. Emerson-Comstock Co.*, 21 Ill.2d 117, 171 N.E.2d 60 (1960) and Dooley, *Modern Tort Law: Liability and Litigation*, Vol. 1, §22.88, 609.
7. *Fidelity & Casualty Co. of New York v. J. A. Jones Construction Co.*, 325 F.2d 605 (8th Cir. 1963).
8. *St. Joseph Hospital v. Corbetta Construction Co., Inc.*, 21 Ill. App.3d 925, 316 N.E.2d 51 (1974), *disagreed with, Hass v. Cravatta*, 71 Ill.App.3d 325, 389 N.E.2d 226 (1979).
9. *Henry v. Britt*, 220 So.2d 917, (Fla.App. 1969), *cert. denied*, 229 So.2d 867 (Fla. 1969).
10. *Bebb v. Jordan*, 111 Wash. 73, 189 P. 553 (1920).
11. *Erskine v. Johnson*, 23 Neb. 261, 36 N.W. 510 (1888).
12. *Fuchs v. Parson Construction Co.*, 172 Neb. 719, 111 N.W.2d 727 (1961).
13. *Manton v. H. L. Stevens Co.*, 170 Iowa 495, 153 N.W. 87 (1915).
14. *S. Blickman, Inc. v. Chilton*, 114 S.W.2d 646 (Tex. Civ. App. 1938).
15. *White v. Green*, 82 S.W. 329 (Tex. Civ. App. 1904).
16. Note, *Liability of Design Professionals—The Necessity of Fault*, 5 Iowa L. Rev. 1221 (1973).
17. *Niver v. Nash*, 7 Wash. 558, 35 P. 380 (1893).
18. Annotation, 25 A.L.R.3d 383 (1969).
19. *Legal Highlights*, Vol. 4, No. 8, *Guidelines for Improving Practice; Architect's and Engineer's Professional Liability*, and James Acret, *Architects and Engineers*, 2d ed. (Colorado Springs, Colo.: Shepards/McGraw-Hill, 1984), 113–120.
20. *Abdul-Warith v. Arthur G. McKee & Co.*, 488 F.Supp. 306 (E.D. Pa. 1980), *aff'd*, 642 F.2d 440 (3d Cir. 1981).
21. *Rozny v. Marnal*, 43 Ill.2d 54, 250 N.E.2d 656 (1969).
22. *Gagne V. Bertran*, 43 Cal.2d 481, 275 P.2d 15 (1954).
23. *Westerhold v. Carroll*, 419 S.W.2d 73 (Mo. 1967).
24. *Carlotta v. Stark & Assoc., Inc.*, 57 Md.App. 467, 470 A.2d 838 (1984).
25. 37 Am.Jur.2d *Fraud & Deceit* §12 (1968), 33–34.
26. *Holy Cross Parish v. Huether*, 308 N.W.2d 575 (S.D. 1981).
27. *Salem Sand & Gravel Co. v. City of Salem*, 260 Or. 630, 492 P.2d 271 (1971).
28. *Alfred A. Altimont v. Chatelain, Samperton & Nolan*, 374 A.2d 284 (D.C. 1977).
29. *Waldinger Corp. v. Ashbrook-Simon-Hartley, Inc.*, 564 F. Supp. 970 (C.D.Ill. 1983), *aff'd. in part, rev'd. in part*, 775 F.2d 781 (7th Cir. 1985).
30. *Kecko Piping Co. v. Town of Monroe*, 172 Conn. 197, 374 A.2d 179 (1977).

5
The Consulting Engineer in Construction: Specific Situations, Damages, and Limitations of Actions

Chapter 3 covered the legal liability for negligence of the consulting engineer working in construction. Chapter 4 discussed other bases of legal liability of the design professional. In this chapter, we will consider some specific situations in which the engineer may be held liable for his negligence. The following situations are discussed:

1. The engineer's responsibility for defective plans and specifications.
2. The engineer's responsibility for making product recommendations.
3. The engineer's responsibility for approving product substitutions.
4. The engineer's responsibility for recommending for use a new design or new products.
5. The engineer's on-site responsibility for observation.
6. The engineer's responsibility for safety.
7. The engineer's responsibility for certifying payouts to the contractor or for certifying construction of the project in accordance with the plans and specifications.
8. The engineer's responsibility for shop drawing review.
9. The engineer's responsibility for cost estimates.
10. The engineer's role in issuing change orders.
11. The engineer's responsibility for bid recommendations.
12. The liability of a consultant to the engineer.

After discussing these situations, we will consider which damages the owner or a third party may recover from an engineer who is found liable for professional negligence or malpractice. Finally, we will discuss the application of statues of limitations and repose to suits brought against engineers.

NEED FOR EXPERT TESTIMONY

As briefly mentioned in Chapter 2, in a lawsuit for professional malpractice, the plaintiff ordinarily must show, through the use of expert testimony, that the services rendered by the design professional did not meet the applicable standards of similar professionals in the community. In a 1979 opinion, the Court of Appeals of Kansas considered this requirement. A school district had sued the general contractor and architect when rainwater flooded a new gym. The gym was constructed below grade. The school district alleged that the architect was negligent in designing a sidewalk which sloped toward an areaway where water collected. Further, it was alleged that during construction, an employee of the general contractor pointed out this problem to the architect, who refused to change his plans and specifications.

The school district did not use any expert to testify against the architect. The architect had three experts testify on his behalf; each stated that the original design met the average standard of care of architects in the community. On appeal, the court stated that the trial court erred in finding the architect liable because the plaintiff had not used any expert testimony. The court noted that drainage design is a technical matter not within the knowledge of the ordinary juror.[1]

Occasionally, however, plaintiffs argue that under the "common knowledge" exception in a professional negligence case, they do not have to provide expert testimony to show that the professional's performance did not meet the expected standard of care of the community. This exception was developed in medical malpractice cases in which the courts have held that a plaintiff does not need to provide expert testimony when a healthy organ rather than a diseased one is removed during surgery or when instruments or sponges are left in the patient's body.

The courts have also recognized the common knowledge exception in cases involving design professionals. Thus, when an architect was aware of flooding in a particular locality and did not take it into account in doing his design, a court held that the plaintiff did not need to have an expert testify against him.[2] Similarly, another court held that the plaintiff was not required to have an expert testify against an architect in a case concerning threshold design. In that case, the plaintiff was injured when she tripped while crossing the threshold of a school entrance.[3]

The plaintiff's experts must also testify as to the standard of care utilized by design professionals in the community in which the project was built. In a Louisiana case, the plaintiff's experts testified about the quality of the work of the architect who was being sued. However, none of them testified about the local standard of care in this situation. Because of this omission, the trial court found for the architect and this finding was affirmed on appeal.[4]

Occasionally, the qualifications of the expert may become an issue during a trial. Usually, the trial judge must first determine whether the expert is qualified to testify, based upon his experience and training, before allowing the expert to give his opinion. Thus, the trial judge will consider the expert's education and work experience, plus his knowledge of applicable standards of care, in determining whether to allow the expert to testify.

Sometimes the question arises of whether a person practicing in one profession may be expert enough to testify against a person practicing in another profession. As an example, can a chiropractor testify as an expert to establish the standard of care when a medical doctor is being sued for malpractice? In such a case, the courts generally would not allow him to testify because of his lack of medical education and probably because he lacks sufficient experience to establish the standard of care used by medical doctors. Similarly, a specialist in one area of medicine usually will not be allowed to testify against a specialist in another area. Thus, an ophthalmologist will normally not be permitted to testify against a cardiac internist because of the former's lack of education and experience in the latter's specialty.

In cases involving design professionals, the courts have been more liberal and have looked at the experience of the experts in determining whether they will be allowed to testify. In a Pennsylvania case, the court considered whether an engineer and a geologist could testify against an architect concerning the design of dry wells at a building site. After construction, the dry wells resulted in sink holes and the owner sued the architect for malpractice. The trial court dismissed the case because the owner did not have an architect testify. On appeal, the court stated that professionals other than architects have experience in designing such systems. Accordingly, the appellate court reversed and stated that an engineer or geologist could testify against the architect.[5]

In a Colorado case, the court held that a chemical engineer who was experienced in designing skylights and a contractor with many years of experience in waterproofing were qualified to testify as experts against an architect concerning the design of skylights for a shopping center.[6]

SPECIFIC SITUATIONS

Defective Plans and Specifications

Numerous lawsuits have been filed against design professionals for defective plans and specifications. A discussion of each of them would require several volumes. However, such cases fall within several broad categories.

First, many suits have been filed alleging defects in the design of roofs, floors, or walls. Roof cases usually involve leaking or collapse. Floor cases typically involve problems arising from settlement. Wall cases usually involve cracking or spalling concrete or masonry walls.

Second, numerous cases have been filed alleging that a building is not watertight. Such lawsuits involve not only leaking roofs, but also penetration of water through walls and windows. In the past few decades, with the development of window curtain wall systems, many claims have been made and suits filed alleging faulty design of the curtain wall because of water intrusion.

Third, many suits have been filed challenging foundation design. Such suits often involve settlement of a building or part of it. They may also focus on cracking of concrete slabs or beams.

Fourth, many claims or suits involving professionals have concerned the design or selection of support systems for a building. As an example, mechanical engineers have been subject to claims and suits arising from the failure of heating, ventilation, and air-conditioning systems to adequately cool or heat a building or portions of it.

A Pennsylvania case provides an example of a suit alleging defective design of a roof. In that case, the architects had been retained to design a weaving mill. The plans provided for a twenty-year roof.

In addition, because of the industrial use of the building, the HVAC system was to provide for constant temperature and relative humidity. Thus, a vapor seal was specified for the roof.

Within a few years after construction, the insulation material failed and the entire roof had to be rebuilt. The plaintiff sued the architects, alleging that the plans were defective because they had not specified a proper vapor seal, drain flushings, or insulation. The jury found for the plaintiff, and on appeal the judgment was affirmed.

In stating its opinion, the appellate court noted that the insulation specified by the architects retained moisture and that a sealant material should have been used around it. Further, an expert testified that the insulation material specified was not generally accepted at the time of the design. Moreover, the expert criticized the design of mechanical fastenings for the roof. The court rejected the architect's defense that the material he originally desired to use was unavailable and that he specified the insulation material ultimately used upon representations of the insulation manufacturer. Further, the court rejected the architect's defense that the insulation was installed by a subcontractor in accordance with the manufacturer's specifications.[7]

As an example of a floor problem, an Oregon case concerned the design of a concrete slab floor for a factory in Milwaukee. The architects had retained structural engineers to design the floor. The engineers designed a floor measuring approximately 350 by 390 feet, consisting of panels 30 feet square and 6 inches thick. The panels were reinforced with ½-inch steel bars placed 12 inches apart and running both ways through the panels. The joints between the slabs were reinforced with steel bars extending 12 inches into each of the slabs. When the manufacturer moved into the new building, cracks immediately appeared in the floor and the floor surface eroded. The manufacturer sued the architects, who in turn sued the engineer. In the case brought by the architects against the engineer, the trial court held the engineers liable, a finding affirmed on appeal.

The appellate court noted that the plaintiff's expert had testified that the cracking was due to the continuously reinforced joint. Another expert testified that because the slabs were tied together, the floor could not move, resulting in cracking. One of the experts testified that the structural engineer was responsible for floor design and its load-bearing capacity.[8]

In an Illinois case, an architect was charged with negligent design of walls for a high school building. Cracks and openings had appeared in the exterior and interior walls after construction, as well as in other locations. The plaintiff's experts testified that the cracks were due to the lack of expansion joints to handle expansion and contraction of walls. Two of these experts also testified that the architect's design did not conform to the standards of practice at the time he did the work. Another expert stated that the cracking was caused by expansion of brick masonry and that the problem could be corrected by placing sixty-five expansion joints in the building. He further noted that the cracks which had appeared after construction could not be used as natural expansion joints, since they could not be sealed properly.

The defendant also had several experts testify for him, some of whom stated that he had met the appropriate design standards. Two of these experts also testified that the construction of new expansion joints would not resolve the problem. The architect had testified that the cracks had widened because the school had not repaired them quickly. On appeal, the court upheld the judgment in favor of the school, noting that this case involved a "classic battle of the experts."[9]

An Alabama case provides an example of an architect being found liable for seepage or water leaking.[10] This architect had been retained to design a college dormitory. His design required aggregate panels for the outside walls. In his specifications, the architect did not require a particular product, but he described specific properties of the epoxy or cementitious matrix to be used for the aggregate panels. The panel subcontractor interpreted the specifications to mean that a specific product was required. At the trial, the architect testified that although he had not named a specific product, he had copied the properties of the matrix from the brochure of the manufacturer from which the subcontractor had purchased the matrix.

After the aggregate panels had been installed, water came through, causing many of them to buckle away from the walls. The court held the architect, the contractor, and the contractor's surety liable. The architect did not appeal the decision, but the contractor and surety did. On appeal, the court reasoned that although the subcontractor had followed the architect's specifications, the general contractor could still be held liable because in his contract with the university he had agreed that the panels would be watertight. Apparently, the leakage was due to a defect in the matrix used by the subcontractor, but the opinion did not state whether the trial court found the architect negligent in writing the specifications.

Many construction cases concern foundation problems arising during and after construction. In those cases, allegations typically are made against either the architect or a structural engineer for the failure to design critical structural elements of the building adequately. In addition, soil engineers frequently are sued in such cases for either testing soils inadequately or giving allegedly negligent advice to the owner, the developer, the contractor, or other design professionals.

In a 1973 opinion, the Minnesota Supreme Court upheld a jury verdict finding the general contractor and the architect liable for damages to the owner and holding a structural engineer liable to the architect for indemnification.[11] The owner had engaged the architect to design an industrial building. Because of the peculiarity of the owner's production process, the design required at least a two-story structure. The architect did not do structural engineering, but retained a structural designer. A site was found which could be used for split-level construction. The property was fairly level, and then dropped twenty feet and continued level. Because of the nature of the drop, fill had to be provided behind the lower level of the two-story portion of the building which abutted the ridge.

At about the time the building was completed, large cracks were noticed in the walls and floors of certain portions of it. In addition, steel columns became out of plumb and bowed. A consulting engineer was retained to determine the cause of the problem and to recommend corrective action. Apparently, the consulting engineer determined that the lower wall of the two-story portion of the building, behind which fill had been placed, could not withstand the horizontal pressures of the fill. The movement of this wall was transferred through the remainder of the building. The consulting engineer also determined that the structural design did not provide adequate lateral support for the wall. Further, he concluded that even if the building had been constructed as designed, eventually it would have collapsed due to the design error.

During corrective construction, portions of the floor had to be removed. It was then discovered that more than two-thirds of the reinforcing steel, which should have been embedded in the concrete flooring, was on the fill. In addition, the fill had not been compacted in accordance with the specifications. This resulted in cracking and settling of the floor, which required even more substantial corrective measures.

In a 1959 Virginia case, the appellate court considered whether the trial court had erred in dismissing a case against an architect for an allegedly defective design of a heating and air-conditioning system for a residence. The mechanical design cases filed against architects or engineers are much more complicated than this one, but this case does provide a simple example of the problems which arise with mechanical systems. The architect initially had furnished plans for a radiant hot water heating system to be placed in a concrete slab floor. A plumbing contractor advised the owner that he could install a combination heating and air-conditioning system for only a small additional cost, and the owner referred him to the architect. The architect advised the owner that the change was acceptable to him, and the architect's design apparently included the plans and specifications for the heating and air-conditioning system. After construction, it was discovered that the system was insufficient. The plans did not encase ducts in concrete and did not provide for a fire wall. In addition, insufficient heat was generated to certain rooms because, due to a defect in either installation or design, the ducts filled with water, cutting off the heat.[12]

Product Recommendations

The design professional usually makes product recommendations to his client. Normally, such recommendations are contained in the specifications. In preparing specifications, architects or engineers may require the contractor to install or use the product of one or several manufacturers. Sometimes, the specifications contain "or equal" provisions. At other times, they may not require that a product of a specific manufacturer or several manufacturers be used or installed. Rather the specifications merely state that the contractor or vendor shall furnish a product which meets specific performance or functional requirements and certain other design requirements, such as size limitations.

When making product recommendations, a design professional faces several problems. First, he must determine to what extent he may be liable for recommending the product of a specific manufacturer or a group of manufacturers which fails to perform as intended. As a corollary, he must determine to what extent he may become liable, if at all, for a mechanical defect in the product which he did not manufacture. Coupled with this, the design professional must determine to what extent he may rely upon the product literature furnished by manufacturers in selecting particular products for use or installation. Second, he must be alert to antitrust law considerations and federal and state statutes and regulations requiring competitive bidding. Third, the design professional must consider to what extent he may be liable to parties other than his client for recommending a product which may malfunction and cause injury or damage to a third person.

When deciding whether the design professional may have erred in recommending a specific product, the courts look to the relevant professional standards of conduct. As an example, in a 1980 Vermont case, a school district had retained an architect to design an addition to a school. His specifications requested alternative bids for the use of a Zonolite Dyzone roofing system in the event that substitutions had to be made to lower costs in order to meet the budget. After the bidding, the school district decided to use the Zonolite Dyzone system. After installation, the roof split and leaking resulted. The school district then sued, among others, the architect.

After the school district had presented its evidence, the architect requested judgment in his favor, which the court granted. On appeal, the Vermont Supreme Court noted that there was no evidence in the record as to what a "reasonable roof designer" would have done in selecting the roofing materials. The school district argued that the architect should have made his own inquiry regarding the Zonolite Dyzone system and should not have relied upon the representations of the manufacturer. However, the court concluded that the architect was not guilty, since the school district had not presented any expert testimony on whether an independent inquiry should have been made or stating that the architect should not have relied upon the representations of the manufacturer.[13]

The Vermont case answers several questions about product recommendations. First, under the law, the design professional is only expected to do what his peers would do in similar situations. Thus, if a design professional would not make an independent inquiry about a product he intends to recommend and would rely upon the manufacturer's representations, he should not be held responsible for the product's failure. However, if a design professional, based on his experience or other information, has learned that the product he is considering for recommendation may have some problems, the courts would probably expect him to make an independent inquiry and not rely upon the manufacturer's representations. Again, the extent of the inquiry would be determined by what his peers would do in that situation. Since the design professional is not the designer or manufacturer of the product, he is probably not responsible for its failure to perform due to a defect in design or manufacture. Also, if the defect was due to improper installation by a contractor or subcontractor, the design professional should not be responsible for the product's failure, because he ordinarily does not control the methods of construction.

Obviously, when specifying a product or products, the engineer must be familiar with the manufacturer's product literature. Such literature contains information not only about specifications and installation but also about recommended uses and warnings. If the specifier has missed a critical warning in the literature, his recommendation of that product may not be acceptable for certain uses.

Generally, an engineer may recommend to the owner and specify any product or products he desires for any reason, and is insulated from the claim of manufacturers that his failure to include their products in his specifications violates the law. In a 1973 federal appellate case, the court held that a purchaser may specify any product he desires. The court noted that the specification of a particular product is not anticompetitive because before that decision is made, all potential sellers are free to urge that their products be used.[14]

Many design professionals prefer to write specifications which allow as many vendors as possible to participate in the bidding process. Such specifications may list the products of many manufacturers and may even include products not listed as acceptable under an "or equal" provision. Usually, when this provision is used, the specifier requires the manufacturer of a product not listed to submit the product for consideration. The design professional may also reject products submitted under an "or equal" provision and still be immune to action by the manufacturer or the contractor who had sought to use the product. However, the law does not give the design professional any guidance on what standards he should use in evaluating an alternative product under an "or equal" provision. The specifier may be required to act as a design professional would generally act under such circumstances in evaluating the product.

In two situations the specifier, when limiting bids to certain products, may run afoul of the law. First, such recommendations may violate competitive bidding statutes or ordinances of the federal or state governments or certain municipalities. In a 1983 Illinois federal court case, the trial judge criticized an engineering firm which had written its specifications so that only the manufacturer of certain sludge-dewatering equipment could meet them and insisted that the mechanical contractor use that equipment.[15] Apparently, the project had received federal funding, and the court noted that the engineer had deliberately violated a federal regulation mandating free competition in bidding.[16] The judge further stated that he had no rational basis for insisting that the preferred manufacturer's subsystems be used. The court also concluded that the design team had presented no evidence to support its conclusion that the preferred manufacturer's product was better. The court though that the design team may not have wanted to switch to another manufacturer because they had already designed a structure to house the sludge-dewatering equipment on the basis of the preferred manufacturer's specifications. The court concluded that this alone would not be sufficient reason for the designer to insist upon using this particular manufacturer's equipment.

The specifier must also be alert to possible violations of federal and state antitrust laws in recommending that the products of certain manufacturers be purchased. The purpose of the antitrust laws is to encourage competition. The design professional must avoid attempts to monopolize or conspiracies or agreements to restrain trade. Section 1 of the Sherman Act, the major federal antitrust statute, forbids contracts, combinations, and conspiracies in restraint of trade. Section 2 of the Sherman Act outlaws monopolization or attempts to monopolize.[17] Many states have similar legislation.

Under the Sherman Act, the courts have held that a product

manufacturer may select his customers and may refuse to deal with anyone provided his refusal does not further a restrictive trade practice; a federal trial court has held that an architect has the same right. In that case, an elevator installer had sued an architect who had stated in the specifications for several buildings that the elevator vendor must be an elevator manufacturer.[18] In a New Jersey case, the court held that the use of an "or equal" provision in a contract for public work defeated a challenge under a state open bidding requirement.[19] Of course, if an architect conspires with a contractor or vendor to limit competition, the design professional could be found liable for violating the antitrust laws, assuming competition had been restrained.

Many trade associations and professional groups set and publish standards for products, which are regularly used by design professionals. Under the law, those standards must be objective and cannot discriminate against the product of any manufacturer unless there is a reasonable basis for the discrimination.[20] Thus, engineers who participate in establishing standards for trade associations or professional societies must ensure that the standards are developed using a rational selection process and that product certification under those standards is nondiscriminatory.

Product Substitutions

The law concerning product substitutions is similar to that governing product recommendations. Generally, the engineer owes a duty of care, in accordance with professional standards, to advise his client about product substitutions. Frequently, such requests for product substitutions come from the contractor or a subcontractor. In the absence of a government regulation or law or conspiracy to restrain the trade of the proferred product, the engineer may deny the request for such substitution for any reason. However, if the specifications contain an "or equal" provision, the engineer is probably obligated to act reasonably when he considers the request for a product substitution, although there are no reported court opinions which clearly delineate the duty of a specifier when considering an alternative product in this situation. Of course, if the request for a product substitution involves a project for a government agency covered by an open bidding statute or regulation, the engineer must also probably act reasonably in judging this request.

New Designs and Products

When contemplating new designs or the use of new products or methods of installation or construction, the design professional is also governed by the applicable standards of his profession. He should follow the same steps that other design professionals use in evaluating innovative designs, products, or methods of installation or construction. Under certain circumstances, those steps may include reading texts and articles and consulting with other design professionals. The engineer may also have to consult with manufacturers. So long as he does what other engineers would do in evaluating new designs, products, or methods of installation or construction, he should not be held responsible if they do not achieve a satisfactory result.

In a Virginia case, an architect had designed a sliding roof for a ballroom. This was a complicated design, and although the roof did not perform as expected, the architect was not held liable.[21]

In a 1977 Rhode Island case, a consulting engineer for a state agency had specified an epoxy paint system for a bridge that had never been used in that application. The paint failed and the agency spent $4 million in remedial work. The agency sued the fabricator-erector of the bridge, alleging that the paint failed because the steel contained mill scale prior to painting and the epoxy-based paint would not penetrate it. The fabricator-erector counterclaimed, contending that the agency's consulting engineer had prepared the specifications negligently. Although the steel fabricator denied that the steel contained mill scale, the trial court found that it did. However, the agency and the consulting engineer countered the steel fabricator's argument that the specifications had been negligently prepared with the testimony of experts who stated that the epoxy system was suitable for the bridge. One of these experts testified that the epoxy system had been used successfully in Marine applications.[22]

On-Site Observation

During construction, the architect or engineer frequently agrees to perform certain on-site duties. These duties may be spelled out in detail in a written contract or document. Thus, the design professional may agree to have one or more representatives on the site during construction at all times or during specified periods. He may also agree to have his on-site representative observe certain critical phases of construction, such as concrete pours. Ordinarily, on-site representatives of the design professional observe the progress of construction to determine whether the work conforms to the plans and specifications. The engineer may also agree that the on-site representative will interpret the plans and specifications for the contractor and subcontractors or relay requests for interpretations to the appropriate designer.

Frequently, the written documents governing the design professional's on-site observation responsibility during construction state that the architect or engineer does not guarantee that the project will be built according to the plans and specifications in all respects. For instance, standard agreements between the design professional and the owner developed by the American Institute of Architects provide that the design professional is not required to make detailed on-site examinations of the work.[23]

When a written contract or document covers in detail the architect's or engineer's on-site observation duties, the courts must first examine it. If there is no written agreement or guide or the writing is general, the court must hear evidence on the relevant standards of the profession to determine whether the designer should be held liable for his failure to observe specific nonconforming work. Thus, the court must first determine whether under the agreement the architect or engineer was responsible for observing this work during construction. Then the court must determine whether the design professional, because of his agreement, had to guarantee that the work would conform to his specifications or whether he should be held liable for the nonconforming work only if he did not perform his duties in accordance with the applicable standards of the profession.

During many construction projects, the design professional does not agree to any clearly defined on-site observation duties. He may merely agree to observe the progress of construction in order to determine whether it conforms to the plans and specifications, or he may only agree to visit the work site at intervals to examine the work in order to certify the contractor's payout requests. In connection with payout requests, architects and engineers frequently examine the work covered by the request to determine whether it conforms to the plans and specifications. In such situations, which occur frequently in simple construction projects, the court, after finding that the architect did have on-site observation duties, should determine whether the nonconforming work should have been noticed by the ordinarily skilled design professional. When making this decision, the court must determine the applicable standards in this situation and should require expert testimony.

In a few cases, the courts have considered whether an architect or engineer was negligent in performing his on-site observation duties. In a 1978 Illinois case, the appellate court found that the contractor had deviated from the architect's plans and specifications in constructing a plaza deck over an underground parking garage. The court further upheld the trial court's finding that the architect had been negligent in "on-site supervision" for failing to notice substantial deviations in the construction of an expansion joint, the omission of expansion strips, and the use of improper mortar mix. The court noted that the architect had had a representative at the site for at least half of each day, but the opinion does not say in what respects the architect was negligent in failing to examine the construction.[24]

In a California personal injury case, the architect had told a contractor not to use certain sheathing in the construction of a roof. The contractor used it anyway, installing it before the architect had returned to the job site. Further, the contractor had covered over the sheathing so that it could not be readily observed. Then a roofer fell through the roof because of the defective sheathing. The court upheld the jury finding in favor of the roofer and against the architect, noting that the architect knew that inadequate sheathing had been taken to the site and that he was negligent for failing to make another examination before the sheathing was covered.[25]

In a much earlier Minnesota case, the court decided that an engineer was not liable for his failure to discover a piling which had not been driven properly. The court noted that the engineer was under a duty to exercise reasonable care, but he did not guarantee that the contractor's work would conform in all respects to his plans and specifications. Further, the court noted that the architect had been on the site two or three times daily, had discussed with the contractor's employees how they had driven the piles, and had been told that they had been driven as required. He had no reason to doubt the veracity of those employees.[26]

However, in an early-twentieth-century New York case in which an architect had agreed to observe construction to ensure that the work conformed to the building code, the court indicated that he was liable for not noticing a method of construction which violated the code. A floor had settled due to improper construction of the floor beams, which did not conform to the building code. The architect had visited the project site once a day, but the improper construction of the floor beams occurred between visits and was concealed from him.[27]

Safety

Probably more suits are filed against design professionals by injured construction workers or on behalf of deceased workers than any other type. Workers may succeed in recovering damages against an architect or engineer for personal injuries because the design professional may have agreed, by either contract or voluntarily, to control the methods of construction or to assume responsibility, for safety. In addition, some local laws place such a burden upon the architect or engineer, and these ordinances can be used by injured workmen to sue design professionals in those localities.

In the typical construction situation, the owner retains the architect or engineer to design a project. He then hires one or more contractors to construct the project, who in turn hire subcontractors. During construction, the owner may contract with the design professional to furnish on-site representatives, on either a part-time or permanent basis, to observe the progress of construction, to determine whether the work is conforming to the plans and specifications, and to handle inquiries from contractors regarding interpretation of construction documents. Normally, the design professional does not assume responsibility for actual construction or safety. This is done by the contractor. Thus, many architects and engineers specify in their contract that they will have no responsibility for the methods of construction or job-site safety. Further, the contract between the owner and the contractor frequently states that the contractor alone is responsible. However, either because of the owner's desire or through inadvertence, design professionals occasionally agree to assume these tasks.

A worker who is injured during construction may sue the design professional. The worker would argue that the professional controlled the methods of construction or safety, either by contract or voluntarily, and that his negligent failure to do so properly was the proximate cause of the worker's injury.

In a 1976 Missouri case, a worker fell to his death through a hole in the roof while a building was under construction. The verdict in favor of the architect was upheld on appeal, with the court noting that he had no contractual responsibility for safety. Further, the owner's contract with the general contractor specifically provided that the contractor would be responsible for safety.[28]

In a 1960 Arkansas case, the architect had agreed to specify the method of shoring and also had the right to stop work in order to ensure proper performance of the construction contract. Three workmen were killed when the shoring of an excavation wall collapsed, and suits were brought against the architect on their behalf. Because of the architect's contractual responsibilities, the court affirmed the judgment against him. In that case, the architect's on-site representative had talked to the contractor about a problem with the shoring before the accident, and the contractor had told him that it would be corrected. However, the on-site representative did not stop the work.[29]

Most of the cases considering the design professional's alleged duty to the injured worker rely upon a determination of whether the professional had contractually agreed either to supervise the methods of construction or to perform certain safety functions. The courts recognize, however, that even if he assumed these responsibilities voluntarily, he may be held liable for injuries to a construction worker.

Several cases have emphasized what the architect or engineer did on site during construction in holding him liable for construction worker injuries. As an example, in Indiana, the state was found liable for damages to an injured employee of a contractor employed by the state. One of the reasons for this finding was that the state's project engineer and project inspector had several times exercised control over the contractor's work. Further, on one occasion, the state inspector had ordered the contractor's employees to stop work when he thought it was dangerous due to heavy traffic upon a state highway. At another time, the state project engineer had ordered that an excavation be made wider so that it would be safe for the workers.[30]

In a California case in which an engineer was retained by a water district, the court affirmed a judgment in favor of an injured construction worker against the engineer. The court noted that the engineer had taken responsibility for the progress and method of construction and safety.[31] And in a Nebraska case involving the construction of an addition to a power plant, the court held an engineer liable for injuries to an injured worker. The court stated that the engineer had made twice-daily safety inspections and had given directions to the contractor regarding safety precautions. In addition, the engineer had conducted weekly safety meetings.[32]

Because of the inherently dangerous nature of construction work, several states have special statutes concerning construction safety. These statutes also afford injured construction workers the right to sue persons who control the work. The worker may recover worker's compensation benefits from his employer for a job-related injury and usually cannot sue the employer for such injuries because such benefits are available. These structural work or scaffolding acts give injured workers the right to sue other persons connected with the construction, including the owner, other contractors, and design professionals. These acts generally state, though, that the injured worker may only recover from a person who is in charge of the work. Further, the courts have held that more than one person may be in charge. The states with such statutes are California, Delaware, Illinois, Montana, New York, Oklahoma, Oregon, and Missouri.

Generally, under the structural work acts, the courts make an analysis similar to that in negligence cases when deciding whether an architect or engineer will be held liable to an injured construction worker. In scaffolding act cases, courts must first determine whether the design professional contractually undertook to supervise or control the method of construction or assume responsibility for safety. If he did, the courts may find him to have been in control of the work and therefore possibly liable under the statute. If the design professional has not contractually assumed either or both duties, the court will consider whether he did so voluntarily. If so, the court may also hold him to have been in control of the work.

As an example, under the Illinois Structural Work Act, the courts have concluded that a design professional is not in charge of the work if he merely performs the traditional on-site duty of an architect and engineer, which is to observe the progress of construction for conformity to the plans and specifications. Moreover, in one case, the Illinois Supreme Court held that if the architect has the right to stop the work under the contract, but only for the purpose of rejecting defective work, then he is not in control of the job.[33] However, if the architect is given the right to stop the work in order to ensure proper performance of the construction contract, then he may be held to be in charge of the work under the Illinois act.[34] Moreover, if he is given broad authority which allows him to control the methods of work, the Illinois courts consider him as a party in charge of the work under the scaffolding act. As an example, in one case where the engineer was held liable under the act, he had the right to stop work and to remove the contractor's employees from the project.[35]

One Illinois case under its structural work act gives an example of an architect voluntarily assuming control of the method of construction, which was one of the reasons the court held him liable. The architect's on-site representative had given directions on how to install acoustical tile, had prescribed the sequence for laying electrical grounds, and had approved the method of fabricating the floor box and girders.[36]

In prosecuted cases under the Federal Occupational Safety and Health Act and under the regulations of the U.S. Occupational Safety and Health Administration (OSHA), the same distinctions are drawn in determining whether the act or the regulations issued under it have been violated as the courts have made in suits filed by injured workmen against architects and engineers. In construction, OSHA is concerned with safety hazards at the job site and can levy penalties upon employers who subject their employees to danger. Special OSHA standards or regulations govern the performance of construction work. These standards apply to all employers who expose any individuals to a hazard, even though only employees of other employers. The critical inquiries are whether the employer is engaged in construction work and, if so, whether the employer controlled the circumstances creating the hazard. If the employer is performing construction work but did not control or create the hazard it must take alternative measures to protect employees to avoid liability. Of course, the architect or engineer should strive to avoid action which would permit a finding that he is engaged in construction work.

Generally, OSHA cases first consider the contractual responsibility of the architect and engineer to determine whether the act will be applied to them for unsafe job site conditions which may affect the employees and contractors or subcontractors at the site. Thus, if the contract gives the engineer safety responsibility, the right to coordinate work, or the right to stop work, he or the architect may be cited for a safety hazard by OSHA and may be given a penalty. Moreover, if the architect or engineer merely has the responsibility to review the safety programs of contractors or subcontractors at the site, they may be penalized by OSHA if unsafe conditions exist. Further, if the engineer assumes any safety responsibility, or voluntarily coordinates the work or tells contractors how to do their work, even though he is not contractually obligated to do so, OSHA probably will try to penalize him for unsafe working conditions.[38]

Certificates

During construction, design professionals frequently undertake to certify the contractor's requests for payment. In cases where the architect or engineer has been sued by either the owner or another party for negligent certification, the courts generally hold that the design professional owes a duty of reasonable care. The courts, however, usually hold that he can only be held to the standard of care of those similarly skilled in his profession in making such certifications. Many cases involving actions brought against an architect or engineer for negligent certification often consider whether he owes a duty not only to his client, usually the owner, but also to other parties, such as lenders.

The first reported U.S. court decision considering the architect's responsibility for negligent certification is a 1877 New York case. There the court concluded that where the architect had agreed to issue certificates of payments upon determining that the work had been done properly, he could be held liable for any defects, but only if those defects were those which an ordinarily skilled architect should have observed.[39]

In an early twentieth-century Manitoba case, the court held that an architect could be liable for certifying a request for payment after he had noticed a defect in construction and so advised the contractor, but issued the certificate without the corrective work being done.[40]

Under certain circumstances, a design professional may also be held liable for damages in negligence due to a failure to determine whether subcontractors and others who have lien rights have been paid prior to issuing the certificate. Thus, in a California case, the court held that an architect could be liable for issuing certificates without ascertaining whether the contractor had paid the subcontractors. The architect argued that the sums owed by the contractor were not due when he had issued the certificates, but the courts stated that large amounts were owed by the contractor at the time of certification and that the architect should have ensured that the bills were paid or that the contractor had obtained lien releases from his subcontractors and material men.[41]

Although early cases held that the design professional could be liable to the owner for negligent certification, because of lack of privity, the architect could not be held to other parties, such as lenders. Thus, in an 1893 English case, a mortgage lender was denied the right to sue an architect retained by the owner for negligently issuing certificates of payment upon which the mortgage lender had advanced money to pay the owner.[42]

In recent cases, U.S. courts have generally abandoned the doctrine of privity and now allow mortgage lenders to sue design professionals for negligence under such circumstances. Thus, in a 1954 Mississippi case, the contractor's surety was permitted to sue an architect for negligent certification. The architect had agreed to determine whether the contractor had met his payroll and paid his material bills before issuing a certificate of substantial completion, but issued the certificate without verifying that this had actually been done. The contractor collected the retainage and then defaulted so that the surety had to complete the work. The court stated that although the architect had no contract with the surety, he could still be liable for negligent certification.[43] In a Missouri case, an architect allegedly had negligently certified that the contractor had completed a certain amount of work. The contractor then defaulted and the surety had to complete the work. In order for the contractor to obtain the performance bond, the surety required him to find someone to indemnify the surety in the event that he defaulted. The indemnitor of the surety sued the architect, and the court stated that the indemnitor's action could not be barred by the lack of privity.[44] And in a North Carolina case, a bank had agreed to lend money to finance the construction of an apartment building and retained an architect to certify payouts. The court stated that although the architect had been retained by the bank, the owners could sue him for negligent certification.[45]

Shop Drawing Review

Design professionals often review shop drawings and other submissions of contractors and vendors. Usually, shop drawing review is limited to ensuring that the drawings or other submissions conform to the professional's design concept. Further, especially with equipment, engineers will check shop drawings for conformity to certain critical dimensions.

The scope of the design professional's shop drawing review is usually specified in his agreement with the owner. Occasionally, he may do a more thorough review than merely checking conformity with the design.

In a lawsuit, allegations are frequently made that the architect or engineer did not catch something during the review of shop drawings that he should have seen. Ordinarily, the question of whether the design professional was negligent in his review should be determined by the applicable standards of care. Would a similarly situated design professional in the community have noticed the error or omission?

Architects and engineers are reluctant to make detailed shop drawing reviews for several reasons. First, much of the engineering work has to be done by the contractor or subcontractors who will build the project. If the design professional must track all the details involved, then his fee to the owner could be astronomical. Second, detailed shop drawing review could involve the architect in methods of construction, something that most design professionals wish to avoid. Third, many design professionals lack expertise in the actual methods of construction, and therefore may not be competent to do detailed shop drawing review.

In a recent South Dakota case, however, the federal court of appeals held that the plaintiff did not have to furnish expert testimony for an architect to be found liable in a case where the architect failed to note a discrepancy between the specifications and the shop drawings.[46] In that case, the architect had been retained to furnish services for the design and construction of an office building. The specifications stated that the steel stair pans could be 14-gauge steel, but the landing pans were to be 10-gauge steel with angle supports. One shop drawing indicated 14-gauge steel for the landing pan, and the architect failed to observe the discrepancy. The landing pan was fabricated with 14-gauge steel and erected at the site. After the erection, two workers walked upon the pan, one of them hauling welding equipment. The pan collapsed, and both workers fell and were injured. They then sued the architect.

The architect's agreement with the owner stated that he would review shop drawings for conformity to the design concepts and compliance with the contract documents.

Judgment was entered against the architect by the trial court. On appeal, the architect argued that the trial judge had erred because the injured workmen had presented no expert testimony on the standard of care which should be exercised when reviewing shop drawings. The appellate court held that no expert testimony was necessary because of the "common knowledge" exception to the rule regarding expert testimony in professional liability cases. The court reasoned that the facts were not beyond the common knowledge of the average juror, implying that the average juror could see the difference between what was specified and what was indicated on the shop drawing.

Liability for Cost Estimates

Many courts have considered the design professional's liability for the failure to design a project which meets the cost estimates or budget set by the owner. Most of these cases deal with situations where the engineer or architect has made an agreement with the owner specifying that the project, when constructed, will not exceed a fixed sum. Only a few courts have considered the design professional's responsibility for cost estimates when his agreement does not establish the cost of construction, and most of them do not agree on his duty under such circumstances.

Many cases have considered the design professional's responsibility for cost estimates when his contract with the owner contains a provision limiting the cost of the project. If the project cost specified in the agreement is *guaranteed,* most courts would not allow the design professional to recover this fee if the probable cost of the project as designed exceeds that price. If the project cost in the agreement is an *estimated* one, the courts of most states would not permit the design professional to recover his fee if the actual or probable cost of construction substantially exceeds that price. Generally, however, the courts will allow the architect or engineer to recover his fee, despite a construction cost limitation in the services agreement, where the excess cost was due to changes made by the owner, where the owner accepts the design and does not object, and where the design professional suggests changes in the design which would bring the construction costs within the budget.

If the estimate of construction costs is greater than the amount agreed to in the services agreement, the design professional, under the law, has the opportunity to redesign the project in order to lower the costs, so long as the general design is not materially modified. Further, if the architect or engineer advises the owner that he is ready to redesign the project to meet the cost estimate, but the owner decides not to go forward with the project, the design professional may also recover his fees.[47]

To illustrate these general rules, we will discuss a few cases. In a Missouri case, an architect verbally agreed to design four buildings for a sewer pipe company, each of which would cost no more than $50,000. The company decided not to go ahead with the project when it learned that the buildings would cost approximately $95,000 each. The court held that under such circumstances the architect was not entitled to his fee, since he had agreed to design buildings that would cost a stipulated sum.[48] In an early Delaware case, the court held that where an architect agreed to do a design for a project, the construction costs of which would not exceed a certain sum, the architect could receive his fee if the estimate of the probable cost did not substantially exceed the maximum cost agreed to by the owner and the architect. The court stated that the estimated cost of construction had to "substantially" exceed the fixed sum because it was impossible for the architect to furnish plans which would result in construction costs no higher than the fixed sum.[49]

In a U.S. district court case in Michigan, an industrial design firm had agreed to remodel a department store at an estimated cost of $57,000. The owner had requested changes which increased the actual cost to $124,000. The court concluded that the owner's changes had substantially altered the project and that he was liable for the designer's fee.[50] In a 1978 Indiana case, a design professional had agreed to design a project with an estimated cost of $70,000. His services agreement also contained a clause stating that he did not guarantee that the bids would meet this estimate. The lowest bid, $128,000, was negotiated down to $105,000. The architect sued the owner when he refused to pay the designer's fee. The court, on appeal, held that the architect could not recover his fee because the actual construction cost substantially exceeded the estimated cost.[51]

Several courts have held that when the owner goes ahead with the project, even though the probable or actual cost exceeds the agreed guaranty or substantially exceeds the estimate, he is liable for the designer's fee if he failed to object in time. As an example, in a Washington case, the owner accepted bids which exceeded the fixed construction cost agreed to with the architect. The court stated that under such circumstances the owner had the right to reject all bids and return the design to the architect, with no liability for paying the designer's fees. The owner, however, was held to have waived his right to object by accepting a bid based upon the architect's documents. Hence, the owner was held liable to the architect for his fee.[52]

What if the agreement between the owner and the design professional is silent about the construction cost? Two cases imply that the architect or engineer is obligated either to advise the owner about the estimated cost or to obtain the owner's budget so that he can design a project within those cost parameters.[53] In addition, a few courts have held that a design professional whose client is a government agency must design a project in such a way that its construction cost will be within the established budget, even though he may not know how much money is available for the project. As an example, in a South Carolina case, an architect had agreed to do the design work for the remodeling of a county courthouse. His agreement with the county did not fix the construction costs. After the architect and the county entered into the professional services agreement, the state legislature authorized $400,000 for the project. Based upon the architect's plan, the lowest bid came in at $863,000. The county decided not to go forward with the project and did not pay the architect's fee; the architect then sued the county. On appeal, the South Carolina Supreme Court held that the architect could not recover his fee. The court reasoned that he was presumed to know the law and that in the appropriate statute the state legislature had set the budget at $400,000.[54]

Cases in Texas and Arizona, however, show that the design professional need not consider construction costs, nor does he have any duty to inform the owner of the estimated costs when the professional services agreement does not establish a budget.[55] In the Arizona case, the architect's agreement with the city for the design of a baseball stadium contained no provision concerning construction costs. The court held that he was entitled to his fee for preparing the plans even though the cost of the project, if constructed, would have been greater than the city was willing to pay.

Change Orders and Extra Work

During construction, changes often occur in the design of a project which may result in either increased or decreased costs. In addition, problems may arise during construction which may increase costs. For example, unforeseen underground conditions may be revealed which would result in extra costs.

In practice, the procedure for handling changes is governed by the contract between the owner and the contractor and also may be covered in the professional services agreement between the designer and the owner. Change order provisions usually require any change in the work or adjustment in the contract price or schedule to be authorized by a change order, which is issued by the owner. Usually, the contractor must submit a request for a change order to the architect, who either rejects it or approves it and sends it to the owner for approval and issuance. Frequently, during this process, the contractor and the owner may agree on the amount by which the contract price will be increased or reduced. Many standard construction contracts also provide that a change order may be issued by the owner, even though the amount of additional compensation or the reduction in compensation to be paid to the contractor is disputed. Under such circumstances, standard documents usually state that the amount of the increase or reduction will be adjusted at a later date, usually in accordance with some prescribed formula. Obviously, such a procedure is necessary to avoid delays in construction while the price of change orders is being negotiated between the owner and the contractor. Moreover, most standard documents usually provide a time limit for filing a request for a change order. Further, many standard contracts state that the contractor must submit the request and receive approval from the owner before the work is done. Naturally, the design professional must process requests for change orders promptly to avoid delays in construction. If not, the design professional may be held responsible for the extra costs due to his delay.

Bid Recommendations

There are two basic ways of awarding contracts to contractors. One method is competitive bidding, which is frequently used for major construction projects and usually for government contracts. The other method is direct selection, whereby the design professional may recommend one or more contractors with whom the owner can negotiate. Or the owner himself may select one or more contractors with whom to negotiate. The owner must decide which method to use, but may ask the architect or engineer for advice. When asked for such advice, design professionals typically consider the type of project, the complexity of the work, the estimated construction cost, and the reputation and background of potential bidders.

Under the competitive bidding method, a bidder does not become a contractor until a contract exists between him and the owner. When the owner selects the competitive bidding method, he usually wants the project completed according to the contract at the lowest price. In receiving bids from a number of bidders, the owner probably will receive the lowest price for the job. Normally, contracts are prepared by the architect, but frequently the owner will have input into the construction contract which normally accompanies the bid documents. In private projects, the number of bidders may be limited by the owner, whereas in government projects it is generally open to all qualified bidders. Under competitive bidding, bidders typically submit their bids at the same time and place.

Frequently, for both private and public projects, a bidder prequalification program is established. Procedures are adopted for potential bidders to submit financial information so that the owner and design professional can judge their financial integrity. In addition, investigations are made of the potential bidders' reputation, past performance, and the scope of their prior projects. These qualification programs may also be set up for subcontractors whom the successful bidder may desire to employ.

Under competitive bidding, after the bids are submitted, the design professional evaluates them. This may be necessary, especially in large projects, because many bidders may have exceptions to the bid documents.

In evaluating potential bidders for prequalification, and also in evaluating the bids themselves, the architect or engineer is protected by a qualified privilege against libel or slander. The few courts which have considered this question hold that the designer has a qualified privilege to advise the owner of derogatory information about potential bidders. However, the privilege does not protect a design professional against actual malice.[56]

Consultant's Liability

Frequently, a design professional will hire a consultant to assist him. Under such circumstances, the hiring professional becomes responsible for the negligence of the consultant. This legal rule arises from the doctrine of *respondeat superior,* which holds that a master is liable for the negligence of his agents and servants.

Under the law, the consultant owes the hiring professional a duty to exercise reasonable care in performing his service. If as a result of the consultant's malpractice the hiring professional is held liable to the owner, he can recover from the consultant the amount of his liability due to the consultant's negligence. In a Colorado case, an architect had hired an engineer and used the consultant's work in preparing his own plans. The court stated that the negligence for which the owner sought to recover may have been that of the consulting engineer, and the hiring professional could seek indemnification from him.[57] Further, because of the abandonment of the doctrine of privity, many states now allow the owner to sue the consultant directly if the consultant's alleged negligence damaged the owner.

DAMAGES

For a design professional to be held liable for malpractice, it is necessary to show that his malpractice was the proximate cause of the damage to the plaintiff. Once the plaintiff establishes this, it is necessary to determine the amount of damages to be awarded to him. Usually, the design professional found guilty of negligence is liable only for the reasonable cost of the corrective work or repair. However, if this cost exceeds the difference between the fair market value of the project as constructed and its fair market value had it been designed properly, the plaintiff is only entitled to the difference between these two values.

In an early-twentieth-century New York case, the court held that the damages to be awarded to the plaintiff due to the architect's negligence would be the cost of the corrective work.[58] In a more recent Washington case, the court held that the cost of the corrective work is the proper measure of damages unless this cost is disproportionately greater than the value of the benefit which would result from the repair. If the value is disproportionate, then the measure of damages is the difference between the market price of the project with and without the defect.[59]

What if the defect cannot be corrected at a reasonable cost? Then the measure of damages is the difference between the value of the building as built and the value it would have had if there had been no negligence in its design. Thus, in an Iowa case, the court stated that the jury should be instructed that if the cost of repair was unreasonable, the difference in the value should be the measure of damages. The owner alleged that the architect had designed private boxes for an opera house which did not give any view of the stage and that an arch was improperly designed, resulting in bulging walls.[60]

Other damages may also be awarded to the plaintiff, depending upon the nature of the case. Frequently, the malpractice of the design professional may cause construction delays. However, for the owner to be awarded damages for such delays he must show those damages with a reasonable certainty of proof. Ordinarily, the owner will not be awarded damages which are too "speculative." Thus, in a 1982 Nevada case, an engineer allegedly had been negligent in surveying the location for a hotel, delaying its completion. The owner filed suit, seeking recovery of the lost profits due to the delay. The court refused to award any such damages, noting that there was no evidence that the parties had specified a particular completion date.[61] In an earlier Florida case, the plaintiff sought delay damages in the form of lost rent. The court also refused to award damages because they were too "remote and speculative."[62] However, a recent California case indicates that condominium buyers may be able to recover loss of use and income due to the alleged malpractice of an architect.[63]

The laws concerning damages which can be awarded in cases of personal injury or wrongful death are discussed in Chapter 2.

STATUTE OF LIMITATIONS

All states have statutes which limit the time in which an injured party must file a lawsuit; beyond that limit, he is forever barred from commencing a suit based upon the damages he sustained. These statutes are referred to as "statutes of limitation."

There are two main reasons for statutes of limitation. First, as the time following the injury increases, it becomes more difficult for the parties, especially the defendant, to gather the evidence needed for the trial. Witnesses may move, disappear, or die, and documents needed for the case may be misplaced or destroyed. Memories also become dim. Thus, our legislatures have decided that as a matter of public policy, persons should be protected from lawsuits filed unreasonably long after the injury has occurred. Second, they have determined that all persons should feel secure so that after a certain period of time following the injury, lawsuits making claims arising from the damage should be barred.

Under common law, there were no statutes of limitation, but the law courts had created similar concepts. Thus, in a suit to collect money owed, the defendant was allowed to claim that if the suit was filed after an unreasonably long period after the obligation became due, there was a presumption that it had been paid. Similarly, in actions involving real property which were also filed long after the claim arose, the courts allowed the defendant to raise a defense based upon the presumption that the necessary documents had been executed but then had been lost.[64]

The chancery or equity courts developed the "doctrine of laches," which could be used to bar a plaintiff's action if, under the circumstances due to the lapse of time, the defendant's case would be prejudiced. The doctrine of laches may still be used in equitable actions. It differs from the statute of limitations in requiring a demonstration of prejudice against the defendant.

The statute of limitations is a complete defense, and the right of a defendant to assert it is vested. However, the defendant may waive this defense.

The legislatures have established different time periods in which the aggrieved party must file his suit, depending upon the nature of the injury or harm that he has suffered. Thus, in many states, actions for negligence or personal injuries must be filed within a few years after the accident occurred. For example, actions for personal injury must be filed in Illinois within two years, whereas in New Mexico the limit is three years. Many states have even shorter filing periods for actions alleging libel or slander. In addition, many states provide a relatively long period of time in which to file a suit under a written contract or challenging title to real property. Some states allow suits under written contracts to be filed ten or twenty years after the cause of action. However, many states which have such relatively long filing periods for suits for breach of written contract provide a much shorter period for filing a suit for breach of an oral agreement.

Even though a statute of limitations applies, a contract may specify a period of time after which a suit for breach of the agreement may not be brought. Often this period is much shorter than the applicable statute of limitations. Generally, the courts will enforce such limiting language, but only so long as the contract provides a reasonable period of time after breach of it to file a suit.

Unfortunately, the language of the statutes of limitations of the various states is not uniform, except where the states have adopted certain uniform or model language. Further, the courts have interpreted the statute of limitations in many different ways. As a result, the statute of limitations that will be used, and its applicability, vary from case to case. Therefore, the design professional should be familiar with the statutes of limitations in the states where he works.

Applying the statute of limitations to the defense of an engineer in a lawsuit involves two basic questions. First, which statute applies? Second, when does the statute commence?

Which Statute of Limitations Applies?

Basically, there are two statutes of limitations which may apply to suits against design professionals. The first limits the time for filing actions for negligence. The second limits the time for filing actions for breach of contract.

In a case where a party other than the client has been injured, the plaintiff generally must sue the architect for negligence, so it is easy to determine which statute applies. However, when the client is injured and sues, he may sue either in breach of contract or in negligence. Unfortunately, the state courts have not uniformly agreed on how to handle this problem. Thus, in Wisconsin, when a client sued an architect, the court stated that the statutes of limitations for negligence and breach of contract would both apply.[65] In Connecticut, a court applied the contract statute of limitations when an architect was sued by his client for negligence. The court concluded that the basis of the complaint was really the breach of the architect's implied contractual duty to render services with a reasonable degree of care.[66] However, in New York and Oregon, courts have held that when a client sues a design professional for negligent design, the case is really a malpractice action and the appropriate negligence statute of limitations would be applied.[67]

When Does the Statute of Limitations Commence?

Generally, the time period in which an aggrieved party must file a suit for breach of contract commences when the agreement is breached, not at the time when damage has incurred because of the breach. Thus, in a suit by a client against a design professional for breach of contract, it may be relatively easy for the court to determine when the negligence occurred and to find that the cause of action accrues upon that date. However, this could lead to inequitable results. For example, many major projects take years to design and complete. The design professional may have made a negligent error early in the design phase, but the error may not appear until late in the construction phase. The damage could appear years after the negligence, and yet a court applying the breach of contract statute of limitations strictly could bar the claim. However, because the statute of limitations for breach of contract in many states is for a relatively long period, only rarely would such an event probably occur.

In applying statutes of limitations for negligence actions, the courts have developed three rules, the application of which depends upon the state where the statute is being applied. These rules are that (1) the statute begins to run at the time of the negligent act, (2) the statute begins to run from the time of damage, and (3) the statute begins to run from the time the plaintiff knew, or in the exercise of due care should have known, of the defendant's possible negligence.

A few states follow the first approach. In those states, the plaintiff's cause of action begins at the time of the negligent act, which is the error or omission in design or the negligent performance of on-site services. Courts following this theory do not consider the time when the damage occurred. They also do not consider the time when the defendant first learned, or in the exercise of reasonable care should have learned, of the negligence. For instance, in a New York case, architects had designed a building prior to 1965. In 1971, the plaintiff filed suit for damages, alleging negligence in its design. The court stated that the statute of limitations had started to run prior to 1965 and concluded that the suit was barred by a three-year statute of limitations.[68]

Under the second theory, the statute begins to run at the time of damage. The courts assume that there are two requirements for negligence action—the negligence and the damage—and the right to sue for negligence does not occur until damage has been done. The courts do not consider when the plaintiff first discovered, or in the exercise of reasonable care should have discovered, the negligence. As an example, in a Georgia case, a roof collapsed as the result of sagging and shifting of a slab. The collapse occurred in 1961 and the court stated that the negligence statute of limitations began to run from that date.[69]

Because of the inequitable results that could occur under the first two rules, the courts of some states have developed a discovery rule. Under this rule, the statute of limitations begins to run at the time plaintiff knew, or in the exercise of reasonable care should have known, of the negligence. This rule obviously is beneficial to plaintiffs because it does not result in the harsh consequences of the first two rules. Under the discovery rule, however, it may be easy for the courts to find that the plaintiff knew, or should have known, after the damage that negligence had occurred. This rule, though, does afford the plaintiff a reasonable period of time after the damage has occurred to investigate in order to determine who may have been at fault. In addition, this rule provides some benefit to design professionals, because it may possibly be used to bar claims of plaintiffs who knew of the negligence before any major damage occurred but did not immediately sue the negligent architect or engineer.

Several cases have considered the application of the discovery rule to design professionals. As an example, in a 1967 Iowa case, the court emphasized that the plaintiff could not have been aware of any negligence until he had suffered injury. This happened when he first noticed water dripping through his ceiling.[70]

A question may arise of whether the plaintiff was diligent in conducting his investigation after he first noticed the damage which allegedly was due to the malpractice of the design professional. As an example, in a 1980 Illinois case, cracks and other defects were observed in the building, but the architect stated that these problems were due to improper maintenance. The plaintiff did not learn of the architect's possible negligence until he received a report from the contractor stating that the problems apparently were due to the lack of expansion joints. In that case, the court concluded that the plaintiff first became aware of the possible negligence of the architect when he received the contractor's report.[71]

A few courts have also considered situations where minor damage was observed by the plaintiff, but plaintiff took no action against the architect or engineer until major or abnormal damage has occurred. In a California case, the plaintiff sued a soil engineer for settlement of his house and the engineer raised a three-year statute of limitations for negligence in his defense. Although the home owner had filed the suit more than three years after the first few hairline cracks were noticed, no appreciable damage occurred until later. The home owner filed the suit within three years after major damage had occurred, and the court refused to apply the statute of limitations.[72] And in a 1973 Minnesota federal case, the plaintiff sued as the result of settlement of a building. The court was applying a two-year discovery rule and noted that the first settlement occurred more than two years before the suit was filed. However, the court stated that as a general matter, settlement of any building would be expected following construction and that the two-year discovery rule began to run when abnormal settlement was discovered.[73]

The Model Act

Under the discovery rule applying the statute of limitations, a design professional faces lifetime liability for malpractice. Thus, an engineer may have designed a structure thirty years ago and, under the discovery rule, may not be allowed to use the statute of limitations as a defense if a party files a suit against him alleging an injury due to his design negligence thirty years previously. Because of this open-ended potential for liability, three professional groups have drafted a model statute of limitations. These groups are the American Institute of Architects, the National Society of Professional Engineers, and the Associated General Contractors. Based upon their efforts, forty-five states have enacted versions of the model statute of limitations. Although the statutes differ as to time period and when the statute of limitations starts to run, they are all aimed at curtailing this open-ended exposure. Under these statutes, the time period begins either at the time of completion of the project or at the time of its acceptance by the owner.

Basically, these statutes provide that after a certain number of years following completion or acceptance all claims are barred, regardless of when the injury or the damage occurs. Further, some states, such as Illinois, have placed a variation in their statutes of limitation which provides that within the period before all actions must be commenced, the claimant must file the suit within a shorter period following discovery of the design professional's negligence. Thus, in Illinois, actions against anyone arising from an error or omission in an improvement of real property must be filed within two years of discovery of the act or omission, but all actions are barred twelve years after the act or omission. This twelve-year period can be extended, however; if a person discovers the act or omission prior to the expiration of the twelve-year period, he has two years after discovery to file suit.[74]

Although the model act provides a four-year limitation as an absolute bar, the states that have adopted it have extended this period as much as fifteen years. Many states have ceilings of ten years. Further, some of the statutes apply only to design professionals and the contractor. Many of them do not apply to the owner or material men. Moreover, several states have barred claims for indemnification by the owner against the design professional or the contractor if the special statute of limitations is run. A few states have provided that the special statute will not apply to actions for fraud.

Of the forty-five states which have adopted special statutes of limitation for the protection of design professionals, between 1961 and 1982 ten states held them to be unconstitutional, whereas sixteen considered them valid. These decisions cannot be easily reconciled because of the differences in the wording of the statutes among the states and the varying interpretations of the state courts. Some states have struck down the statutes because they protect only design professionals and builders, not owners and material men. These courts see no reason for the distinction and hold that such a statute violates the equal protection clause of the U.S. Constitution or similar clauses of various state constitutions. Further, some of the statutes were struck down because they were found to be vague and violative of the due process clause of the U.S. Constitution.[75]

Tolling

Many states have provisions for "tolling" the statute of limitations. During such a period, the statute of limitations does not run. For example, most states provide that the statute of limitations for personal injury actions is tolled when the injured person is a minor or is mentally incapacitated. After majority is reached or the incapacity is removed, the person is allowed a fixed number of years to file the suit. Of course, during the period of minority or incapacity, the states usually provide a means by which a suit can be filed on the person's behalf. Usually, this is done by a parent or a court-appointed guardian, depending upon the applicable state law.

NOTES

1. *Seaman Unified School District No. 345 v. Casson Construction Co., Inc.*, 3 Kan.App.2d 289, 594 P.2d 241 (1979).
2. *Seiler v Levitz Furniture Co.*, 367 A.2d 999 (Del. Super. 1976).
3. *Hull v. Enger Construction Co.*, 15 Wash. App. 511, 550 P.2d 692 (1976).
4. *Maloney v. Oak Builders, Inc.*, 224 So.2d 161 (La. App. 1969), *modified*, 256 La. 85, 235 So.2d 386 (1970).
5. *National Cash Register Co. v. Haak*, 233 Pa. Super. 562, 335 A.2d 407 (1975).

6. *Perlmutter v. Flickinger*, 520 P.2d 596 (Colo. App. 1974).
7. *Bloomsburg Mills, Inc. v. Sordoni Construction Co.*, 401 Pa. 358, 164 A.2d 201 (1960).
8. *Owings v. Rose*, 262 Or. 247, 497 P.2d 1183 (1972).
9. *Society of Mt. Carmel v. Fox*, 90 Ill.App.3d 537, 413 N.E.2d 480 (1980).
10. *United States Fidelity & Guaranty Co. v. Jacksonville State University*, 357 So.2d 952 (Ala. 1978).
11. *Northern Petrochemical Co. v. Thorsen & Thorshov, Inc.*, 297 Minn. 118, 211 N.W.2d 159 (1973).
12. *Willner v. Woodward*, 201 Va. 104, 109 S.E.2d 132 (1959).
13. *South Burlington School District v. Calcagni-Frazier-Zajchowski Architects, Inc.*, 138 Vt. 33, 410 A.2d 1359 (1980).
14. *Security Fire Door Co. v. County of Los Angeles*, 484 F.2d 1028 (9th Cir. 1973).
15. *Waldinger Corp. v. Ashbrook-Simon-Hartley, Inc.*, 564 F.Supp. 970 (C.D.Ill. 1983), *aff'd. in part, rev'd. in part*, 775 F.2d 781 (7th Cir. 1985).
16. 40 C.F.R. §§35.936-3 and 35.936.13.
17. 15 U.S.C.A. § 1 and 2 (Supp. 1985).
18. *Kendall Elevator Co. v. LBC & W Associates of South Carolina, Inc.*, 350 F.Supp. 75 (D. S.C. 1972).
19. *Fisher v. Borough of Longport*, 135 N.J.L. 217, 53 A.2d 210 (1947).
20. *Radiant Burners, Inc. v. People's Gas Light & Coke Co.*, 364 U.S. 656 (1961) and *American Society of Mechanical Engineers Inc. v. Hydrolevel Corp.*, 456 U.S. 556 (1982).
21. *Surf Realty Corp. v. Standing*, 195 Va. 431, 78 S.E.2d 901 (1953).
22. *Rhode Island Turnpike & Bridge Authority v. Bethlehem Steel Corp.*, 119 R.I. 141, 379 A.2d 344 (1977).
23. AIA Document B141, Standard Form of Agreement between Owner and Architect (Washington D.C.: American Institute of Architects, 1977).
24. *Corbetta Construction Co. v. Lake County Public Bldg. Commission*, 64 Ill. App. 3d 313, 381 N.E.2d 758 (1978).
25. *Paxton v. County of Almeda*, 119 Cal. App.2d 393, 259 P.2d 934 (1953).
26. *Cowles v. Minneapolis*, 128 Minn. 452, 151 N.W. 184 (1915).
27. *Straus v. Buchman*, 96 App. Div. 270, 89 N.Y.S. 226 (1904), *aff'd*, 184 N.Y. 545, 76 N.E. 1109 (1906).
28. *Brown v. Gamble Construction Co.*, 537 S.W.2d 685 (Mo. App. 1976).
29. *Erhart v. Hummonds*, 232 Ark. 133, 334 S.W.2d 869 (1960).
30. *Indiana State Highway Commission v. Thomas*, 169 Ind. App. 13, 346 N.E.2d 252 (1976).
31. *Stilson v. Moulton—Niguel Water Dist.*, 21 Cal. App.3d 928, 98 Cal. Rptr. 914 (1971).
32. *Simon v. Omaha Public Power Dist.*, 189 Neb. 183, 202 N.W.2d 157 (1972).
33. *McGovern v. Standish*, 65 Ill.2d 54, 357 N.E.2d, 1134 (1976) *overruled, Emberton v. State Farm Mutual Auto Ins. Co.*, 71 Ill.2d 111, 373 N.E.2d 1348 (1978).
34. *Emberton v. State Farm Mutual Automobile Insurance Co.*, 71 Ill.2d 111, 373 N.E.2d 1348 (1978).
35. *Kirk v. Walter E. Deuchler Assoc. Inc.*, 79 Ill. App.3d 416, 398 N.E. 2d 603 (1979).
36. *Emberton v. State Farm Auto Mutual Insurance Co.*, 71 Ill.2d 111, 373 N.E.2d 1348 (1978).
37. 29 C.F.R., Part 1926, §§ 1926.1–1003 (Rev. 1984).
38. *In re Skidmore, Owings & Merrill*, 1977–8 OSHD (CCH) ¶22101, *In re A.C.& S. Inc.*, 1976–7 OSHD (CCH) ¶20,955, *In re Smith and Mahoney*, 1980 OSHD (CCH) ¶24,759, *In re Bertrand Goldberg Assoc.*, 1976–7 OSHD (CCH) ¶20,995, *Bechtel Power Corp. v. Secretary of Labor*, 548 F.2d 248 (8th Cir. 1977), *In re Walsh Construction Co.*, 1975–6 OSHD CCH) ¶20,127, and *In re Weinap Construction Corp.*, 1975–6 OSHD (CCH) ¶20,072.

39. *Gilman v. Stevens*, 54 How. Pr. 197 (N.Y. 1877).
40. *Bruce v. James*, 23 Manitoba L 339, 12DLR 469 (1913).
41. *Palmer v. Brown*, 127 Cal. App.2d 44, 273 P.2d 306 (1954).
42. *LeLievre v. Gould*, 1 QB 491 (1893).
43. *National Surety Corp. v. Malvaney*, 221 Miss. 190, 72 So.2d 424 (1954).
44. *Westerhold v. Carroll*, 419 S.W.2d 73 (Mo. 1967).
45. *Browning v. Maurice B. Levien & Co., P. C.*, 44 N.C. App. 701, 262 S.E.2d 355 (1980).
46. *Jaeger v. Henningson, Durham & Richardson, Inc.*, 714 F.2d 773 (8th Cir. 1983).
47. Richard N. Seybold, *Liability of Architects and Engineers to Their Clients* (Milwaukee: Defense Research Institute, Inc., 1982), 2–23, and Annotation, 20 A.L.R.3d 778 (1968).
48. *Campbell v. Evens & Howard Sewer Pipe Co.*, 286 S.W.2d 399 (Mo. App. 1956).
49. *Brinckle v. England*, 25 Del. 16, 78 A. 638 (1910).
50. *Loewy v. A. Rosenthal, Inc.*, 104 F.Supp. 496 (D. Mich. 1952).
51. *Malo v. Gilman*, 177 Ind. App.365, 379 N.E.2d 554 (Ind. App. 1978).
52. *Bissell v. McCormack*, 162 Wash, 482. 298 P. 697 (1931).
53. *Zannoth v. Booth Radio Stations*, 333 Mich. 233, 52 N.W.2d 678 (1952) and *Durand Associates, Inc. v. Guardian Investment Co.*, 186 Neb. 349, 183 N.W.2d 246 (1971).
54. *Beacham v. Greenville County*, 218 S.C. 181, 62 S.E.2d 92 (1950).
55. *Baylor University v. Carlander* 316 S.W.2d 277 (Tex. Civ. App. 1958) and *Guirey, Srnka & Arnold, Architects v. Phoenix*, 9 Ariz. App. 70, 449 P.2d 306 (1969).
56. *Vojak v. Jensen*, 161 N.W.2d 100 (Iowa, 1968) and *Kecko Piping Company, Inc. v. Town of Monroe*, 172 Conn. 197, 374 A.2d 179 (1977).
57. *Naiman v. Warren A. Flickinger & Assoc., Ltd.*, 43 Colo. App. 279, 605 P.2d 63 (1979).
58. *Schwartz v. Kuhn*, 71 Misc. 149, 126 N.Y.S. 568 (1911).
59. *Eastlake Construction Co. v. Hess*, 102 Wash.2d 30, 686 P.2d 465 (1984).
60. *Trunk & Gordon v. Clark*, 163 Iowa 620, 145 N.W. 277 (1914).
61. *Daniel, Mann Johnson & Mendenhall v. Hilton Hotels Corp.*, 98 Nev. 113, 642 P.2d 1086 (1982).
62. *Bayshore Development Corp. v. Bonfoey*, 75 Fla. 455, 78 So. 507 (1918).
63. *Cooper v. Jevne*, 56 Cal. App.3d 860, 128 Cal. Rptr. 724 (1976).
64. 5 Am. Jur.2d *Limitation of Actions* §2 (1970).
65. *County of Milwaukee v. Schmidt, Garden & Erikson*, 43 Wis.2d 445, 168 N.W.2d 559 (1969).
66. *Skidmore, Owings & Merrill v. Connecticut General Life Insurance Co.*, 25 Conn. Supp. 76, 197 A.2d 83 (1963).
67. *Bales For Food, Inc. v. Poole*, 246 Or. 253, 424 P.2d 892 (1967) and *Naetzker v. Brocton Central School Dist.*, 50 App. Div.2d 142, 376 N.Y.S.2d 300, *rev'd.*, 41 N.Y.2d 929, 363 N.E.2d 351 (1977).
68. *Sosnow v. Paul*, 43 App. Div.2d 978, 352 N.Y.S.2d 502 (1974), *aff'd.*, 36 N.Y.2d 780, 369 N.Y.S.2d 693, 330 N.E.2d 643 (1975).
69. *Wellston Co. v. Sam N. Hodges, Jr. & Co.*, 114 Ga. App. 424, 151 S.E.2d 481 (1966).
70. *Chrischilles v. Griswold*, 260 Iowa 543, 150 N.W.2d 94 (1967).
71. *Society of Mt. Carmel v. Fox*, 90 Ill. App.3d 537, 413 N.E.2d 480 (1980).
72. *Oakes v. McCarthy Co.*, 267 Cal. App.2d 231, 73 Cal. Rptr. 127 (1968).
73. *Continental Grain Co. v. Fegles Construction Co.*, 480 F.2d 793 (8th Cir. 1973).
74. Ill. Code of Civ. P., § 13-214, Ill. Rev. Stat. ch. 110, § 13-214 (1984).
75. William T. Birmingham and Ted A. Schmidt, *Architects, Engineers and the Statute of Limitations: Liability of Architects and Engineers* (Milwaukee: Defense Research Institute, Inc., 1982), 24–35.

6
The Manufacturer: Legal Liability
for Product Defects

In this chapter, we focus on the responsibility of manufacturers. The laws used to determine the liability of a manufacturer for products defective in design or manufacture are different from those applied to consulting engineers working in construction. Unfortunately, the law of product liability, due to its historical development, is not as favorable to a manufacturer as the law of professional liability or malpractice is to a construction engineer. Under the law, a manufacturer today ensures or guarantees that a product manufactured and sold by him is not defective.

Product liability law covers the various theories of law which have been used when a person is injured or his property is damaged due to a defect in manufacture or design. In this chapter, we shall concentrate upon those cases arising from such injuries or damage. In Chapter 9, we will discuss those situations where a seller or manufacturer of a product may be liable for a defect which does not necessarily cause bodily injury or damage to property. These are commonly referred to as "breach of warranty" cases and typically involve a situation where a vendor sells a product or products which are defective and cannot be used, do not perform as intended, or must be repaired.

We are all familiar with newspapers accounts of injuries due to an allegedly defective product. For example, a person may have been injured in an automobile accident due to the failure of the steering mechanism in the car in which he was the driver or a passenger. Or a person may have been injured when a space heater malfunctioned due to a defect in its design or manufacture.

Hundreds of liability suits are filed every day. Some of them have resulted in multi-million-dollar verdicts against manufacturers. Because of the number of these suits and the potential for high damages due to serious personal injuries, all manufacturers of consumer and industrial products are justifiably concerned. Although most of them can obtain product liability insurance, the cost can be relatively high.

PRIVITY

In the nineteenth century, product manufacturers were not overly concerned about product liability suits, since they were protected by the doctrine of privity. Under this doctrine, only someone who had purchased the product directly from the manufacturer could sue him. Subsequent purchasers or other parties who were injured by a defective product could not sue because they were not in "privity of contract" with the manufacturer. Starting approximately 100 years ago, however, the courts began chipping away at the citadel of privity. Within the last decade or two the requirement for privity product liability suits ended.

Historically, when resolving the question of privity, the courts have dealt with two types of cases: those for breach of warranty and those for negligence. However, court decisions striking down the requirement for privity in both types of cases have run in parallel. In recent years, with the adoption of the doctrine of strict liability in product liability cases, the question of privity also arose, but because of the abandonment of the privity defense in breach of warranty and negligence cases, this requirement in strict liability cases was abandoned early in the development of the theory of strict liability.

Prior to the adoption of the Uniform Commercial Code by forty-nine of the fifty states, the general rule was that privity was required in an action for injury seeking recovery for breach of warranty. Most of the states had such an appellate court decision and applied the rule to actions for breach of both express and implied warranty. This rule had some exceptions. Privity was not required for breach of warranty actions alleging defects in food, beverages, and drugs. It was not necessarily required when the injured party had relied upon express warranties made by the manufacturer. In addition, some courts allowed a suit to be maintained, even though there was no privity between the plaintiff and the defendant, where the purchaser of the product acted as an agent of the injured party. Thus, in a 1929 Washington case, the plaintiff had filed a suit for damages to an apple crop because of the use of a certain spray purchased through a retailer. The court concluded that the retailer was acting as the plaintiff's agent and rejected the defense based upon the doctrine of privity.[1]

Other exceptions were allowed when the injured party was a guest of the product's purchaser or when a brother or sister had purchased the product and one of his or her siblings was injured by it, but not necessarily when one spouse was injured by product purchased by the other. Cases involving a parent's purchase of a product that injured a child have gone both ways. Some cases have held that the child is not in privity with the manufacturer, and others have concluded the opposite.

With the adoption of the Uniform Commercial Code, the requirement of privity was abrogated or modified for breach of warranty actions. The drafters of the code provided three alternatives. The first one states that the doctrine of privity does not apply to express or implied warranties to persons who reside with the buyer or who are guests in his home and it is reasonable to expect that such persons may use the product. The second alternative goes further and states that the doctrine of privity is not required for suits for breach of express or implied warranty if the plaintiff is reasonably expected to use the product. However, this alternative refers to only living persons. The third alternative goes even further and abrogates the doctrine of privity for all entities, including businesses and corporations.

Most of the states have adopted the first provision although some have even modified it. Alabama, Colorado, Delaware, Kansas, South Carolina, South Dakota, and Vermont have adopted the second alternative. The third alternative has been adopted by North Dakota and Iowa. Hawaii, Maine, Minnesota, Rhode Island, Virginia, Arkansas, Massachusetts, and New Hampshire have adopted provisions which have an effect similar to that of the third alternative. In addition, some of the states which have adopted the first and second alternatives have amended their language to make them broader and similar to the third alternative.

Even without the adoption of the Uniform Commercial Code, a 1960 New Jersey case foretold the death of the defense of privity in breach of warranty cases.[2] The court's reasoning probably would have been adopted by courts of many other states, but the acceptance by most states of the Uniform Commercial Code and the theory of strict liability for product liability cases following that New Jersey opinion meant that they did not have to consider the issue.

In that New Jersey case, a husband purchased a new automobile. His wife was driving it when it suddenly went out of control and she was injured. Initially, the husband and wife sued for both negligence and breach of implied warranty. The negligence action was dismissed, apparently because the plaintiffs had no evidence that either the dealer or the automobile manufacturer had been negligent. The trial court, however, permitted the plaintiffs to sue for breach of warranty. The jury found in their favor, and judgment was entered accordingly. On appeal, the New Jersey Supreme Court affirmed the judgment. The court reasoned that in a modern industrial society, consumers are dependent upon the manufacturer and can no longer bargain equally. When a manufacturer promotes and sells a new automobile to the public, the court stated, an implied warranty that is reasonably suited for its use passes to the purchaser. Further, the court held that the wife of the purchaser can also sue the manufacturer. The court implied that the manufacturer could reasonably expect that persons other than the purchaser would be driving the automobile. Thus, using a breach of warranty theory, plaintiffs were able to recover from the manufacturer and the dealer merely because of an unexplained accident.

The demise of the requirement for privity in negligence cases was initially discussed in Chapter 2. For many years, the courts held that an injured party could not sue a manufacturer or seller of a product for negligence for product liability if there was no contract between them.[3] However, in the latter part of the nineteenth century, the courts developed some exceptions to this rule. One exception stated that if the defendant knew that the product was dangerous, and did not so advise the buyer, the injured party need not be in privity with the manufacturer.[4] The other exception applied if the defendant negligently manufactured or sold a product which was inherently dangerous. Thus, plaintiffs were not required to be in privity with the defendant in cases involving the negligent production of food, beverages, drugs, firearms, and explosives. Then, in a 1916 case involving the manufacturer of an automobile with a defective wheel, Judge Benjamin Cardozo held that there was no need for privity of contract between the plaintiff and defendant in a negligence suit against an allegedly defective manufacturer of a product that would reasonably cause harm if negligently made.[5] Even after this decision, however, the courts still became embroiled in privity arguments, especially in determining whether a product could reasonably cause harm if it was negligently made or inherently dangerous. Finally, in a 1946 Massachusetts case, the court completely abandoned the requirement for privity in negligence cases.[6]

To date, many other states have also rejected the need for privity in negligence actions. Among these states are Georgia, Indiana, Iowa, Kentucky, Louisiana, Michigan, Minnesota, New Mexico, North Carolina, Ohio, Tennessee, Washington, Wisconsin, South Carolina, and maybe Florida, Illinois, Maryland, Mississippi, New Jersey, North Dakota, Oregon, Pennsylvania, Vermont, Kansas, Montana, Texas, and West Virginia. In addition, Arkansas, Georgia, Maine, Tennessee, and Virginia, as well as Massachusetts, have abrogated the requirement for privity in negligence cases by statute.[7]

Besides abandoning the requirement of privity in warranty and negligence cases, the courts have rejected this doctrine in strict liability cases. A product liability suit seeking recovery for damages under the theory of strict liability merely requires the plaintiff to show that the product was defective in design or manufacture. He need not show that the defect was negligently caused.

The modern doctrine of absolute or strict liability was created in a 1963 California case, which will be discussed later.[8] Because of the adoption of strict liability at a time when the courts had already made headway in abandoning privity of contract in negligence actions, it was easy for the courts in strict liability cases to hold that the plaintiff need not be in privity of contract with the defendant in order to sue him under that theory.

Thus, the doctrine of privity has been abrogated by the courts or legislatures in most states for breach of warranty, negligence, and strict liability actions. However, in breach of warranty actions, some states still have not completely rejected the doctrine of privity.

NECESSARY ELEMENTS

Any product liability case, whether for breach of warranty, negligence, or strict liability, has two common elements. First, the seller or manufacturer must be identified. Second, a defect in the product must be shown.

In breach of warranty and strict liability cases, anyone in the chain of distribution is a potential defendant. However, in negligence cases this is not so, because of the plaintiff's need to show that the defendant was negligent in order for him to be held liable. Thus, a retailer or vendor who has no reason to question the safety of a product cannot be held liable merely for selling what turns out to be a product which was negligently manufactured. However, there are two exceptions to this general rule. First, restaurants and druggists are held to the same standard of care as manufacturers. Second, if the retailer assembles the product, he is responsible for using the same skill as the manufacturer.

In most product liability cases, the retailer or manufacturer is readily identifiable. Usually the product contains a trade name or other markings which can be used to identify the manufacturer. Further, it may be possible to identify the manufacturer through the business records of either the manufacturer, the retailer, or other companies in the chain of distribution. In addition, the retailer who advertises himself as a manufacturer of a product, even though he did not actually produce it, is held by the courts to be the manufacturer and is estopped from denying it.[9]

In recent years, the courts have been groping for ways to handle situations in which the product is destroyed by the alleged defect and the plaintiff cannot identify the manufacturer. In a landmark case, a federal district court in New York held that under certain circumstances all the manufacturers of the product may be held liable, except for those who can show specifically that their product was not the one involved. That case involved eighteen different accidents in which children had been injured by blasting caps. The plaintiffs sued all the manufacturers of blasting caps and a trade association for failure to warn purchasers and to take proper safety precautions. The plaintiffs could not identify the manufacturer of any of the caps which had caused injury. The court stated that in industries with only a few manufacturers who are all cognizant of the risks and have a means to reduce it (such as using the trade association), each of the manufacturers may be found liable.[10]

In a later case involving this doctrine of "enterprise liability," the court was faced with actions brought by two women who had suffered injuries due to their mothers' taking the drug diethylstilbestrol (DES) during pregnancy. Neither of the women could identify the manufacturer, since the drug had been produced by several companies. The court concluded that the plaintiffs could sue all the manufacturers without showing which specific firms had supplied the DES, since all had used an identical formula.[11]

In two other cases, however, the courts have questioned the use of the doctrine of enterprise liability. In one New York case, the plaintiff was injured when a beer bottle exploded. The beer producer filed a third-party action against the bottle manufacturers who had furnished the bottles and who were the sole suppliers. The court stated that the manufacturers could be found liable only if they had adhered to industry standards which were inadequate.[12] In a 1980 Tennessee case arising from a jail fire in which several inmates were killed, the plaintiffs sued all the manufacturers of the type of inflammable material in the padded cells which had given off poisonous fumes during the fire. The court refused to apply the theory of enterprise liability.[13] In an earlier Texas case the court allowed a plaintiff to recover from certain asbestos insulation manufacturers for asbesteosis, but each of the manufacturers had supplied the asbestos which the plaintiff had breathed in over a number of years.[14]

Generally, product liability suits involve the sale of a product. However, some courts have allowed recovery under product liability theories when a product has not been sold, such as when persons have been injured while testing a product prior to purchase.[15]

Another requirement of all product liability suits is the need to show a defect in the product which was the proximate cause of the injury. The defect must be shown to have existed at the time the product left the defendant's possession or control. A critical question in many cases is whether the plaintiff has presented sufficient proof that a defect existed.

The mere occurrence of an injury does not necessarily prove that the product was defective when it left the defendant's control. However, the malfunctioning of a product under normal use may be evidence of its defectiveness without the need to show the defect.[16] Often plaintiffs are able to show the defect through circumstantial evidence which consists primarily of factual testimony and an expert opinion eliminating all other possible causes of the accident. Of course, the plaintiff always has a stronger case if, through the testimony of expert witnesses or other evidence, he can show the actual defect which proximately caused the accident.

As examples of proving a defect by circumstantial evidence, we shall consider a few breach of warranty, negligence, and strict liability cases. In a case for breach of the implied warranty of merchantability under the Uniform Commercial Code, the plaintiff had purchased a used truck which had an engine failure four days after delivery. The court stated that the plaintiff did not have to prove a specific defect. He only needed to show that there had been proper maintenance and operation of the truck between the date of delivery and the date of the failure. This, along with the failure, was sufficient circumstantial evidence to show that there had been a defect in the engine at the time of delivery.[17]

In an action for both negligence and breach of warranty, the plaintiff showed that he had leased an automobile and had driven it for almost 10,000 miles when it veered off the road, causing injury. The plaintiff also showed that the automobile had performed adequately from the first day of the lease and that he had not been negligent while driving at the time of the accident. The court concluded that those facts alone provided enough circumstantial evidence from which the jury, if it so desired, could find the lessor liable.[18]

In a strict liability action, a cable was used for a winch which should have had a breaking strength of 8,000 pounds. The working strength of the cable should have been 1,700 pounds. However, the cable broke at 800 pounds. The court concluded that since there was no evidence of improper maintenance of the cable or damage to it, sufficient circumstantial evidence existed for the defendant to be held responsible for a product defect.[19]

In product liability suits, the injured plaintiff may want to use evidence of accidents similar to the one in which he was injured in order to show a product defect. In their defense, manufacturers may want to show that the continued use of the product for a number of years without any reports of similar accidents shows that there was no defect in the product. Some courts have allowed the use of such evidence by both the injured plaintiff and the defendant manufacturer. However, the courts have stated that the mere occurrence of similar accidents is not absolute proof of the product's defect, but only evidence that the defect exists. Similarly, in cases where manufacturers have tried to use evidence of lack of accidents, the courts have held that the mere lack of similar occurrences is not absolute proof that there was no product defect, but only as evidence that there may have been no defect.

In a 1978 Illinois Appellate Court case, the court held that the trial judge erred in not admitting evidence of similar occurrences in a product liability suit against the manufacturer and seller of a metal ladder.[20] In a subsequent opinion, this court allowed a manufacturer to introduce evidence that there were no reported occurrences similar to the accident in which the plaintiff was injured to show that there was no defect in the design of a truck.[21]

Finally, in any product liability action, regardless of which theory or theories are used by the plaintiff, the defendant can be held liable only if the jury finds that the plaintiff's injuries were the proximate cause of the alleged defect in the product.

PRODUCT LIABILITY THEORIES

Breach of Warranty

One of the theories which may be used by a plaintiff in a product liability case is breach of warranty. In such a suit, the plaintiff alleges that he has been injured by breach of an express or implied warranty by the product manufacturer or seller.

In this section, we will consider breach of warranty actions in cases of personal injury or property damage. In Chapter 9, we will discuss in further detail the law pertaining to claims that the product does not work, must be repaired, or does not meet the purposes for which it has been purchased.

A warranty action differs from a negligence action because it originates in the law of contracts, whereas negligence is part of the law of torts. Further, negligence actions require the buyer to show negligence by the seller or manufacturer; warranty actions do not. Rather warranty actions concentrate upon the failure of the product to meet either expressed or implied warranties. Thus, in a suit for breach of warranty, the plaintiff need not show that the seller or manufacturer was negligent—a definite advantage to the plaintiff. All the plaintiff need show, besides his injury and damage, is the existence of either an express or implied warranty and the product's failure to meet it, which frequently is a defect in the product.

There are two kinds of warranties: express and implied. Express warranties are promises or representations made prior to the sale about the characteristics of the product. As an example, a statement that an automobile is new or has only 10,000 miles of use is an express warranty.

Implied warranties are creatures of law. Under the Uniform Commercial Code, there are two types of implied warranties: the implied warranty of merchantability and the implied warranty of fitness for the particular purpose. The implied warranty of merchantability states that the product is acceptable in the trade and can be used for ordinary purposes. The implied warranty of fitness for a particular purpose states that if the seller knows for what purpose the product will be used and knows that the purchaser has relied upon the seller's skill to select the proper product, then the product selected and sold by the seller should be fit for the specific purpose.

Four defenses have frequently been used in breach of warranty actions. In cases where the plaintiff did not purchase the product from the defendant, defendants have used the privity defense. However, as noted above, this defense is no longer viable in all breach of warranty actions. Second, defendants have argued that the plaintiff in an express warranty case did not rely upon the warranty. This argument often arises in a suit by a party who was not in privity with the defendant. Third, the defendant may argue that the plaintiff did not give notice of the breach of warranty or did not give prompt notice. Under the Uniform Commercial Code, the buyer must notify the seller of any breach within a reasonable time of discovery. Apparently, however, in a personal injury action, notice may not necessarily be required, especially where the injured party was not the buyer.[22] Fourth, the seller's contract may contain provisions either eliminating or limiting certain or all of the warranties. These provisions frequently are referred to as "exculpatory clauses"; they will be discussed in further detail in Chapter 9.

Occasionally in a breach of warranty action, defendants may use the doctrine of contributory or comparative negligence. In theory, this defense would not seem to apply in a breach of warranty case, which is really a suit for breach of contract, whereas the contributory and comparative negligence are used in negligence actions. A few courts have allowed the defense of contributory negligence to be used in a breach of warranty case. However, most courts reject this defense in such a case but do recognize as a defense the product's misuse by the plaintiff.[23]

In recent years, legal scholars have wrestled with the question of whether implied warranties of sale apply to used goods, leased goods, or service contracts. Under the common law, implied warranties were not part of the purchase of used goods or service contracts. However, many courts recognized that there was an implied warranty of quality for leased goods. Today, most courts which have considered whether the implied warranties under the Uniform Commercial Code apply to used products sold by a merchant hold that they do. The rulings on leased goods are not consistent under the Uniform Commercial Code, but some courts have held that they do involve warranties of quality. To determine whether service contracts really contain any implied warranties, most courts today consider the nature of the transaction. If they conclude that it involved primarily the sale of good, they apply the Uniform Commercial Code's implied warranty provisions. However, if they determine that the nature of the transaction was really service, they will not take this action.[24]

Conceivably, express warranties may be made in advertisements by the manufacturer or seller. However, for a plaintiff to recover under such warranty statements, he must show that he relied upon those statements in purchasing or using the product.[25]

Negligence

As discussed in Chapter 2, an action for negligence requires that the plaintiff show (1) a duty which the defendant owed him to conform to certain standards of conduct as prescribed by law, (2) a breach of the legal duty by the defendant, (3) that the breach of the duty was the proximate cause of injury to the defendant, and (4) damage suffered by the plaintiff.

In a product liability action in which the plaintiff uses a negligence theory, he must show all of the above elements. A negligence suit is different from a product liability suit for breach of warranty because it requires the plaintiff to show negligence. Negligence introduces the concept of fault into product liability cases, whereas it is not necessary in either a breach of warranty or a strict liability suit. Today, due to the rejection of the privity doctrine in breach of warranty and strict liability cases, along with the general acceptance of strict liability for product liability cases, pure negligence actions against manufacturers are relatively rare. However, negligence actions still frequently appear in lawsuits because the plaintiff's attorney often drafts a complaint against the manufacturer alleging breach of warranty, negligence, and strict liability.

Negligence actions are not dead. There are cases where a person has been injured by a product and seeks recovery from a party other than a retailer or manufacturer. For example, plaintiffs have proceeded against testing firms which have tested products and certified that they meet certain standards.[26] Further, a negligence action may be the only one a plaintiff can pursue when he has been injured by a product due to faulty maintenance.

In a typical negligence action for injury due to a product defect, the plaintiff must show both that the defendant manufactured the product and that he manufactured it negligently. In other words, he must show that the defendant failed to use due or reasonable care to prevent an unreasonable risk of harm to any person who might reasonably be expected to use the product in a manner in which it might reasonably be expected to be used. Further, the plaintiff must be a person who is reasonably expected to use the product and must show that his injuries were caused by the manufacturer's negligence.

A mere defect in a product is not sufficient to show negligence in its manufacturer. The plaintiff must show the negligence which resulted in the defect.

Historically, product liability actions in negligence concentrated upon three main areas: (1) the inspection and testing of the product and its components, (2) the design of the product, and (3) the failure of the manufacturer to warn potential users of a possible hazard.

Under negligence law, a manufacturer has a duty to inspect and test not only the products manufactured by him, but also the components of those products. Inspections and tests should be reasonable and designed to uncover both obvious and latent defects in the product. The type of testing depends upon the product, how it will be used, and the safety hazards which may result from a defect. Whether all products should be inspected and tested or whether sampling may be used depends upon the product and the hazard. For example, not all castings can be destructively tested. However, it may be the custom of the foundry industry to perform quality control inspections on all castings and to test one or two destructively from a given batch.

Industry custom concerning testing is relevant. The manufacturer's failure to adhere to it may be evidence of negligence. Further, his adherence to industry custom regarding inspection or testing may be evidence of due care.

Manufacturers also have a duty to make reasonable inspections and tests of components received from vendors. If those inspections and tests indicate that the use of the components would make the finished product reasonably safe, then the manufacturer has not been negligent. Naturally, the inspections and tests must be performed in a reasonable manner.[27]

Generally, retailers or wholesalers have no duty to make any inspections or tests of products they sell, unless for some reason they know that a product may be defective. However, the seller who does not merely resell the goods, but also installs or repairs them, may have a duty to reasonably test and inspect them.[28]

Manufacturers and sellers who have a duty to inspect and test a product, are not relieved of these obligations merely because someone else assumed them. Frequently, manufacturers require vendors to have quality control programs involving inspection and testing, often sending certificates to the manufacturer stating that this has been done. However, the fact that the vendor has done the inspection and testing does not relieve the manufacturer of his duty to perform these tasks. Further, any testing or inspection by the purchaser does not relieve the manufacturer of his duty.[29]

Under the law, the purpose of inspection and testing by the manufacturer is to determine whether the product has any patent or obvious defects. The manufacturer is not responsible for inspecting and testing a product for latent or hidden defects unless for some reason he learns that they may exist. Thus, if the manufacturer acts reasonably in testing and inspecting a product, under the negligence theory of product liability law he cannot be responsible for any injuries due to a latent or hidden defect in the product.

Another theory used in product liability negligence cases is that of negligent design. In designing a product, a manufacturer must use reasonable care, considering the risk involved if someone is injured due to the design. The manufacturer must use reasonable care to avoid not only obvious design defects, but latent or hidden defects as well. Further, in designing a product, the manufacturer must consider its expected uses. However, the manufacturer is liable only to those he expects would be harmed by the product's failure.[30]

The mere occurrence of an injury does not show that a product is defective, and the fact that the accident would not have occurred with a differently designed product does not show that there was any negligence in the design. The use of the product for a long period of time without any injuries and the conformance of the design to normal design for such products are evidence of due care in the product's design.

A manufacturer has no duty to design a product which is accident proof. However, he must consider emergencies which may arise in the use of the product and design it to meet those emergencies.

Generally, the manufacturer who uses components also has a duty to use reasonable care in designing them. But if the component manufacturer determines the design, then the manufacturer using the component product is not liable.[31]

The manufacturer, when designing a product, must consider the necessity for safety devices, but he need not design a machine with all possible safety devices. Moreover, he has no duty to use a safety device or guard which will destroy the machine's usefulness. In considering safety device design, the manufacturer need only determine the expected normal use of the machine. Further, he need not furnish safety devices if the danger is obvious.[32]

Usually, the reasonableness or unreasonableness of a product's design is shown by the use of expert testimony. The expert, based upon his education and experience, testifies about general engineering standards and the compliance or noncompliance of the design with those standards, normally in the field of design for safety.

Two design defect cases may be helpful in understanding the above principles. In a New York case, a 1969 Ford Falcon was struck in the rear. A fire resulted, causing death and injuries. The plaintiffs argued that the use of a flange-mounted gas tank without a protective fire wall was the design defect and recovered damages.[33] In a North Carolina case, clothes in an electric clothes dryer caught fire and burned part of the plaintiffs' house. The plaintiffs argued that there should have been a fail-safe device on the dryer;

however, the court refused to allow this theory to be presented to the jury because the plaintiffs' own expert testified that he had never seen such a device on a dryer and he did not know of any industry standard requiring its use.[34]

In a product liability action grounded in negligence, the defendant seller or manufacturer may raise the defenses of contributory negligence and assumption of the risk. Thus, the injured person may be found to be contributorily negligent when he (1) uses the product, knowing it to be defective, (2) uses a product without proper inspection that could have disclosed the defect, (3) uses a dangerous product, knowing of the danger, or (4) fails to be cautious in using the product.[35]

Another theory often used in product liability negligence cases is the purported failure of the manufacturer to warn of a known hazard. Assuming that the product's design or manufacture could make it unsafe, the manufacturer or seller has a duty to warn potential users of the hazard when (1) the manufacturer or seller is aware of the danger, (2) the danger is not obvious to the user, and (3) the danger arises from a cause other than an unexpected use of the product.

The duty to warn runs not only from the manufacturer or seller to the buyer of the product, but also to expected users. Thus, manufacturers frequently put warning labels or decals on equipment or machinery, so that the employees of the purchaser who operate the machinery receive reasonable notice of various safety hazards. There is no need to warn of obvious dangers or to warn someone who may not reasonably be expected to use the product.[36]

The duty to warn usually arises when the product is sold, but the seller and manufacturer are under a continuous duty to warn. For instance, if the seller or manufacturer learns after the sale of the product that a hazard does exist, he must take reasonable steps to warn potential users. As an example, after the manufacture of power brakes used in automobiles, the manufacturer learned of a failure of which he had previously been unaware. Although he furnished repair kits to his dealers, he took no steps to notify users of the automobiles. Hence, he was found liable for his failure to warn them.[37]

Even though a manufacturer or seller has given a warning, he may still be found liable if the warning was not adequate. The adequacy of the warning is determined by its reasonableness, which is a question for the jury to consider. Under the law, the warning must be unambiguous and easily seen. Thus, warning labels are usually printed in bright colors and large letters with appropriate underlining. Further, they must warn not only of the safety hazard, but also of the possible effects that may result from failure to follow them, such as potential injury to a hand or eye.[38] If appropriate, the warnings should not only be included in the instructions for the product, but should also be placed on the product itself.

Today, many statutes and regulations, most of them federal, require warnings to be placed on certain products. Among such statutes are the Federal Food, Drug and Cosmetic Act, the Federal Hazardous Substances Act, the National Traffic and Motor Vehicle Act, the Poison Prevention Packaging Act, and the Federal Insecticide, Fungicide and Rodenticide Act. Regulations under the Consumer Product Safety Act require warnings on certain consumer products. Commonly, these acts establish standards for products which must be labeled and provide guidance on how the label must be written. Further, the acts typically provide for recalls, warnings, and/or fines or penalties if a product which should contain a label does not or has been mislabeled.

Strict Liability

In the 1960s and 1970s, with the development of the law of strict liability, plaintiffs in product liability actions gained an effective weapon to use in suits against sellers and manufacturers. Strict liability was recognized for the first time in 1963 in a product liability case in California.[39] In that case, the court stated that a manufacturer becomes strictly liable when he markets a product which contains a defect resulting in injury.

In a strict liability case, it is not necessary for the plaintiff to prove that the defendant was negligent. Further, since strict liability is a tort theory, warranty defenses, such as the plaintiff's failure to notify the defendant of the alleged defect which resulted in injury to the plaintiff, may not be used.

The doctrine of strict liability is a creation of the courts, which as a matter of public policy decided that injuries from defective products should be borne by the sellers and manufacturers, not by the injured parties. Strict liability is applied to both sellers and manufacturers. Thus, anyone who sells a product in a defective state which could be unreasonably dangerous to a user or his property, provided that the seller sells such products regularly and the product remains in the same condition as it is sold, may be held liable for selling a defective product. The seller or manufacturer is liable even though he used all due care. Further, the injured party need not show privity with the defendant.[40]

A product liability case in strict liability has obvious advantages over either a negligence or breach of warranty theory. In a negligence case, it is often very difficult for the plaintiff to show that the seller or manufacturer was negligent. In such a case, the defendant may use the defense of contributory negligence or assumption of the risk. Further, a manufacturer defendant could show that the negligence was really in a component purchased from another manufacturer and that he had no way of discovering the defect. Strict liability also has obvious advantages over a breach of warranty case, because in the latter case the defendant has certain defenses, such as the plaintiff's failure to notify about the breach of warranty, disclaimers of liability, and the plaintiff's failure to rely upon the warranty.

Strict liability applies only to products which are defective and unreasonably dangerous. A handsaw may result in injury to its user, but ordinarily it is not defective. Thus, the manufacturer or seller of the handsaw would not be liable for the injury unless, for example, there was some defect in the manufacture of the blade.

In order for the plaintiff to recover in a strict liability case, he must first show the relationship of the defendant to the product. The defendant must have been either the manufacturer or a member of the chain of distribution. Second, the plaintiff must show that the product was defective and unreasonably dangerous. Third, he must show that the defect was the proximate cause of his injuries. Fourth, he must show his injuries or damages.

The defect may be in the actual manufacture of the product, such as in the manufacture of a casting or forging. Or the defect may be in the design of the product, such as the failure to provide adequate safety guards. Further, the defect may be the failure to furnish a required warning with the product.

To prove that a product was unreasonably dangerous, the plaintiff must show that he used it in the manner intended and that it was unsafe for that use. The plaintiff must also show that there was no substantial change in the condition of the product after it left the manufacturer's or seller's hands. Of course, if the defendant argues that there was a substantial change in the product after it left the defendant's control, the jury must find that this modification must somehow have created the defect which caused the possibility of injury to the plaintiff in order for the defendant to be found innocent.

In a strict liability case, the plaintiff can seek recovery for both personal injuries and damage to property. However, some courts have refused to apply strict liability to cases seeking recovery purely for commercial loss. Neither contributory negligence nor assumption of the risk may be used by the defendant in most states.

Proving a defect in the actual manufacture of a product is relatively easy for a plaintiff in a strict liability case. Some manufacturing defects in castings for forgings are readily apparent to a trained metallurgist. Further, circumstantial evidence can be used to prove the defect. For example, in a Pennsylvania case, a truck driver was injured when driving a truck eighteen days after its delivery to the owner. The plaintiff presented evidence that the truck had been maintained properly during those eighteen days, when the brakes suddenly failed. The court stated that this was sufficient evidence to conclude that the product was defective.[41]

Cases involving design defects have probably resulted in the greatest number of appeals in strict liability actions. Generally, the courts now hold that the plaintiff must show that the design was "not reasonably safe." The jury may consider alternative designs, the obviousness of the safety hazard to the plaintiff, and the cost of making the product safer.[42] Thus, proof of a design defect in a strict liability case is similar to that in a negligence case. However, in a strict liability case, the jury looks at the product to determine whether it is defective, whereas in a negligence case it considers the actions of the manufacturer to determine whether he acted reasonably in the design process.

In a design defect strict liability case, the defendant may introduce evidence on the "state of the art," the industry customs or standards for the design of the product, when it was manufactured. However, the fact that the defendant may have followed industry design norms at the time the product was manufactured is not a complete defense. The plaintiff may still show that feasible alternative designs were available which would have eliminated the design defect. Moreover, some courts today allow the plaintiff to introduce evidence on changes in product design *after* manufacture, not to show that the original design was defective, but only as proof of an alternative feasible design which would have eliminated the safety hazard.

PRODUCT RECALLS

When a manufacturer or seller learns of a product defect after manufacture or sale, he is required by law to take reasonable steps to warn potential users of the potential hazard. Although the manufacturer or seller is not necessarily under a duty to recall the product, many do so to minimize the chances of injury. Of course, this should also minimize exposure to potential lawsuits. Unfortunately for the party initiating a warning or recall letter, the letter may be used as evidence to show that a defect was present in the product before it left the manufacturer's control.[43]

In recent years, Congress has passed several acts covering certain products, providing for mandatory recalls pursuant to an order of the appropriate federal agency. These acts are the National Traffic and Motor Vehicle Safety Act, administered by the National Highway Traffic Safety Administration; the Consumer Product Safety Act, administered by the Consumer Products Safety Commission; the Food, Drug and Cosmetic Act, administered by the Food and Drug Administration; the National Mobile Home Construction and Safety Standards Act, administered by the Department of Housing and Urban Development; and the Federal Boat Safety Act, administered by the U.S. Coast Guard.

Under the National Traffic and Motor Vehicle Safety Act, a manufacturer who learns of a safety defect in a motor vehicle must notify the Secretary of Transportation and remedy the defect free of charge. However, a manufacturer need not take any steps if he determines in good faith that the defect is not substantial.

Pursuant to the Consumer Product Safety Act, when the manufacturer or seller determines that the product does not comply with a commission safety standard or contains a defect, he must notify the Consumer Product Safety Commission. The commission may then, if appropriate, order the manufacturer or retailer to engage in a recall campaign, which could include repair or replacement of the product or even a refund of the purchase price.

The Food, Drug and Cosmetic Act specifically provides that the Food and Drug Administration may recall defective medical devices and products which emit radiation. However, the administration has also ordered recall campaigns for other products under the Food, Drug and Cosmetic Act.

The Department of Housing and Urban Development, under the National Mobile Home Construction and Safety Standards Act, may order mobile home manufacturers to notify purchasers of defects. The U.S. Coast Guard, under the Federal Boat Safety Act, may order repair of boats that do not comply with certain safety standards or are otherwise defective. The manufacturers must pay for the repairs. However, the act does not apply to defects or failures to comply with a safety standard which are discovered by the manufacturer more than five years after the date of certification or manufacture. Finally, the Environmental Protection Agency may order recalls of vehicles and engines which do not meet its emission standards.

SUCCESSOR LIABILITY

As discussed below, in many states the statute of limitations in a product liability action does not start to run until the plaintiff has been injured. Accordingly, manufacturers may be defendants in product liability lawsuits arising from the use of products manufactured decades prior to the injury. Further, under certain circumstances, the corporation which is the successor to the corporation which manufactured the product may be held liable for its defect(s).

Generally, a corporation can be acquired by one of three methods. First, persons may acquire the shares of stock showing ownership of the corporation, which continues to operate as the same corporation. Since the corporation is a continuous entity, it always remains liable for the products it has manufactured, except for a special statute of limitations.

Second, a corporation may be acquired by merger with another corporation. Under such circumstances, the surviving corporation becomes a successor to the corporation which was merged into it. The successor corporation may also be held liable in a product liability lawsuit arising from the malfunction of a product manufactured by the prior corporation.

Third, the corporation may be acquired by purchasing its assets. Technically, the corporation which acquires the assets is not a successor corporation. However, the courts in recent years have wrestled with the question of whether the acquiring corporation will be treated as a successor corporation under product liability law. Generally, the courts look at the surviving entity and its similarity or dissimilarity to the corporation whose assets it bought. Thus, if the same basic shareholders and management group control the corporation which acquired the assets, the courts may find the second corporation to be the successor corporation under product liability law and responsible for the products manufactured by the first corporation.

STATUTES OF LIMITATION

Product liability actions may be filed either in contract for breach of warranty, in negligence, or strict liability. The state statute of limitations generally distinguish between actions brought in negligence, which include strict liability cases. Usually, the statute of limitations for a breach of contract action is longer than that of suits in negligence or strict liability. However, with the adoption of the Uniform Commercial Code, most of the forty-nine states which have accepted the code have adopted a four-year statute for breach of sales agreements. Section 2-725 of the code provides that actions for breach of contract must be brought within four years after the right to sue has accrued. The right to sue accrues at the time the breach of contract occurs. In a breach of warranty case, however, the right to sue generally begins at the time of delivery of the product. Thus, typically, a party who was injured and wants to file a suit for breach of warranty against the seller or manufacturer must do so within four years after delivery of the product.

For negligence actions, the majority of state courts have stated that the statute begins to run on the date of injury. The minority rule holds that it begins to run on the date of sale of the product. Further, a few states have adopted a discovery rule which states that the statute begins to run from the time the plaintiff knew, or by the exercise of due care should have known, that he has been injured.

In strict liability actions, the courts generally hold that the statute starts to run on the date of injury. In situations where the injury is not obvious, some courts hold that the statute begins to run at the time the plaintiff discovered, or by the exercise of due care should have discovered, the injury. In asbestos cases, some courts have held that the statute begins to run from the date of the last exposure to the asbestos or when it is determined medically that the plaintiff has asbesteosis.

Because of the possibility of a manufacturer being held liable in a product defect suit for a product produced by him decades earlier, some states have passed "statutes of repose" which provide that regardless of when the plaintiff was injured, no suit can be filed against a manufacturer after a stated number of years. Some states have voided these statutes for constitutional reasons. Other states have upheld them.

In Georgia, the legislature has declared that no product liability suit may be filed more than ten years following the first sale or use of the product.[44] The Oregon statute provides that strict liability suits must be commenced two years following the date of injury; however, no suit may be commenced more than eight years following the first sale of the product.[45]

DAMAGES

In Chapter 2, we considered the remedies or damages which an injured plaintiff may obtain in a negligence case. Those rules apply to the damages which may be recovered in a product liability suit for either negligence or strict liability.

Punitive damages may also be awarded in a product liability case prosecuted in negligence or in strict liability. Most often, punitive damages are sought in cases where the manufacturer is alleged to have knowingly breached the duty to warn. For example, the plaintiff may allege that the manufacturer had prior knowledge of the defect and took no steps to warn potential users of the hazard.

In a product liability case for personal injury in which damages are sought for breach of warranty, the Uniform Commercial Code's rules regarding award of damages apply. The code provides that the plaintiff in a breach of warranty action who has been personally injured may seek recovery for injury to his person.[46]

NOTES

1. *Wisdom v. Morris Hardware Co.*, 151 Wash. 86, 274 P. 1050 (1929).
2. *Henningsen v. Bloomfield Motors, Inc.*, 32 N.J. 358, 161 A.2d 69 (1960).
3. *Winterbottom v. Right*, 10 M & 109, 11 L.J. Ex.415 (1842).
4. *Huset v. J. I. Case Threshing Machine Co.*, 120 F. 865 (8th Cir. 1903).
5. *MacPherson v. Buick Motor Co.*, 217 N.Y. 382, 111 N.E. 1050 (1916).
6. *Carter v. Yardley & Co.*, 319 Mass. 92, 64 N.E.2d 693 (1946).
7. Robert D. Hursh and Henry J. Bailey, *American Law of Products Liability*, 2d ed. (Rochester, N.Y.: Lawyers Co-operative Publishing Co., 1974) §10:38 p. 413.
8. *Greenman v. Yuba Power Products, Inc.*, 59 Cal.2d 57, 27 Cal. Rptr. 697, 377 P.2d 897 (1963).
9. *Davidson v. Montgomery Ward & Co.*, 171 Ill. App. 355 (1912) disapproved, *Suevada v. White Motor Co.*, 32 Ill.2d 612, 210 N.E.2d 182 (1965).
10. *Hall v. E. I. Dupont de Nemours & Co.*, 345 F. Supp. 353 (E.D.N.Y. 1972).
11. *Sindell v. Abbott Laboratories*, 26 Cal.3d 588, 607 P.2d 924 (1980), *cert. denied sub nom, E.R. Squibb & Sons, Inc. v. Sindell*, 449 U.S. 912 (1980).
12. *Centrone v. C. Schmidt & Sons, Inc.*, 114 Misc.2d 840, 452 N.Y.S. 2d 299 (1982).
13. *Davis v. Yearwood*, 612 S.W.2d 917 (Tenn. App. 1980).
14. *Borel v. Fibreboard Paper Products Corp.*, 493 F.2d 1076 (5th Cir. 1973), *cert. denied*, 419 U.S. 869 (1974).
15. 63 Am. Jur.2d *Products Liability* §192 (1984), 181–182.
16. *Workstel v. Stern Brothers*, 3 Misc. 2d 858, 156 N.Y.S. 2d 335 (1956) and *MacDougall v. Ford Motor Co.*, 214 Pa. Super. 384, 257 A.2d 676 (1969).
17. *Worthey v. Specialty Foam Products, Inc.*, 591 S.W. 2d 145 (Mo. App. 1979).
18. *Abramowitz v. Chrysler Corp.*, 61 App. Div.2d 913, 402 N.Y.S.2d 818 (1978).
19. *Lachney v. Motor parts & Bearing Supply, Inc.*, 357 So.2d 1277 (La. App. 1978).
20. *Beihler v. White Metal Rolling & Stamping Corp.*, 65 Ill.App.3d 1001, 382 N.E.2d 1389 (1978).
21. *Darrough v. White Motor Co.*, 74 Ill.App.3d 560, 393 N.E.2d 122 (1979).
22. 63 Am.Jur.2d *Products Liability* §103 (1984).
23. 63 Am.Jur.2d *Products Liability* §63 (1984).
24. George I. Wallach, *The Law of Sales Under the Uniform Commercial Code*, §11.05 (Boston: Warren, Gorham & Lamont, 1981), 11-22 to 11-32.
25. 63 Am.Jur.2d *Products Liability*, §§193–195 (1984).
26. *Hempstead v. General Fire Extinguisher Corp.*, 269 F. Supp. 109 (D. Del. 1967).
27. Colorado Jury Instructions 2d—Civil, 2d ed., (San Francisco: Bancroft-Whitney, 1980), 14:2.
28. 63 Am.Jur.2d *Products Liability*, §38 (1984).
29. 63 Am.Jur.2d *Products Liability*, §41 (1984).
30. Restatement (Second) of Torts §395 (1965).
31. 63 Am.Jur.2d, *Products Liability* §63 (Rochester: Lawyers Co-operative Publishing Co., 1984).
32. 63 Am.Jur.2d, *Products Liability* §65, (1984).
33. *Oberman v. Alexander's Rent-A-Car*, 56 App.Div.2d 814, 392 N.Y.S.2d 662 (1977).

34. *Zahren v. Maytag Co.*, 37 N.C. App. 143, 245 S.E.2d 793, (1978), *cert denied*, 295 N.C. 557, 248 S.E.2d 735 (1978).
35. 63A Am.Jur.2d, *Products Liability* §§931–940 (1984).
36. 63 Am.Jur.2d, *Products Liability* §§42, 43, 47, 48, 50–52, (1984).
37. *Comstock v. General Motors Corp.*, 358 Mich. 163, 99 N.W.2d 627 (1959).
38. 63 Am.Jur.2d, *Products Liability* §53 (1984).
39. *Greenman v. Yuba Power Products Inc.*, 59 Cal. 2d 57, 27 Cal. Reptr. 697, 377 P.2d 897 (1963).
40. *Restatement (Second) of Torts*, §402A (1965).
41. *Clarke v. Brockway Motor Trucks*, 372 F.Supp. 1342 (E.D. Pa., 1974) and 63 Am.Jur.2d *Products Liability*, §123–151 (1984), 126–155.
42. *Voss v. Black & Decker Manufacturing Co.*, 59 N.Y. 2d 102, 463 N.Y.S. 2d 398, 450 N.E.2d 204 (1983).
43. Louis R. Frumer and Melvin I. Friedman, *Products Liability*, Vol. 2A, §17A.05 (New York: Matthew Bender, originally published 1960, last updated 1984), pp. 4A-23 to 4A-24.
44. Ga. Code Ann. §51-1-11 (1982).
45. Or.Rev.Stat., §12.115[1] (1983).
46. Uniform Commercial Code, §2-715 (1976).

Part III
CONTRACTS

7
Contract Law

During his career, an engineer usually becomes involved with contracts. An engineer working in the construction industry may have to sign an agreement drafted either by his attorney or the attorney for his client to render professional services. He may also become involved in drafting contracts to be used by his client for the contractor, including the writing of general terms and conditions. The engineer working for a manufacturing company may become involved with contracts. Occasionally, a manufacturing company may enter into a contract with a vendor for a long period of time to furnish components for a product to be manufactured and sold by the manufacturer. The drafting of such a contract may require the engineer's input. Further, engineers working in both the construction industry and manufacturing often become involved in interpreting contract provisions.

In this chapter, we will discuss some of the basic principles of contract law. In Chapter 8, we will discuss construction contracts, including the professional services agreement typically made between a design professional working in the construction industry and his client. In Chapter 9, we will look at the Uniform Commercial Code's provisions dealing with sales agreements, and in Chapter 10 we will consider government contracts.

In these chapters dealing with contracts, we can only skim the surface. A thorough investigation of contract law would take volumes. Hence, because we must deal with broad, sweeping generalities. Many of the rules we will discuss have exceptions and permutations which may affect any question concerning contract drafting and interpretation.

Contracts can take many forms. They can be simple verbal agreements. They can be written letters. They can be formal contracts drafted by attorneys and executed by the parties involved.

Regardless of the form a contract takes, the same general rules apply.

As an example, I may agree to sell you my 1963 DeSoto for $200. However, because my new car will not be delivered for another week, I will not give you the DeSoto until next week. You reply that you will be happy to buy my DeSoto for $200 and pick it up next week at my house. This simple exchange of words may result in a binding contract.

Or you come to my appliance store looking for a new freezer. I show you a number of freezers and you finally decide that you like a certain one. I state that I will sell it to you for $300. You indicate that you are willing to pay this amount and inquire when it will be delivered. I say that it will be delivered the day after tomorrow and you reply, "Fine. I will take the freezer." Under such simple circumstances, a binding contract has also resulted.

Or, you send me a letter stating that you want to purchase a specific amount of sheet metal for use in your business and inquire about the price and shipment date. I reply by letter, offering to sell you the sheet metal at a specific price and advising you of the date when it will be delivered. You write back, stating that you will take the sheet metal at that price and under the terms of shipment. Again, a contract has resulted.

Or, on behalf of your truck manufacturer, you inquire whether my company would be willing to manufacture a chassis for a special truck. I answer "yes" and we enter into a long series of negotiations and discussions about the proposed venture. During those discussions, you may furnish specifications and drawings of the truck. I, in turn, may provide drawings and specifications for the proposed chassis. After much discussion, we begin negotiating the terms and conditions of the contract, which we agree will be in writing. We each contact our respective lawyers and ask them to draft a contract. One lawyer may do a draft and the other one may make changes in it. That process may continue through a number of drafts, with both of us giving instructions to our lawyers. Finally, we agree upon a specific contract, which may run for many typewritten pages. We then have the appropriate officers of each of our companies sign the contract and place the corporate seals of the respective firms on it. Again, a contract has resulted.

Regardless of the form a contract takes, whether verbal or written, to be enforceable it requires some form of agreement between the parties, who must be competent and who must have assented to the agreement. Further, the agreement must be supported by consideration, it must be legal, and it must meet the formal demands of the law.

If I tell you I will sell you my 1963 DeSoto for $200, but you say that you'll pay only $100, and nothing further is said about the price, there is no agreement between us. If I agree to sell a minor or a mentally incapacitated person my DeSoto, there is also no agreement. If we both agree that I will sell you my 1963 DeSoto for $200, neither of us realizing that my sixteen-year-old, highly irresponsible son has just driven it off a cliff, totally destroying it and rendering it worthless, there is also no agreement. If I tell you that I will give you my house and you say you will take it, there is no agreement because there is no consideration. If I tell you that I will pay you $10,000 if the Chicago Cubs lose the World Series, there is no agreement because under the law of most states such gambling contracts are illegal and unenforceable. Further, if I tell you that I will sell you my house for $50,000 and you agree, the law of most states will not enforce this agreement because it has not met the requirement that contracts on the purchase of real estate be written.

These are the concepts we will discuss in the remainder of this chapter.

DEFINITIONS

At the outset, we shall consider the definition of some terms commonly used in the law of contracts. First, a "promise" is a statement of an intent to act or not act in a specific manner and makes it clear that a commitment has been made. The person making the promise is referred to as the "promissor" The person receiving the benefit of the promise is called the "promissee." If the performance of the promise benefits a person other than the promissee, that person is known as the "beneficiary.[1]

When I tell you that I will sell you my 1963 DeSoto for $200, I have made clear to you my intention to sell you the car at that price. Under those circumstances, I am the promissor and you are the promissee.

Some promises are merely illusory or statements of intention. A statement that I will employ you as an engineer if I get a certain contract is a statement of intent. Although it is a promise, it depends on whether I obtain the contract.

A promise must also be distinguished from a statement of opinion. If I tell you that my 1963 DeSoto is in good condition, that may not necessarily be a promise, but rather a statement of opinion. If you have a mechanical problem with the car after buying it from me, my statement may not be sufficient for a court to hold that I have warranted the car's mechanical condition in all respects.

A promise may be in writing, may be verbal, or may be inferred from conduct. Thus, my promise to sell you my DeSoto for $200 is verbal. If I wrote you a letter making the same promise, this would be a written promise. Or if I tell you I will sell you my car for $200, holding out the keys, which you then take, your action may imply a promise on your part to pay $200 for the automobile.

Contracts are occasionally referred to as "formal" or "simple." A formal contract is a creature of common law, an executed document under seal, frequently using a wax seal. All other contracts are simple, including verbal contracts and contracts in writing, but without a seal.

Contracts may also be "expressed" or "implied." If the parties state their agreement in either written or verbal form the contract is referred to as being expressed. Or if I call a repairman to come to my house and fix my refrigerator, and do not discuss the cost of the service with him, an express contract results in which I have agreed to pay him a reasonable fee.

An implied contract is one that is implied as a matter of law. Thus, when an unconscious patient is brought to a hospital by an ambulance service, the law implies that the patient will pay a reasonable fee for services rendered to him in connection with his care at the hospital.

Contracts may also be "executed" or "executory." An executed contract is one which is performed. Thus, when I promise to sell you my car for $200 and you pay me the money, taking delivery of the car, the contract has been executed.

An executory contract is one under which something must still be performed. As an example, if I promise to sell you my car for $200 with payment and delivery next week, neither payment nor delivery has been performed and the contract is executory.

Contracts may also be "enforceable," "void," "voidable," or "unenforceable." An enforceable contract is one which is binding and may be enforced in a court of law, with the aggrieved party receiving either damages or, under some circumstances, specific performance due to breach of the contract.

A voidable contract is one in which one of the parties may avoid the obligations of the contract. For example, when a minor enters into a contract, he has the option either to accept or reject it.

A void contract is one under which the promisor has no legal obligation.

An unenforceable contract is one which may not be enforced by law due to certain defenses, such as the statute of limitations.

OFFER AND ACCEPTANCE

An offer and its acceptance are two of the main ingredients creating a contract. An offer is simply a statement by which the offeror promises something to the promisee. The acceptance is the promisee's acceptance of the offer. Thus, if I say that I will sell you my car for $200, that is an offer. If you say that you will buy my car, you have accepted the offer. Essentially, both of us have indicated our intent to form a contract.

For years, legal scholars and the courts have debated whether the intent should be determined by an objective or subjective standard. What if I say I will sell you my car for $200, not really intending to do so? Will the court, in determining whether there has been an intent to make a contract, attempt to look into my mind? Generally, the courts have concluded that they will not follow such a subjective standard. Rather, they have determined that they will look at what a reasonable man in the position of the offeree would have concluded from my statement.

What exactly is an offer? Is my statement really an expression of an opinion, an intention, or an intent to enter into preliminary negotiations?

In one case, a father asked a doctor how long his son would be in the hospital following an operation. The doctor said that he thought it would be no more than four days and that the boy would be able to return to work after a few days of recuperation at home. However, it took the boy a month to heal. In that case, the court said that the doctor was not liable since he had offered an opinion and had not made a promise.[2] However, a statement by a doctor guaranteeing that a patient's hand would be perfect was interpreted as a promise.[3]

If I tell you, "I think I *may* want to sell my car for $200," and you reply, "I *will* pay you $200 for your car," no contract results. This is because the courts have concluded that my statement is an intention, not a promise.[4] Similarly, a request to enter into negotiations is not an offer.

In recent years, businessmen have been agreeing to "letters of intent," which often outline the broad general agreement to a transaction but which envision the execution of a written contract. Whether a letter of intent really has no binding effect depends upon the language used in it. It is possible that a letter of intent itself is a contract.

The courts usually hold that an advertisement which offers to sell a product at a specific price is not an offer, but rather an invitation for an offer. This principle evolved from cases where either the newspaper or the advertiser had made a mistake in the advertisement on the price of a product. However, under some circumstances, an advertisement may be construed as an offer by the court—where, for example, a person states in an advertisement that he will purchase each share of a company's common stock for a specific price.[5]

Normally, a price quotation is considered to be a statement of intent. Frequently, the seller will receive an inquiry from a buyer on the price of a product. If the seller responds with the price, the court considers this to be a statement of intention because usually no quantity is stated in the price quotation. However, under some circumstances, a price quotation may be considered an offer when a definite quantity is discussed.

An offer must be definite. If it is vague, so that the courts have no standard by which to interpret it, the offer will not result in a contract. Thus, the mere statement that an employer will pay an employee a bonus based upon the profits of a business is vague and will not be considered a definite offer.[6] In such a case, the court has no way to determine what share of the profits should be paid. However, if an engineer agrees to render professional services to a client and does so without any agreement on the fee to be paid, the engineer is entitled to a reasonable fee. The reason for this rule is that although no price was agreed to, the engineer has performed services and should be compensated for them.

Frequently, the offer involves performance by the offeree over a period of time. If an engineering firm offers an engineer a job for one year and the engineer accepts, a contract of employment for a year has occurred. However, if an engineering firm simply offers an engineer a job, without a statement regarding its duration, the employee can be terminated "at will." Of course, today, state and federal legislation and court decisions govern the reasons for which an employee may or may not be terminated, such as statutes dealing with race, age, and sex discrimination.

In situations involving dealers or distributors of products, the courts generally hold that when there is no agreement specifying the length of the business relationship, the dealer or distributor may be terminated at will. However, the courts further state that the dealer or distributor must be given reasonable notice of termination and must be allowed a reasonable period of time before being terminated, unless some justifiable reason exists for immediate termination, such as the nonpayment of bills from the manufacturer. The courts have held that a reasonable period of time must be allowed prior to termination in such situations in order to permit the dealer or distributor to attempt to obtain a new source of supply. Further, the courts have ruled that in situations where the dealer or distributor has not had a reasonable opportunity to recoup his investment, he may receive as damages in a wrongful termination case the amount of his unrecovered investment, even though he may still be terminated.

An offer may be terminated by several methods. First, it may be revoked by the offeror. This simply means that the offeror informs the offeree that he is withdrawing the offer.

In order for revocation to be effective, it must be received by the offeree. Thus, a letter revoking an offer is not effective until the offeree has received it. Of course, the offeror may give an option or a firm offer which states that the offer will remain open for a certain period of time. Under such circumstances, the offer remains open until this period of time has passed.

If it has not definitely been stated how long the offer will remain open, then it lapses after a reasonable period of time. What is reasonable depends upon the facts of each situation.

Rejection of the offer by the offeree also terminates the offer.

Similarly, a counteroffer by the offeree terminates the offer, as does the death or disability of either the offeror or the offeree. An offer may also be terminated by a subsequent law barring the subject of the offer.

For a contract to be created, the offeree must accept the offer. There are no particular words which must be used to signify acceptance. However, if the offeree qualifies his acceptance, there is no contract. A qualified acceptance becomes a counteroffer and a contract will not result until the original offeror accepts the counteroffer.

Only the person to whom the offer is made may accept. However, if a offer is made to a class of individuals or to the public, the acceptance of any member of the class or the public creates a contract.

If the offer specifies a particular method of acceptance, such as a letter of reply, that method must be used for the contract to be effective. Usually, silence cannot be interpreted as acceptance of an offer.

In a "unilateral" contract, acceptance occurs with performance by the offeree. A unilateral contract is an agreement by which a promise is made in exchange for performance by the offeree. Thus, if I state, "I will pay you $10 to cut my grass," and you cut my grass, a unilateral contract has occurred.

A "bilateral" contract exists when two promises are exchanged. For instance, if I say that I will pay you $10 to cut my grass and you say that you will cut my grass, a bilateral contract has been made.

An offer can be accepted by any means of communication. The acceptance can be by mail, telegraph, or telephone. Generally, acceptance by mail takes effect when the letter containing the acceptance is mailed and is properly addressed. The acceptance is effective when the letter is mailed, even though the offeror may have sent a letter revoking the acceptance before he receives the letter containing the acceptance by the offeree.

INCAPACITY

Under the law, certain persons do not have the legal capacity to enter into a contract. These are primarily minors and those with certain mental disabilities. A contract with a minor is not void; it is voidable. The minor may elect to perform the contract. However, an adult who has entered into a contract cannot void it. A minor may void a contract any time during his minority. If the minor has received money or property under the contract, he must return it if it is still in his possession. However, if he does not have control over the money or property, he may void the contract without making restitution.

After reaching legal age, the person still has a reasonable time to void any contracts he entered into as a minor. Or he may ratify any contracts entered into when he was a minor.

A minor is always liable for any necessities he purchased under a contract. Such contracts cannot be voided by the minor.

During minority, a contract between a minor and an adult may be approved by a court. Such contracts then become binding. Usually, the contract is entered into on behalf of the minor by a court-appointed guardian.

Some persons may lack the mental capacity to enter into contracts. Contracts between such persons and those who are competent are voidable by the person who is mentally disabled. However, contracts entered into on his behalf by a duly appointed guardian with a competent person are valid.

Generally, a person who is intoxicated is bound by the contracts he makes while drunk, except if he was in such a state of intoxication that he could not have realized what he was doing. Under those circumstances, upon recovery, that person may ratify the contract to which he entered.

MISTAKES, FRAUD, AND DURESS

At times, courts must determine whether one or both of the parties genuinely intended to enter into a contract. This raises questions of fraud, duress, mistake, undue influence, and unconscionability.

Historically, the law has considered mistakes as being of two kinds—unilateral and mutual. If only one party made a mistake concerning a fact pertaining to the contract, he was bound by the contract and could not obtain relief. However, if both parties had made a mutual factual mistake, they could obtain relief.

For example, if I had agreed to sell my 1963 DeSoto for $200, not knowing it was worth considerably more, I would be bound by the contract. However, in the situation referred to earlier, where both of us have agreed to the sale while being unaware that my son had just demolished it, the courts would state that no contract existed because there was a mutual mistake of fact, the existence of the automobile.

Today, some courts allow relief in certain cases where a unilateral mistake has been made. In such situations, the court balances the advantages and disadvantages to both parties if the contract is to be declared void. First, the court determines whether enforcement of the contract would be oppressive to the party who made the mistake. Second, the court decides whether voiding it would result in a substantial detriment to the other party.

As an example, traditionally when a subcontractor or contractor made a mistake in a bid he was not allowed relief, because the court looked upon such a mistake as unilateral. Now some courts will grant relief in such a situation, but only if certain facts exist. First, the agreement must be executory. Second, the mistake must be substantial. Third, the mistake cannot be an error in judgment, but must be a mistake in computation, misunderstanding of specifications, or a mistake of similar input.[7]

If one party has fraudulently induced another party to enter into a contract, the party who has been defrauded may set aside the contract. In order to do this, the party seeking to terminate the contract must show the same elements as a tort action for fraud. Thus, in the lawsuit, the plaintiff must prove that the defendant made a representation while knowing it to be false or concealed certain crucial facts from the plaintiff. In addition, the plaintiff must show that this was done with the intent to deceive and to induce the plaintiff to act upon the representation or concealment of the fact. Further, the plaintiff must show that he relied upon the representation or concealment and was induced by it to act.[8] Essentially, the plaintiff must show that the defendant knew of the misrepresentation and intended to deceive the plaintiff. Usually, the courts require that the misrepresentation be of a material fact.

Making a promise to perform without the intent to do so is also considered by most courts to be a misrepresentation of fact. However, giving an opinion is not necessarily fraudulent. Further, a misrepresentation of the law is not considered fraudulent, since all parties are presumed to know the law.

Failure to disclose a fact is not a misrepresentation. However, the concealment of a fact with the aim of hiding it from the other party may be a sufficient misrepresentation to constitute fraud. Further, in certain situations, the party concealing the fact may have a legal duty to disclose it. For example, in a case where city officials knew of abnormal subsoil conditions but did not inform the contractor, the city was held liable to the contractor. The city had advised the contractor to examine the conditions of the work site prior to bidding on the contract. The court reasoned that because the contractor did not know of the potential subsoil problems due to the concealment of the city officials, the city should be liable to reimburse him for his loss.[9]

The party who uses fraud to set aside a contract must also show that he was deceived by the misrepresentation and relied upon it when entering into the contract. Although in a tort action for fraud the plaintiff must show that he has suffered damage, no such requirement is necessary in a contract case to terminate an agreement due to fraud.[10]

In fraud actions, the courts also hold that if the plaintiff could have reasonably investigated to determine the truth or falsity of the misrepresentation, he should not win the case.

Ordinarily, the law places a party under a duty to read any document or contract he executes. He cannot object that he did not read or understand it. However, there are some exceptions to this rule. If the document or provision is illegible, the courts may find it not binding. Further, under certain circumstances, a party may owe a duty to another party to call certain provisions to his attention, such as standard printed provisions on the reverse side of a purchase or sales order. Some courts also allow the doctrine of fraud or mistake to be used as an exception. Thus, some courts have allowed relief to a party allegedly defrauded when the other party misrepresented the terms of the contract.

In recent years, some courts have been reluctant to enforce "contracts of adhesion." Such contracts result primarily when both sides have unequal bargaining power and the party with greater power has drafted a contract which contains terms favorable to him. Usually cases involving contracts of adhesion center on the attempt by the party with greater bargaining power to enforce a provision of the contract. Under some circumstances the courts have refused to enforce such a provision, reasoning either that there had been no real bargaining over the provision or that enforcement of it would violate public policy or be unconscionable.

In cases involving contracts of adhesion, the courts do not necessarily throw out the entire contract. The cases usually involve interpretation of one provision, which, if interpreted favorably to the party with greater power, could be extremely detrimental to the other party.

CONSIDERATION

For a contract to be made, there must be "consideration." Consideration is the thing which the promisor acquires in exchange for his promise. Thus, in a simple situation where I tell you that I will sell you my car for $200 and you pay me that amount, the payment is the consideration.

A promise can be exchanged for a promise which gives sufficient consideration to support the existence of a contract. As an example, when I tell you that I will sell you my car and deliver it to you next week in exchange for $200, and you agree to buy my car and pay me $200 next week when you take delivery, my offer to you, which is a promise, is supported by the consideration of your promise to pay for the car.

As stated earlier, a unilateral contract is one in which the promisor makes a promise in exchange for performance by the promisee. Thus, when I tell you that I will pay you $10 to cut my grass, and you cut my grass, the act of cutting my grass is performance and consideration.

Some courts have looked at consideration in terms of legal detriment, which occurs when the promisee promises either to do something he legally need not do or refrain from doing. A California case provides an example of consideration where the promisee had refrained from doing something he legally could do. In that case, the contractor and the earthwork subcontractor both made a mistake about soil conditions in connection with the construction of an airfield. Because of the mistake, the subcontractor, if he had wished, could have avoided performing the contract. However, the contractor told him that he would pay him an extra sum if he performed the subcontract. Following performance of the subcontract, the contractor refused to pay. The subcontractor sued him and the court decided in favor of the subcontractor, stating that he was entitled to the extra payment because he forebore his right to not perform the contract due to the mutual mistake.[12]

Neither motive nor past consideration will support consideration for a promise. Thus, when I state that I will give you $50 next week and ask nothing of you in return, my motive may be good, but because you have not suffered any detriment, no binding contract has resulted. Further, If I tell you that I will pay you $50 because you helped me move last week, you have not given up anything, and therefore there is not sufficient consideration to enforce my promise.

In order for there to be adequate consideration, the promise should be binding. In some cases, this involves a subtle distinction. For instance, when a manufacturer agrees to purchase all the components he orders during the year from a vendor at a stated price, there is no consideration because the manufacturer's promise is not binding. The manufacturer is not under any obligation to purchase any components from that vendor during the year. However, when the manufacturer tells the vendor that he will purchase all the components he needs during the year from that vendor, a binding contract exists.

The courts do not consider the adequacy of the consideration. The payment or the agreement of $1 may be sufficient consideration resulting in a valid contract.[13]

An existing obligation is not consideration which will support a contract. When a party agrees to do something or refrain from doing something which he is already obligated to do or not do, there has been no detriment and hence no consideration. As an example, a police officer has a duty to enforce the law. Accordingly, although an ordinary citizen may be able to claim a reward for furnishing information which leads to the apprehension and conviction of a person for a crime, a police officer cannot do so because he is already under a legal obligation to enforce the law. Similarly, if I have agreed to sell you my car for $200 and to deliver it next week, if prior to that time I change my mind and tell you that I want $300 and you agree, I cannot enforce my contract against you to purchase the car for $300. The reason is that I was already obligated to sell you the car for $200. A few courts, however, would hold that your agreement to pay me $300 for the car, instead of $200, resulted in a new contract and that you would be bound by it. These few courts which follow this minority rule reason that our first contract was mutually rescinded and that the detriment you paid for it was giving up your right to sue me for breach of contract.

Suppose I have borrowed money and have agreed to pay it back 90 days from today, but when that time comes, the promissee, knowing that I have only limited funds, agrees to take a lesser amount? Can the promissee then sue me for the difference between what I paid and what I should have paid? Under the law, the promissee can recover because there has been no consideration or detriment on my part for paying the lesser sum. However, if I agree to do something in addition to paying the lesser sum, then the courts will find adequate consideration. Thus, if I owe $10,000 but the bank agrees to reduce this sum to $8,000 in exchange for a mortgage upon some of my property, the courts accept the mortgage as sufficient consideration to support a new contract.[14]

In certain situations, consideration is not required to create a binding contract. For example, voluntary subscriptions to a charity are legally enforceable. Numerous people may pledge funds for the construction of an addition to a church or a new college building. Under the law, all the pledges are legally enforceable, because the courts consider the promise of one pledger to have been supported by the promises of the other pledgers.

Under common law, sealed instruments did not have to be supported by consideration to be legally binding. This rule has been either abolished or modified in most states.

Under the Uniform Commercial Code, "firm offers" by merchants are also legally enforceable, even though not supported by consideration. A firm offer is a written statement that written offer will be held open for a stated period of time.

Finally, the consideration must be legal. Thus, no binding contract will result when I agree to pay you $50 if you break into someone's house.

LEGALITY

Generally, the courts will not enforce an illegal contract. For example, due to antigambling statutes, gambling, including lotteries, is illegal in many states. Contracts to influence government action through corruption are illegal and unenforceable. However, insurance contracts usually are legal because the purchaser has an insurable interest in the property or life being insured. Generally, any contract to commit a crime is unenforceable.

By statute in most states, usury, a rate of interest above some legally prescribed maximum, is illegal. In most states, if a contract is usurous, all the interest is forfeited. In other states, only the illegal portion of the interest is forfeited. Further, some states assess penalties in addition to forfeiture of interest.

Under common law, contracts in restraint of trade were unenforceable. However, the contract had to be an unreasonable restraint of trade. For example, many employment contracts contain provisions barring the employee from competing with the employer for a certain period of time after termination of employment. The enforceability of such contracts is a matter of state law, and depends upon the work that the employee did for the employer and the extent of the restraint. In addition, agreement to fix prices, divide territories, limit production, or pool profits were held to be illegal restraints of trade under common law.

FORM

The next requirement for a valid contract is that the agreement comply with the form required by law. A contract may be either written or verbal, except in those instances where a contract is required by statute to be in writing. Such statutes are called "statutes of fraud."

Statutes of fraud began with a 1677 act of the English Parliament entitled the "Act for the Prevention of Fraud and Perjuries." This act contained twenty-five sections and stated that certain documents had to be in writing. For contracts, these included agreements to answer for the debt of another, marriage agreements, agreements concerning the sale of land or interest in land, agreements on the sale of personal goods above a certain value, and agreements which could not be performed within one year.

One reason for requiring certain contracts to be in writing was to prevent perjury. Further, Parliament obviously realized that certain contracts were so important that in order for them to be enforceable in the courts, they had to be in writing. Basically, by enacting the statute of frauds, Parliament was seeking independent verification of the contract, rather than relying upon the testimony of witnesses, which might be perjured or faulty.

Usually, when someone promises to pay the debt of another, the law refers to the person making the promise as a "guarantor" or "surety." Typically, in most states, such promises must be in writing in order to comply with the statute of frauds. However, if the person making the promise to pay the debt is doing so primarily for his own benefit, then there is no need for a written contract. As an example, an aircraft manufacturer contracted with a company to manufacture a wind tunnel. Another company was selling material to a subcontractor for construction of the wind tunnel, and the aircraft manufacturer and contractor both advised the subcontractor's vendor that he would be paid. When he was not paid, he sued the manufacturer and the contractor, who alleged that their promises were not in writing. The court found for the subcontractor's vendor, holding that the primary beneficiaries of the promise to pay the debt of another were the promissors, that is, the aircraft manufacturer and the contractor for the wind tunnel.[15]

All contracts to convey or sell land or interest in land, such as buildings or leases, must be in writing. However, the statute of frauds of most states ordinarily applies only to the agreement pertaining to the land. Thus, a contract between the seller of the land and a real estate broker to solicit perspective purchasers of the land does not necessarily need to be in writing. Further, once the contract is performed, that is, once the seller has conveyed the land or the interest in the land to the buyer, an oral contract for the sale of either is enforceable.

Generally, contracts for the sale of goods or products above a certain sum must be in writing. Today, the sale of goods is covered by Article II of the Uniform Commercial Code, which provides that there must be evidence in writing of a sale of goods worth more than $500. We will discuss this provision of the code in Chapter 9.

A contract which cannot be performed within one year from its date must be in writing. However, under the interpretation of the statute of frauds followed by the courts of most states, if it is possible to perform the contract within one year, it need not be in writing. Thus, a promise made today to cut and deliver a certain amount of timber prior to a date two years hence need not be in writing, because it would be possible to perform the contract within one year.[16] However, an agreement to work for someone for two years must be in writing, because the work cannot possibly be performed in one year.[17] Further, promises which may be performed within one year but are conditioned upon an uncertain event need not be in writing. Thus, a promise to pay a commission upon the sale of certain property need not be in writing, because the sale could occur within one year.[18]

Under the statute of frauds, the written evidence of the contract need not be a formal document. It can simply be a note or memorandum consisting a number of documents, such as a series of letters. Further, it may not necessarily be made at the time of the original agreement; it may be made subsequently. However, it must contain sufficient identity of the parties and a description of the subject matter of the agreement, and must identify the terms and conditions of the agreement, including who promised what to whom. Further, the document does not have to be signed by both parties. Only the person who is being charged with breach of the agreement must have signed it.

According to the majority rule, a contract which is not in compliance with the statute of frauds is voidable. The minority rule is that the contract is void. Under the majority rule, if an action is brought upon a contract which should be within the statute of frauds, the defendant may raise this statute as a defense. Further, in some situations, when the contract does not comply with the statue of frauds, the courts will enforce it if there has been partial performance showing that a contract had been made.

PAROLE EVIDENCE RULE

Under the Parole Evidence Rule, the last writing evidencing a contract is considered the final document showing the agreement of the parties. Evidence of earlier negotiations or agreement upon earlier terms cannot be used to alter the meaning of any provision of the last written document containing the contract terms. However, evidence may be introduced at trial to show that the last document was not intended to be the final contract. Under the Parole Evidence Rule, once the court decides that the written document is the final version of the contract, and was intended to be so by the parties, other evidence, such as evidence of statements made during negotiations, cannot be admitted to alter the written document.

The Parole Evidence Rule does not apply under certain circumstances. First, one of the parties may argue that the written document is not a complete statement of the agreement. If so, other evidence may be admitted by the court to determine what other provisions were agreed to by the parties. Second, parole evidence may be used to show that the act of entering into the contract was fraudulent or that certain provisions of it were accidental or mistaken. Further, if the written document contains an ambiguity, the court may hear evidence or look at other documents in an attempt to interpret it. Moreover, the party may introduce other evidence to show that the written document was modified or terminated after it was written.

A common situation arises when two parties execute a contract to construct a building, but later the owner makes changes in the work without any written evidence about these changes. In such cases, the Parole Evidence Rule may not be applicable. The contractor can introduce other evidence to show that the written contract had been modified.[19]

INTERPRETATION

Over the years, the courts have set down certain basic rules of interpretation for contracts, besides those pertaining to parole evidence. First, words are to be given their plain meaning. Technical words should be interpreted technically. Words should be interpreted to meet the intention of the parties.

The contract document should be interpreted as a whole. The terms of the contract should be interpreted to give meaning to all of the provisions, so that none of the terms are in conflict with each other.

If when applying the above rules a court is unable to interpret a contract, it relies upon other rules. Obviously, clear mistakes in writing or grammar will be corrected by the court. For example, if a contract term refers to the "seller" when it obviously meant the "buyer," the court will correct the contract accordingly in interpreting it. Specific words will modify general words. Conflicts between terms should be resolved by interpreting the terms in such a way that there is no conflict. The contract should be interpreted so that it will be reasonable and will be construed against the person who wrote it. The parties' interpretation of a specific term will be used in interpreting the contract. Further, when a contract contains both printed and typed terms, the latter will take precedence over the former. Where a term has a certain meaning under trade or custom, the court will hear evidence on trade and custom in the relevant business to interpret the contract provision.

THIRD-PARTY BENEFICIARIES

Under the law of most U.S. states, the third-party beneficiary to a contract has certain rights to enforce provisions of the contract. A third-party beneficiary is not a party to the contract but is someone who may benefit from its performance. The intent of the parties to the contract determines whether a person is a third-party beneficiary entitled to certain rights. As an example of third-party beneficiary contracts, the beneficiary of a life insurance policy is not a party to the contract but is a third-party beneficiary entitled to payment under the policy. Typically, owners are not party to a performance bond, but are beneficiaries of it if the contractor defaults on performance. Similarly, material men and subcontractors are third-party beneficiaries of payment bonds.

ASSIGNMENT

Under common law, a person could not assign a contract right or duty. Today, however, rights and duties under a contract may be assigned under certain circumstances. First, there must be an intent of the person holding the right to assign it. The assignment does not have to be in writing. An assignment, however, is ineffective against the other party if his duty owed to the assigning party is materially changed, if the burden to the other party is materially increased, or if the other party's chance of obtaining return performance is materially impaired.

As assignment of the right to receive money or delivery of goods is not considered material. However, under certain circumstances, an assignment of an employment contract may be invalid.

If someone sells a house and assigns an insurance policy covering it to the buyer, the risk to the insurer may be materially altered, so that the assignment may be void. Or the assignment of an agency to promote the sale of certain products may be invalid.[20]

Assignment of duties is ineffective if the other party has a justifiable reason for relying upon the performance of the assignor. Thus, where an owner enters into a contract with a contractor for the construction of a building, the assignment of the contract to another contractor may be invalid because of the owner's reliance upon the first contractor.

Basically, if the assignment of a right can make no difference to the other party, it is considered valid.

Generally, when a contract is assigned, the assignee accepts it with all the defenses which could be raised by the other party. After notice of assignment is given, defenses against the assignor which arise after the assignment are not effective against the assignee.

DISCHARGE

A contract may be discharged by performance, by agreement of the parties, by impossibility of performance, or by law. If a contract is fully performed by both parties, obviously it is discharged. If one party tenders performance by stating that he is ready to perform, but the other party does not accept the tender, then the party offering to perform is discharged from any obligation under the contract.

The contract need not be performed in every respect. The courts will accept substantial performance. This issue usually arises in construction cases, where the contractor did not meet all the requirements of the contract documents. However, the noncompliance may be minor, and the courts will allow an offset for the cost of correcting the minor defects.

The parties may also agree to terminate the contract. Further, one party may agree to waive performance by the other party. The parties may also agree to terminate the first contract and substitute a second one.

The parties may also agree to substitute a different form of performance under the contract, which is referred to as an "accord." When the substituted performance is done, then the courts say there has been an "accord and satisfaction." Under an accord and satisfaction, the original contract considered is discharged.

A contract may be discharged due to the destruction of the subject matter, a change in the law, the death or disability of one of the parties, or the act of the parties to the contract. As an example, if an owner refuses to pay a contractor, the contractor's performance may be excused or discharged.

Under the law, when one party makes a material alteration in a written contract without the approval of the other party, the party who did not make the alteration is discharged from performance. The statute of limitations may also discharge a contract. Further, under the bankruptcy laws, contracts may be discharged by order of the bankruptcy court.

BREACH AND REMEDIES

Any failure to perform a contract is a breach of it which entitles the aggrieved party to damages. In some circumstances, the injured party may also obtain specific performance from the other party.

If the breach is minor, courts refer to it as a "partial breach," and the aggrieved party may obtain damages for the minor breach alone. However, if the courts determine that the breach is "material," the injured party need not continue to perform the contract; he may consider the contract terminated and file a suit for damages. In a case of material breach, the injured party is no longer bound to perform under the contract. As an example, a contractor had retained a subcontractor to work on a construction project. The contractor was to make monthly payments to the subcontractor. The subcontractor, in doing his work, damaged a wall under construction by the contractor. The contractor did not pay him the monthly installment due after the damage. The subcontractor walked off the job and sued the contractor. The court held that the subcontractor's negligence in damaging the wall excused the contractor from failure to make the monthly installment and stated that the subcontractor could not cease performance. Hence, the subcontractor was liable to the contractor for damages resulting from the subcontractor's breach.[21]

If a party breaches the contract more than once, the injured party may file a suit for each breach. However, at the time he files the first suit, he must seek damages for any prior breaches or his right to recover for those breaches may be lost.

In a situation where a contract is to be performed over a period of time in installments, a material breach of any one installment allows the injured party to treat the contract as totally breached and to sue the defendant for not performing the contract in its entirety. Thus, where a vendor has agreed to deliver components to a manufacturer at certain time intervals, and in one installment delivers a product which completely fails to conform to the contract specifications, the manufacturer can treat the material breach of that installment as a breach of the entire contract.

In a situation where one party states that he will not continue to perform the contract, the injured party must treat this as a complete breach. The act of refusing to perform the contract further is referred to as "repudiation."

When, prior to the time of performance, one party states that he will not perform, that party has repudiated the contract. The courts refer to this as "anticipatory repudiation." The injured party may treat this as a total breach of the contract and bring a suit for breach of the contract prior to the time set for performance.

Under certain circumstances, one party's failure to perform may not be a breach of contract. These situations are referred to as "impossibility of performance." They arise due to an unexpected occurrence which would render performance unreasonable based upon the cost and the risk or contingency has not otherwise been allocated between the parties to the contract. As an example, if a farmer had agreed to deliver potatoes to be grown upon his farm, which subsequently were destroyed due to disease, under the law, the farmer, may be excused from performance.[22]

The rules concerning impossibility of performance are complex. For example, in the building construction field, the contractor bears the risk of loss if a new building under construction is destroyed by fire. Although the contractor may look upon the fire as resulting in the impossibility of performance, the courts apparently have adopted this rule of law as a matter of public policy based primarily upon the contractor's control of the entire construction process.

In a situation where a contractor is making repairs or modifications to a building and the building is destroyed by fire, the courts hold that the owner should bear the risk and that the destruction of the building renders the contractor's performance impossible under the law, excusing his further performance.[23]

When a contractor is given plans by the owner showing the intended result but not containing sufficient details to indicate how it is to be reached, the contractor is bound to construct a building that achieves the desired effect. However, if the contractor is given plans by the owner which were done by professional engineers or architects retained by the owner, the owner bears the risk of the failure of the building to meet the desired or intended result if the contractor follows the plans and specifications.

For breach of contract, the aggrieved party's traditional remedy is to seek damages in a lawsuit. Under certain circumstances, he may bring an action in equity to rescind the contract or to obtain specific performance of it.

Under the law of damages, the purpose of the rules is to place the injured party in the same position he would have achieved had the contract been performed. Such damages are referred to as "compensatory damages." Compensatory damages include the difference between the contract price and what it would have cost the plaintiff to perform. In addition, the plaintiff may recover many of his losses or gains lost due to the defendant's breach of contract.

In a New York case, the plaintiff had agreed to manufacture automobile bodies for the defendant. The defendant repudiated the contract after production had started and approximately one-fourth of the bodies had been delivered. The plaintiff had no other market for the bodies, since they were of a special design. The court held that the plaintiff could recover his lost profit (the difference between the price and the cost of performance). In addition, the plaintiff could recover other losses, such as the costs that could not otherwise be recovered.[24]

If the plaintiff has not sustained any damage due to breach of the contract, the jury or court may still award him nominal damages. Ordinarily, punitive damages are not available to the plaintiff in a breach of contract action.

The plaintiff, however, cannot recover damages which are remote. The damages which he may recover must be those which normally arise from a breach of contract of the sort at issue, and they must have been in reasonable "contemplation" of both parties.

The damages must also be reasonably certain. The jury or the court must be able to determine them. Thus, lost profits may be recovered for an established business, whereas lost profits for a new business may be so speculative or uncertain that they may not be recovered.

The parties to a contract may have established a specific sum which will be awarded upon breach of contract by one or both of the parties. These are referred to as "liquidated damages." The courts usually enforce liquidated damages provisions in contracts, but only so long as the amount is not a penalty. In other words, the liquidated damages agreed to by the parties must be a reasonable estimate of what the loss may be due to a breach of the contract.

Under the law of damages, the plaintiff is under a duty to mitigate his damages. For instance, in the case of the automobile manufacturer mentioned above, if the body manufacturer had had another customer for the bodies and the cost of producing them would have been less than his loss due to stopping manufacture, then he may have been under a duty to look for alternative purchasers of the bodies.

If a party to a contract has totally breached it, or the contract was induced by fraud or entered into under a mutual mistake of fact, the aggrieved party may also sue in equity for "rescission" and "restitution." In an action for rescission, the plaintiff requests the court to legally terminate the contract. In rescission, the plaintiff is to be placed back into his original position and if he requires the award of any money, he seeks restitution.

Finally, under certain circumstances, the plaintiff may obtain specific performance of the contract. However, he cannot obtain specific performance if he has an adequate remedy of law. If a court can reasonably assess damages for the breach, the plaintiff will not be awarded specific performance of the contract. Generally, contracts for the purchase of land can be enforced by specific performance, since each piece of land is considered unique. However, specific performance will not be awarded when the court cannot supervise performance of the contract.

NOTES

1. *Restatement (Second) of Contracts* §2 (1981), 8–9.
2. *Hawkins v. McGee*, 84 N.H. 114, 146 A. 641 (1929).
3. *Robins v. Finestone*, 308 N.Y. 543, 127 N.E.2d 330 (1955).

4. *Cutler-Hammer, Inc. v. United States,* 441 F.2d 1179 (Ct. Cl. 1971).
5. *R. E. Crummer & Co., v. Nuveen,* 147 F.2d 3 (7th Cir. 1945).
6. *Gray v. Aiken,* 205 Ga. 649, 54 S.E.2d 587 (1949).
7. John D. Calamari and Joseph M. Perillo, *The Law of Contracts,* 2d ed., § 9-27 (St. Paul, Minn.: West, 1977), 306–308.
8. 37 Am.Jur.2d, *Fraud and Deceit* §12 (1968), 33–34.
9. *City of Salinas v. Souza & McCue Construction Co., overruled, Helfend v. So. Calif. Rapid Transit Dist.,* 2 Cal.3d 1, 84 Cal. Reptr. 173, 2165 P.2d 61 (1970), 66 Cal.2d 217, 57 Cal. Reptr. 337, 424 P.2d 921 (1967).
10. Calamari and Perillo, *The Law of Contracts* §9-16 281–282.
11. *Bob Wilson, Inc. v. Swann,* 168 A.2d 198 (Ct. App. D.Col. 1961), disagreed with as stated in *King v. Industrial Bank of Washington,* 474 A.2d 151 (Ct.App.D.Col. 1984).
12. *Healy v. Brewster,* 251 Cal. App. 2d 541, 59 Cal. Rptr. 752 (1967).
13. *Smith v. Smith,* 340 Ill. 34, 172 N.E. 32 (1930).
14. *Post v. First National Bank,* 138 Ill. 559, 28 N.E. 978 (1891).
15. *R. H. Fretag Mfg. Co. v. Boeing Airplane Co.,* 55 Wash.2d 334, 347 P.2d 1074 (1959).
16. *In re Estate of Hargreaves,* 201 Kan. 57, 439 P.2d 378 (1968).
17. *Carroll v. Palmer Mfg. Co.,* 181 Mich. 280, 148 N.W. 390 (1914).
18. *Sullivan v. Winters,* 91 Ark. 149, 120 S.W. 843 (1909).
19. *Harrington v. McCarthy,* 91 Idaho 307, 420 P.2d 790 (Idaho 1966).
20. *Paige v. Faure,* 229 N.Y. 114, 127 N.E. 898 (1920).
21. *K & G Construction Co. v. Harris,* 223 Md. 305, 164 A.2d 451 (1960).
22. *Ontario Deciduous Fruit Growers' Ass'n. v. Cutting Fruit Packing Co.,* 134 Cal. 21, 66 P. 28 (1901).
23. Calamari and Perillo, *The Law of Contracts* §13-2, 482–484.
24. *Lieberman v. Templar Motor Co.,* 236 N.Y. 139, 140 N.E. 222 (1923).

8
Construction Contracts

In this chapter, we will discuss construction contracts. We will briefly consider some of the common terms and conditions in such contracts, as well as some of the problems which may arise in drafting various contracts used in the construction industry. We will not discuss particular contracts or provisions in depth, but we will analyze some of the more common provisions and problems which arise.

The contracts we will consider in this chapter are:

1. The professional services agreement.
2. The agreement between the design professional and his consultant.
3. The construction management contract.
4. Joint ventures.
5. Fast-track jobs and contracts.
6. The construction contract with the general or prime contractor.
7. Subcontracts.
8. Turn-key or design-build jobs and contracts.

In Chapter 10, we will consider some of the common provisions of government contracts and bidding, plus some of the problems which arise in government contracts and claims made against government agencies.

PROFESSIONAL SERVICES AGREEMENTS

The agreement between the design professional and his client, the professional services agreement, can take many forms. It may be a verbal contract, a simple letter agreement, or a formal contract document. Design professionals may enter into professional services agreements using one of the standard forms prepared by either the

American Institute of Architects or the American Consulting Engineers Council. Finally, the engineer may have developed his own agreement or his client may draft an agreement for the engineer to execute.

To some extent, the nature of the services to be performed by the professional dictates the form of the agreement. An agreement to design a minor modification for an existing structure need not be as detailed as the agreement to design a large building or complicated structure. Further, not all of the duties to be performed by the engineer need be covered in the professional services agreement; some of them may be specified in an additional document, such as a scope of work agreement. Regardless of the form of the written contract, all agreements should cover the duties and responsibilities of the engineer and the method of payment.

Scope of Services

The professional services agreement should state exactly what the design professional is to do. The more specific the description of the scope of services, the less likely it is that there will be any ambiguity or that the design professional will be charged with a design error for which he never intended to be responsible. Thus, the scope of services should state not only what the design professional is to do, but also what he is not to do. With a well-defined statement, not only will ambiguities be minimized, but the engineer will be able to present claims for extra work not covered by the scope of services which will be readily apparent to the client as legitimate.

For certain construction projects, because of the routine nature of the services to be performed by the design professional, it may be relatively easy to write a scope of services. For other projects involving new, unique, unusual, or process engineering, it may not be possible to describe the full scope of services precisely. Instead, a description of the design parameters may be necessary, such as the inputs and outputs of a process plant. Of course, it may not be feasible to cover all the services to be furnished. In such cases, the custom and practice of the professional may be considered in determining what work falls within the scope of his services.[1]

AIA Document B141, Standard Form of Agreement Between

Owner and Architect, 1977 edition, contains a detailed statement of the services and responsibilities of an architect in a contract with his client. The architect's scope of services are described by various phases, such as the schematic design phase, the design development phase, the construction documents phase, the bidding or negotiation phase, and the construction phase. The services beyond those described in the scope of services are considered to be extra services for which the architect is to be compensated, in addition to the sums provided for in the basic agreement.

The services to be rendered during the design phase of a construction project may, under most circumstances, be relatively easy to state. However, this may not be true of the services to be rendered during the construction phase. Of course, in both the design and construction phase provisions of the scope of services, as well as in other provisions of the professional services agreement, the design professional must be careful not to assume any responsibility for safety or the right to direct the work of the contractor or contractors. If he does, he increases his exposure to suits brought by workmen injured during construction.

Three areas of the scope of work during the construction phase typically present drafting problems. These are the provisions covering the engineer's on-site observation, pay-out certification, and shop drawing review responsibility.

The scope of services should clarify the circumstances under which the engineer is to visit the construction site and what he is to be responsible for as a result of those visits. Frequently, especially with smaller construction projects, the owner does not want to pay the design professional for observation visits during the construction period. If he is not to be paid for this and not to have any responsibility for such visits, the scope of services should specifically so state.

Traditionally, when a design professional visits a construction site, he does so periodically to determine whether the contractor's work is in accordance with the plans and specifications. However, he does not ensure that this will be done in all respects. When undertaking on-site observations, the design professional under the law is only expected to act reasonably and can only be held liable for his failure to observe a defect or nonconformance if his failure was negligent according to the applicable professional standards.[2]

Thus, if the design professional is to provide on-site observation services, the scope of services should state this, specifying how often he is to observe and what he will be held responsible for noticing. As an example, AIA Document B141 makes it clear that during his visits to the site, the architect is not responsible for making in-depth inspections.

Frequently, the design professional's site visits are designed to observe the progress of the work in connection with a contractor's request for a pay-out. If the engineer is to make such certifications, the scope of services should so provide and should also state the nature of his responsibility in connection with those visits. For example, AIA Document B141 states that when issuing a certificate for payment, the architect renders his opinion that the work conforms to the contract documents to the *best of his knowledge.*

The design professional must also be sure that the certificate used to approve the owner's payment to the contractor does not contain language which broadens his responsibility for observing the progress of the construction. Occasionally, certificates may be used which require the design professional to certify that the construction conforms to the design and specifications *in all respects.* Such certificates are often used by financial institutions. They must be completed by the engineer in order for the owner to obtain advances under the construction loan so that the contractor may receive progress payments. Clearly, a certificate with such broad language goes beyond the engineer's traditional duty of on-site observation and may be a guaranty. Obviously, he should avoid executing any such certificates, and if he has any questions about its language or requirements, he should consult his attorney.

The scope of services for the construction phase should also make clear the limited responsibility of the engineer in reviewing shop drawings and other submittals of the contractor. Generally, the engineer is not responsible for verifying the dimensions or the engineering used to generate the shop drawings. They are done by the contractor in order to construct the project. Traditionally, the engineer's only duty in reviewing them is to determine whether they conform to the general design concept.

Frequently, professional services agreements provide that the design professional shall have no responsibility for controlling the method of work. Such a provision is contained in AIA Document

B141. An agreement with this provision may be helpful to a design professional in a case filed against him by an injured workman or by the client when the problem is due to a defect in the contractor's work.

Standard of Care

The engineer must always be alert to ensure that his professional services agreement does not contain any provisions which broaden the traditional duty of care owed by him to his client and third parties. Any language which could be interpreted as a guaranty would do this and should be avoided. Further, since professional liability policies ordinarily do not cover guarantees, the engineer may not have any insurance protection for such an undertaking.

A provision stating the design professional's traditional standard of care may also be helpful in minimizing disputes with owners. Often owners do not understand the concept of professional liability and expect the engineer to guarantee that his services will be "perfect." However, a design professional is only responsible for rendering services in accordance with the applicable professional standards used locally, unless he expands this duty by contract or other means. An engineer does not guarantee a project result. Reminding an owner of his traditional legal responsibility may help limit frivolous claims made by the owner.

There are several ways to state such a provision. A simple way is:

Engineer shall render services hereunder pursuant to generally accepted engineering principles.

Another way to describe this concept, which is more consistent with the court's statement of the concept of professional liability, is:

Engineer shall render services hereunder in accordance with the standard of care followed by engineers regularly practicing in the community in which the project is to be constructed at the time services are rendered by the engineer.

The engineer should avoid entering into agreements which state that he will act in accordance with the "highest" or "best" standards of care. Such language could impose a higher standard of care upon the engineer than that for which he would ordinarily be liable.

Besides avoiding making any warranties or guarantees in professional services agreements, an engineer may explicitly deny making them. Occasionally, agreements contain statements such as:

Engineer makes no warranties or guarantees, whether expressed or implied.

Owner's Responsibilities

The owner obviously has certain responsibilities under the professional services agreement. For example, he must cooperate with the engineer so that the latter can do the necessary design work. And if the owner does not pay him, the engineer can terminate the contract.[3]

AIA Document B141 contains a lengthy description of the owner's responsibilities, including the obligation to furnish necessary assistance, to designate a representative who may authorize on his behalf (if needed), to furnish a legal description of the property and necessary surveys, to furnish soil services, and to advise the architect of any defects in the work or discrepancies in the contract documents discovered by him.

Payment

Usually, the professional services agreement describes the amount and manner of payment to the engineer. If it does not contain a provision for payment, the engineer is still entitled to be paid a reasonable amount, based upon the customary fees charged by design professionals in his community.[4]

If the written agreement contains provisions for payment, the fees may be based upon one of several methods: a lump sum, the engineer's cost plus a fixed fee and reimbursement of certain expenses, a percentage of the estimated cost of completion, or a percentage of the actual construction cost. In the cost plus fixed fee contract, payments are frequently based upon hourly labor costs times a fixed multiple. In addition, the contract can provide for payments at particular intervals, either monthly or on completion of various phases of the project.

The engineer is entitled to a payment upon substantial completion of his work. If minor items have not been provided, his fee will be reduced accordingly. However, if he is in material breach of the contract, he is not entitled to his fee.[5]

Estimates

In Chapter 5, we discussed the problems which arise when a design professional makes cost estimates. Similar problems may arise when he estimates the time of completion or works out a project schedule. Because of their exposure under the law, many design professionals disclaim any responsibility for estimates in written agreements.

AIA Document B141 contains a lengthy description of the construction cost estimating process and contains a specific disclaimer of the architect's responsibility, including the statement that the architect does not guarantee that any bids or prices will vary from the budget or the architect's estimate of the cost.

Code Compliance

Frequently, professional services agreements provide that the design professional will prepare his design and specifications in compliance with all applicable laws. Those laws include building codes, zoning laws, zoning ordinances, and federal and state statutes, such as those concerning environmental protection. Today, with the ever-expanding number of construction regulations and laws, the typical engineer may not be an expert in all the applicable rules and may therefore not want to agree to broad statements of legal compliance. Accordingly, the engineer may want to meet with his client and his client's attorney prior to executing the agreement in order to reach an understanding on which legal statutes, ordinances, and regulations of law will apply to the project. If possible, the engineer should attempt to limit the language of the agreement to a statement that he only will comply with those codes, ordinances, regulations, and laws to which the parties have specifically agreed.

During both the design and construction phases of a project, an engineer is called upon to interpret codes and regulations, and his interpretation may differ from those of government officials. Government officials may insist that certain aspects of the design or construction be done in a certain way, although this is not clearly called for by the applicable law. In the written agreement, the engineer should make it clear, if possible, that any conflicting interpretations by government agencies with which the engineer or the owner must comply may result in additional costs to the owner for which the owner should be responsible.

Indemnification

Frequently, owners will request that the professional services agreement contain an indemnification or hold-harmless provision. Such a provision is intended to hold harmless the owner from errors or omissions of the design professional. However, the owner often drafts broad indemnification clauses which may make the engineer liable to him for damages for which the engineer would not ordinarily be liable. For example, some hold-harmless provisions can be interpreted to make the engineer liable not only for indemnification of the owner for the engineer's malpractice but also for damages sustained by the owner or third parties which may not be due to the engineer's negligence. Indemnification clauses should be reviewed by the engineer's attorney so that the engineer can determine whether he is liable for something for which he would not otherwise be responsible. Further, hold-harmless clauses should be reviewed by the design professional's insurance broker, since some professional liability policies may not cover certain indemnification provisions.

The subject of indemnification will be discussed in further detail in Chapter 13.

Insurance

The professional services agreement may also contain a provision stating that the engineer will maintain insurance covering certain risks. Occasionally, the agreement will list the specific policies required and the monitor limits of each. Obviously, such provisions should also be reviewed by the design professional's insurance broker. The topic of insurance will be discussed in Chapter 14.

Document Ownership

Under the law, once an architect or engineer has prepared plans or other construction documents and has been paid by the owner, the owner or client owns this material.[6] Design professionals are often reluctant to give up ownership of their plans, which may contain innovative work, especially in engineering.

Because of the general rule giving the owner ownership of the plans, AIA Document B141 specifically states that drawings and specifications are the architect's property and should not be reused by the owner without permission. The standard agreement between the owner and the engineer for professional services prepared by the American Consulting Engineers Counsel contains a similar provision.

Occasionally, design professionals state in the services agreement that if the client reuses the plans and specifications in a project for which the engineer is not the designer, the engineer will not be liable for their reuse and the client will hold the engineer harmless.

Limitation of Actions

As discussed in Chapter 5, architects and engineers, through their professional organizations, have been urging state legislatures to pass laws limiting the time period in which a plaintiff can file a suit arising from malpractice. Although the validity of such statutes has been upheld in many states, the engineer may still face an inordinately long period of time after completing his work in which the owner or third party may sue him. In a written agreement with his client, the engineer may shorten this period, but any such provision would not affect the statute of limitations applicable to third parties. Generally, the courts will enforce provisions shortening the statute of limitations so long as the period in which the client may sue is reasonable.

AIA Document B141 contains a provision stating that the statute of limitations will begin to run no later than the date of substantial completion and no later than the date of final certification for payment for matters arising after the date of substantial completion.

Limitation of Liability

In recent years, design professionals have been inserting provisions limiting their monetary liability if they are found liable or responsible for a professional error. Such provisions have also been used by manufacturers.

In the design field, limitation of liability provisions originated in two separate problems. First, some engineers work on massive projects for which millions, if not billions of dollars worth of damages could be incurred by the owner due to a professional error. For example, in the electric utility industry, an error by an engineer or manufacturer could result in the failure to complete a power plant on time or in the need to take a plant off line. Under such circumstances, the utility may have to buy power from another utility, which could cost millions of dollars. Because of this exposure, both design professionals and manufacturers in that industry commonly insert provisions stating that they will not be liable for "consequential damages."

Second, the fee received by the design professional may be miniscule compared to the amount of damage which may result from his error. As an example, a structural engineer working as a consultant for either the architect or the client may receive only a few thousand dollars to structurally design a building which may cost several million dollars to construct. A design error by the engineer could result in hundreds of thousands of dollars worth of corrective work. Since there is no relationship between the fee received by the engineer and the potential exposure, the engineer prefers to limit his liability to some specific amount of his fee.

The typical limitation of liability provision states that the design professional shall not be liable for consequential or incidental damages. A consequential damage could be the owner's loss of profit due to a delay in completing the project. An incidental damage could be the expenses incurred by the owner in retaining consultants to investigate alleged errors or omissions.

Besides attempting to limit their liability to the fee or a percentage of the fee, some design professionals are attempting to limit their liability to the cost of redoing deficient plans and specifications. In other instances, they are attempting to limit their liability to the cost or a percentage of the cost of corrective work.

Obviously, the exact limitation of liability provision to be used in a professional services agreement depends upon several factors. First, it depends upon the risks involved. Second, the client's bargaining power may make it very difficult for a design professional even to have such a provision. Third, the attorneys for both the client and the engineer will determine in part the breadth of the limitation of liability clause.

Although a limitation of liability provision may be effective against the client, it cannot be used against third parties, who ordinarily are not a party to the professional services agreement.

Arbitration

In recent years, there has been a growing movement in the construction industry to provide for compulsory arbitration of construction disputes. Generally, the AIA contract documents, including Document B141, provide for compulsory arbitration. Arbitration will be discussed in Chapter 16.

CONSULTANTS' AGREEMENTS

When rendering services under an agreement, it may be necessary for the design professional to retain a consultant. Essentially, the consultant performs a portion of the services which the design professional has agreed to perform for his client. As a result, under the law, it may be necessary for the design professional to obtain the permission or consent of his client before delegating any of his work to a consultant. Further, under the law, the design professional remains liable for the errors of consultants retained by him. Thus, it is important that the hiring professional have a written agreement with the consultant.

This agreement usually contains many of the provisions of a standard professional services agreement. Obviously, the hiring engineer should be sure that his consultant is bound by the same terms and conditions by which he himself is bound with this client. In the agreement, it is extremely important for the consultant to hold harmless both the hiring professional and the client from any of the consultant's negligent acts, errors, or omission. Further, the agreement should list the consultant's mandatory insurance coverage. In addition, arrangements should be made to obtain evidence of that coverage, such as a certificate of insurance.

Frequently, the owner will enter into a contract with a design professional to render specific services, but not all of the design services, for a construction project. For instance, the owner usually retains the soils engineer directly. Further, some owners prefer to retain their own specialists, such as structural or mechanical engineers. Under such circumstances, each design professional should have a separate services agreement with the owner. Occasionally, the owner will ask the design professional to retain a consultant specified by the owner. Design professionals usually do not like to do this, since they want to avoid being responsible for the negligence of a consultant with whom they have never dealt or have no continuing relationship.

When the owner retains several consultants for a construction project, the professional services agreement for each consultant should clearly delineate his responsibility. Further, the architect may have responsibility for coordinating the work of some of the consultants. In such situations, the architect's duty should be clearly defined. Usually, it consists of coordinating the work to avoid interferences. If so, the architect's agreement should so clearly state.

CONSTRUCTION MANAGEMENT AGREEMENTS

In recent years, "construction management" has become a popular term in the construction industry. Many firms, including engineering firms, enter into contracts as "construction managers." Despite the popularity of this concept, there is no clear definition of it. What a construction manager is and what he does depends upon the agreement pertaining to a particular project. Sometimes a construction manager acts as a general contractor. At other times he acts purely as a consultant, undertaking no responsibility for construction. Finally, he may assume both roles, acting as a consultant and performing some of the duties of a contractor.

Construction management was and is relatively easy to sell to some owners, because of their dissatisfaction with the traditional construction process. Some owners think that by using a construction manager, they receive the benefit of certain economies that would not otherwise be available. They believe that a construction manager may be more efficient in scheduling and reducing costs than a general contractor.

Typically, the owner starts working with the construction manager during the design phase, so that the manager becomes involved in scheduling not only the actual construction but also the design phase. Further, the manager can give advice to the owner and the design professional on design concepts which may appreciably reduce construction costs.

A construction manager may not perform any actual construction tasks. He may work with the general contractor or with several primes. He may go so far as to make contracts on behalf of the owner as his agent with the contractor or contractors. Further, a construction manager may become involved in purchasing material which will be used by the contractors. Occasionally, he may assume responsibility for safety and may even perform work in one or more of the trades used in the construction project.

Many engineers act as construction managers; others are reluctant to do so. Many engineers do not have experience or ability in construction work and thus prefer to avoid this responsibility. Others are concerned that by being construction managers they may extend their traditional area of responsibility to overseeing the methods of construction and ensuring that the project will conform in all respects with the plans and specifications.

Construction managers consider themselves as part of a team involving the owner, the design professional, and them. Ideally, construction managers want to be retained by the owner at the start of the design phase so that they can be available to consult with the owner and the engineer at all times. However, construction managers typically do not render purely engineering or design services. Thus, in making agreements, they usually disclaim any liability for design.

When the construction manager does execute agreements with the contractors as the owner's agent, he must be sure that all parties are aware that he is acting as an agent. Otherwise, the construction manager risks a court finding that he is an independent contractor, not the owner's agent, and thus, liable on the contract to the contractor.[7]

Contractual relationships among the owner, the design professional, and the construction manager may take various forms. First, the design professional himself may agree to be construction manager, so that only one basic agreement may be made between him and the owner, covering construction management as well as other responsibilities. Occasionally, in such situations, the design professional may enter into two separate agreements, one covering the traditional design obligations and the other covering construction management.

In other situations, the owner will sign agreements with separate design professional and construction manager. Occasionally, he will make an agreement with the construction manager, who then retains the design professional. Further, the design professional and construction manager may enter into a joint venture. In this situation, these persons may execute a separate joint venture agreement and then make an agreement with the owner to furnish design and construction management services.

The wording of construction management agreements varies widely. Many construction managers are large companies, and accordingly have taken the time to draft agreements which they prefer to use. In addition, both the American Institute of Architects and the Associated General Contractors of America have drafted standard form agreements to be used between owners and construction managers. AIA Document B801 is the AIA's Standard Form of Agreement between the Owner and the Construction Manager. AGC Document No. 8 is the Standard Form of Agreement between the Owner and the Construction Manager adopted by the Associated General Contractors. There are distinct differences between these standard forms.

Under the AGC form, the construction manager acts as a consultant and administrator, with no liability for costs in excess of the budget, scheduling, or the manner in which the contractors perform the work. However, this form contains a guaranteed maximum price provision which allows the construction manager and the owner to establish a fixed price for completion of the project and the construction fee. The guaranteed maximum is established at the time the design is "sufficiently complete" so that a reasonable cost of construction may be estimated. Under the AGC form, if the owner and the construction manager agree to a guaranteed maximum price, the construction manager enters into the contracts with the trades. However, if the owner makes these contracts, they must contain provisions giving the construction manager the right to control the work of the trades.

The AGC documents further provide that during construction, the construction manager will coordinate the work of the trade contractors. Further, the manager will perform any construction not done by any of the trades. He also agrees to inspect the work of the trades, but does not assume any of the responsibility of the architect or engineer for on-site observation. Further, the construction manager agrees to review the trade contractor's safety programs.

Essentially, the AGC document may make the construction manager a contractor, with all of the responsibilities involved. Further, because of the construction manager's right to control the work, he may become responsible to the owner for satisfactory completion of the project, just as a contractor would.[8] In addition, he may be held liable in suits brought by injured workmen because he has assumed control of the methods of work and some responsibility for safety.

AIA document B801 contains some significantly different concepts than the AGC form. The AIA document provides that the construction manager makes recommendations to the architect regarding certification of payment requests from the contractor or contractors. The AGC document merely states that the construction manager administers the process. The AIA form requires the construction manager to inspect the work, whereas the AGC document as mentioned above, states that although the construction manager will inspect the work, he will not assume any of the architect's obligations of on-site observation. The AIA document limits the construction manager's safety responsibility to ensuring that the construction contracts documents contain safety requirements. Further, it states that the construction manager will help answer the contractor's questions pertaining to an interpretation of the contract documents, whereas under the AGC form, the construction manger refers all requests for interpretation to the design professional.

JOINT VENTURE AGREEMENTS

Joint ventures are becoming increasingly common in the construction industry. Contractors form joint ventures to construct a project, and professionals do so to furnish design and construction services.

Joint ventures are primarily a marketing tool by which the co-venturers, by pooling their resources and capabilities, make their services more attractive to the owner or client than each would be separately. Joint ventures are also formed because one of the co-venturers may have excellent contacts with the proposed client, but not the expertise or resources of the other co-venturers.

Joint ventures may arise when an architect joins forces with certain engineers in an attempt to obtain the architectural and engineering design work for a project. Further, a local architect or engineer may form a joint venture with an out-of-state colleague who can provide the client and the services he does not necessarily possess.

Joint ventures are also frequently used in projects in foreign countries; the U.S. design professional will associate with a domestic engineer. Obviously, in such work, the foreign client, which is frequently a government agency, will insist or prefer that a domestic engineer be part of the design team. Further, foreign countries encourage such associations in order to develop needed engineering expertise among their domestic professionals.

A joint venture takes different forms. In its purest form, it is a partnership between two firms, which may be sole proprietorships, partnerships, or corporations, for the purpose of carrying out one project. However, if the joint venture is a partnership, each of the co-venturers is liable to its clients and third parties for any negligence of the joint venture. Thus, an architect may be liable for the professional errors of any of his co-venturers, even though he had nothing to do with the negligence which resulted in the damage. As a result, in order to limit their liability, some co-venturers form a corporation. The insurance aspects of joint venture liability will be discussed in Chapter 12.

In the typical joint venture, an agreement is made between the co-venturers. Then the joint venture executes a professional services agreement with the client.

The joint venture agreement usually covers the basic relationship between the parties. It establishes what each party will do, a means for governing the joint venture, the method of determining capital contributions, the method of accounting, and the payment of expenses by and distribution of the profits of the joint venture.

The ordinary joint venture agreement starts with the name of the joint venture. Then it states the purposes of the joint venture and the obligation of each co-venturer. It may establish a separate office and staff or merely specify the use of the existing facilities of the co-venturers. If there are any joint venture assets, their use is restricted to the joint venture. Control of the joint venture is normally established by setting up a board to which each co-venturer will name a certain number of members. The board usually establishes general policy for the venture and makes major decisions. The day-to-day operation of the venture is designated to be in the hands of one or more project managers selected by the board or the co-venturers.

In a joint venture between two participants, each one will probably want to have an equal voice in any decisions. Occasionally, one co-venturer will have the right to make a decision in a certain operational area if the participants cannot agree. The joint venture agreement usually provides for each party to furnish capital for the venture's operations. Also, a clause may be provided for the contribution of additional capital.

If one or more of the co-venturers will be working with his own staff and resources, the agreement provides for his reimbursement. Further, each of the participants may agree to hold each other harmless for any of their professional errors. Moreover, the agreement may establish a way of allocating liability in cases of joint negligence. In addition, the agreement may provide for each of the parties to maintain specific insurance coverage and may require the joint venture itself to maintain certain coverage.

Since one or more of the participants may be contributing a trade secret or proprietary information to the joint venture, a confidentiality provision is usually included. Further, if the venture involves participants from more than one country, provision is made for handling currency exchange fluctuations. There also must be an outline of how profits will be determined and distributed. Finally, either the joint venture itself or one of the participants may maintain the accounting records for the project. Joint venture agreements typically provide that any party shall have the right to audit such records.

The AIA has prepared a joint venture agreement for professional services. It is AIA Document C-801.

FAST-TRACK PROJECTS

In recent years, due primarily to the relatively high interest rates for construction loans, developers of major projects have looked for ways to shorten the design-construction process. This has led to the "fast-track" approach. Using this method, the owner negotiates with and retains a contractor before the design professional completes the plans and specifications. Construction usually starts before these documents are completed for the entire project.

As an example, for a large office building, the architect and engineer furnish preliminary design information to the owner and the contractor, who then reach an agreement under which the contractor can proceed to build. This agreement may contain either a fixed price or a cost plus fixed fee payment to the contractor. The architect or engineer then completes the drawings and specifications needed for the contractor to start subsoil work, including the foundation. As the contractor's work proceeds, the design professional continues to work, keeping ahead of the contractor.

Generally, the same professional services agreement can be used for a fast-track job as for any construction project. However, some modifications are necessary. For example, the agreement should specifically outline what types of plans the architect or engineer must furnish at various stages.

CONSTRUCTION CONTRACTS

During the construction process, the owner usually makes an agreement with either a general contractor or prime contractors to do the construction work. A general contractor assumes responsibility for complete construction. However, the owner may decide to use multiple prime contractors instead. For instance, he may have separate contracts with the heating and ventilation contractor, the electrical contractor, the plumbing contractor, the structural steel erector, and the contractor for the other or general work. Often, the prime contractor concept is used in conjunction with construction management.

Regardless of the legal relationships governing the construction work, the design professional often becomes involved in drafting the construction contracts. Indeed, in some large engineering firms, these contracts are typically drafted by the design professional and merely adopted by the owner or client.

In the typical construction scenario, the owner retains the design professional to prepare the plans and specifications. Then the owner either obtains bids from general contractors to do all the work or negotiates with specific contractors. Under the traditional arrangement, the owner warrants the plans and specifications, and the contractor, provided he follows them, has no responsibility for the results.

Construction contracts take three basic forms: fixed price, unit price, and cost-plus. Under the fixed price contract, the contractor agrees to do the work pursuant to the construction documents for a lump sum.

Under the unit price contract, contractors are paid pursuant to the quantities of certain materials, such as concrete or structural steel. The unit price for each item is established. Thus, concrete would be paid for by the cubic yard and structural steel by the pound.

Under a cost-plus contract, the contractor is paid for the cost of the work plus an additional sum covering overhead and profit. The determination of costs can become detailed and involve such items as labor plus fringe benefits, cost of materials, and cost of rental of equipment. The "plus" amount is usually a fixed percentage of the actual cost which is designed to cover overhead and profit.

Because of the open-ended nature of a cost-plus agreement, owners often insist that the contractor agree to do the work for a maximum or upset price. Under this contract, the contractor agrees to do the work at a cost-plus basis not to exceed a set price.

Occasionally, a fixed-price agreement will contain a "shared-savings" clause. Under such a provision, if the contractor is able to perform the work for less than the fixed price, savings are divided on a percentage basis between him and the owner.

Various contract forms are used as construction contracts. The most frequently used forms are probably the AIA documents. These include AIA Document 101, Standard Form of Agreement between Owner and Contract, and AIA Document 201, General Conditions of the Contract for Construction.

Contract Documents

Usually the contract documents contain the agreement between the contractor and the owner, the drawings, the specifications, and other relevant documents, such as general and special terms and conditions. Addenda to the specifications may also be included, as well as any amendments to the contract or change orders.

Many contracts contain a clause listing the order of priority of the contract documents in the event that there is a conflict between them.

Licensing

Most states have statutes governing the licensing of contractors; these statutes vary by states. The owner should determine whether there is a licensing statute covering contractors for the type of work to be done and should make a contract only with a licensed contractor. If the state has a licensing statute, it is important that the contractor comply with it to avoid any penalties. As an example, some states do not permit an unlicensed contractor to use their courts to recover any sums due him.[9]

Notice to Proceed

Occasionally, a contract will contain a notice to proceed provision. Frequently, these clauses are used in government contracts. Under such a provision, the contractor does not start to work until he is notified by the owner or the owner's representative to do so. A notice to proceed is often used in a contract in which the contractor agrees to complete the work within a specific number of days. With a notice to proceed, the time period commences with the date of the notice.

Scope of Work

Most construction contracts contain a "scope of work" provision, which describes the work to be done by the contractor. This provision should give a clear description of the work to be performed.

It must be read in conjunction with the plans and specifications, which may contain the details of the work.

Of course, not all of the contractor's work can be covered in the contract documents. Thus, these documents usually contain a scope of work provision which states that the contractor will do all the work, including furnishing all the necessary labor, materials, and equipment, to complete the project. Generally, when determining what work is covered by the scope of the work, the courts look not only at the specific requirements of the plans and specifications, but also at the work that is "reasonably implied" by them.[10]

Changed Conditions

One of the perplexing problems in drafting construction contracts is how to handle unexpected job site conditions. During construction, the contractor may discover site conditions unforeseen by any of the parties. Totally unexpected subsoil conditions may occur, undiscovered by the soil-testing firm, usually retained by the owner, which did not discover them. Such conditions, unanticipated by the contractor, could result in substantial unforeseen expenses.

Construction contracts may contain clauses covering changed conditions which may be onerous to the contractor. A provision whereby the contractor is relieved of any responsibility for a condition not disclosed in the contract documents would probably be most favorable to him. However, in contracts, owners have placed the burden for undiscovered conditions upon the contractor. Typically, in such a provision, the owner requires the contractor to verify the site conditions prior to submitting a bid or making a contract. The owner disclaims responsibility for any information he gives the contractor, such as the results of soil tests. Such disclaimers have been upheld by the courts.[11]

Some courts, however, have held that when this information is inaccurate, that disclaimer is not effective. Such cases typically involve disputes over the interpretation of government contracts.[12]

Warranties

A construction contract may contain two types of warranty clauses. Typically, the first clause states that the contractor will perform the work in a "workmanlike" manner. It may also specify that the contractor will use new materials and equipment. The second clause normally states that the contractor will guarantee his work for a stated period of time.

Workmanlike clauses generally are interpreted in accordance with the type of construction involved and the standards of practice in the local community. Thus, in a New York case, the court held a contractor liable for structural problems when the plaintiff's expert testified that the foundation's construction was substandard, noting that many of the columns exceeded plumb standards. Further, the expert testified that the foundation was not square.[13]

Warranty provisions should clarify whether the contractor is relieved of further obligation or responsibility for the quality of the work after the warranty period. For example, if there is one-year warranty, is the contractor relieved of responsibility for any latent defects which may be discovered later? Some courts have held that following the warranty period, the contractor has no further obligation.[14] Others have stated that the warranty provision is not an exclusive remedy and have allowed the owner to sue for damages due to defects in the work following the warranty period. Those courts apparently look upon the warranty period as one in which the contractor will remedy the defect, whereas following this period, the contractor need not perform repairs but may still be held liable for damages.[15]

Occasionally, a construction contract will state that the work will be done to the satisfaction of the owner. However, some courts have stated that the owner's rejection of the work under this provision will be judged by a "reasonable man" standard. Other courts have not accepted the reasonable man standard but have held that the owner's dissatisfaction must be in good faith.[16]

Discrepancies

Many construction contracts require the contractor to notify the design professional of any discrepancies or ambiguities in the construction documents. Such clauses usually require the notice to be given in writing or the contractor will have waived any claim for a discrepancy or an ambiguity.

Or-Equal Provisions

Frequently, a construction contract will contain an "or-equal" provision, which allows him to substitute material and equipment with the approval of the design professional. Such provisions are often used in private contracts where bidding has occurred or in public contracts. In a public contract, an or-equal provision is used to meet the competitive bidding requirement of state or federal law. In a private contract, this provision can be used by the contractor to substitute material equal in quality to that specified, which allows him to take advantage of price or availability. Further, in some circumstances, if a lower price is obtained, the contract may provide that it be passed on to the owner. This usually involves following the change order procedure of the construction contract.

Of course, when a contractor asks to substitute a named product, it must meet the technical specifications. In determining whether a substitution will be permitted under an or-equal provision, the engineer should act reasonably; he probably cannot arbitrarily reject the contractor's request.

Shop Drawings

Shop drawings include any submittals made by the contractor to the owner or the design professional describing the contractor's work. Ordinarily, the design drawings do not contain sufficient information for the contractor to use in constructing the project. The contractor must prepare shop drawings from which his staff will work. Frequently, shop drawings are prepared by subcontractors and submitted through the general contractor. Besides drawings, the contractor may submit samples of material to be used.

Normally, the contract provides that the approval or review of any shop drawings by the contractor or design professional does not relieve the contractor of the responsibility for meeting the requirements of the contract.

Inspections

Most construction contracts contain provisions concerning inspection of the construction by the engineer. Usually, the type, manner, and number of inspections depend upon the project. In large projects, the design professional may have one or several representatives on the site throughout construction to observe the contractor's work. In smaller projects, the design professional or his representative may visit the site periodically, such as weekly or monthly. Often, these infrequent inspections are coupled with a walk through the site by the engineer's representative to assess the progress of the work in order to certify pay-out requests by the contractor. Further, many contracts provide that upon substantial completion, the engineer will inspect the work.

The contract usually provides that the contractor will cooperate with the design professional in his inspections, making the site and assistance available when necessary. Further, many contracts state that if work has been covered between inspections, the engineer may order the contractor to uncover the work he wants to examine. Moreover, most contracts provide that the engineer's inspection does not relieve the contractor of his obligation to perform the work in accordance with the contract.

Interpretations and Decisions

Construction contracts frequently provide that the design professional will interpret the contract documents at the request of the contractor and that these interpretations will be binding. Such contracts normally state that at various times in the construction process, the architect or engineer will decide whether the contractor's work conforms to the contract documents. This will be certified by him, usually at the time of substantial completion. Typically, such provisions state that his determination will be binding and conclusive upon the owner and the contractor.

Under such circumstances, the courts will enforce such provisions and will not set aside the decision of the architect unless it has been fraudulent or arbitrary. The architect acts as an arbitrator and receives immunity from his decisions. Of course, as pointed out in Chapter 3, he does owe a duty to his client, usually the owner, to render decisions which are reasonable according to the applicable standards of his profession.

Under the law, the decision of the design professional is binding only in regard to patent or observable defects; it does not cover latent defects which he could not have reasonably observed. However, the design professional's decision on certain issues may not be conclusive, such as his interpretation of the legal import of contract documents. For instance, in one case where a dispute arose as to whether a contractor was to perform certain work, the courts concluded that this was a matter of contract construction and not within the scope of the design professional's powers under the contract.[17]

Change Orders

Generally, construction contracts provide for a change order procedure. A change order recognizes a modification in the contract documents regarding the contractor's work. A change may involve either the contract price or the time of performance. Normally, if a material change in the work or an adjustment to the contract price or time of performance is involved, the contractor must submit a written request for a change order. The design professional then reviews the change order and transmits it to the owner with his recommendation to accept or reject it. Normally, however, the change order must be executed and issued by the owner before it becomes part of the contract documents. Many contract provisions state that a contractor is not entitled to make any change in the price unless he has received an approved change order from the owner.

Payment

When we first talked about construction contracts, we discussed the three common methods of paying the contractor. These are the fixed price, unit price, and cost-plus methods. Once the basic price and form of payment are settled by the owner and the contractor, several ancillary questions arise, which are usually covered in the construction contract. First, most contracts cover a lengthy period of time, and the contractor expects progress payments. The contract ordinarily establishes a procedure by which such payments are made. Often the contractor must give an affidavit to the engineer and a request for partial payment. The engineer then reviews the progress of the work and determines whether the request is acceptable. If it is, he certifies the request and delivers it to the owner for action.

Second, with the request for payment, the contractor may be expected to provide a waiver of lien, not only from himself but also from all subcontractors, vendors, and materialmen.

Third, the contract may provide for an amount to be retained from each payment. The retainage, which frequently is 10 percent, is held by the owner and paid to the contractor upon final acceptance of the job. Owners prefer to use a retainage to ensure that the contractor will complete the job and correct all defects during construction or at observation of the completed project, when the final certificate of substantial completion is issued by the engineer and a "punch list" is produced. A punch list is a list of construction deficiencies which must be corrected by the contractor.

Occasionally, a contractor will refuse to continue with his work and demand additional payment in order to complete it. The majority of courts which have considered this situation hold that the owner's agreement to pay additional compensation is not binding, due to lack of consideration, unless the contractor has encountered substantial difficulties in performance which were not anticipated by either the owner or the contractor. A few jurisdictions hold that the agreement for additional payment is binding because the consideration was the contractor's refusal to continue working and his decision to be liable for damages.[18]

Assignment

Construction contracts typically contain clauses forbidding the contractor to assign either his rights or his obligations under the contract. He is barred not only from assigning the work to another contractor but also from assigning any future payments to be received by him. Although a contractor may use subcontractors, technically he is not assigning any of his rights or obligations under the contract. The contractor who employs subcontractors remains liable to the owner for their work.

Suspension

A construction contract may contain a clause allowing the owner to suspend the work at any time for any reason. Such a clause is advantageous to the owner because conditions may arise during the work which make it advisable to stop. A suspension provision protects the owner, especially in cases where a government agency which has licensing authority over the project may halt construction. Such cases may involve the Nuclear Regulatory Commission, which occasionally halts the construction of a nuclear power plant so that it may investigate alleged safety problems.

A typical suspension provision may permit the owner to stop construction for a relatively short period of time without making any additional payment to the contractor. However, under such a provision, if the contractor is to complete work on a specific date, there may be a corresponding extension of the deadline. Some suspension provisions also state that if work is to be suspended for an unreasonably long period of time, extra payments may be made to the contractor covering additional costs incurred by him in closing down the project.

Termination

Many construction contracts contain a clause permitting the owner to terminate the contract for any reason. Frequently, these clauses provide that if termination is due to the contractor's default, the owner need not pay him any sums due, but may hold those sums until the project has been completed, using them to offset any increased construction costs due to the default. Further, a termination clause may permit the owner to take possession of the contractor's equipment or material on the site in order to complete construction.

The termination clause may also give the owner the right to terminate the contract for his own convenience, even though the contractor may not be in default. Owners prefer such a provision because it allows them to terminate a project which may be uneconomical to complete. Generally, if the owner has this right, the termination clause usually provides that the contractor will be paid for the work performed so far and may also be allowed profit to the date of termination. Further, the clause may provide that the contractor will be paid for any reasonable expenses incurred in termination which would not otherwise have arisen.

Occasionally, termination provisions may permit the contractor to terminate a contract, but usually only when the owner is in material default of his obligations, such as payment.

Arbitration

As mentioned above, many construction contracts, including those with the general contractor or other contractors, contain compulsory arbitration provisions. Arbitration will be discussed in Chapter 16.

SUBCONTRACTS

Most contractors use subcontractors to perform part of the work to be furnished by the contractor. A contract between a contractor and a subcontractor can take many forms. It may be merely verbal, or it may consist of a written quotation for the subcontractor's work. The contract may also be an exchange of letters or a purchase order issued by the contractor to the subcontractor. Finally, many contractors and subcontractors enter into formal written subcontracts.

A formal contract may parallel the contract between the owner and the contractor. The subcontractor then becomes bound by the same terms and conditions as the contractor. Alternatively, a subcontract may be quite different from the prime contract. It may not incorporate, by reference, the terms and conditions of the agreement between the owner and the contractor. If a subcontract is unrelated to the general contract, it may have many of the terms and conditions ordinarily contained in a general contract.

Frequently, subcontracts contain a contingent payment clause by which the subcontractor's payment is contingent upon payment to the contractor. This clause provides that if the contractor is not paid, neither is the subcontractor. To avoid such a harsh result, the courts of several states have stated that contingent payment clauses do not completely bar payment to the subcontractor. These courts hold that if there is a contingent payment clause but the subcontractor is not paid within a reasonable period, he is entitled to payment from the contractor.[19] The subcontract forms written by the AIA and the AGC state that if a contractor is not paid for a reason which was not the fault of the subcontractor, then the contractor will pay the subcontractor.

DESIGN-BUILD CONTRACTS

Centuries ago, the architect was the "master builder," who not only designed a project but often supervised its construction. Over the years, as architecture and engineering developed into independent professions, design professionals intentionally limited their activities to design. However, in recent years, there has been a return to the concept of the master builder in the form of design-build or turn-key contracts.

Under a design-build contract, the party who will construct the project undertakes not only the construction work but also the necessary design and engineering. Such contracts frequently are referred to as "turn-key contracts" because their intent is to give the owner a completed project for which he need only put the key in the door and turn it. Turn-key projects are frequently used in process engineering for sophisticated industrial plants.

Design-build contracts may involve either a professional design firm—often a large sophisticated engineering firm—a contractor, or a joint venture of a design firm and a contractor. If the contractor has the contract, he may retain an independent design firm to do the architecture and/or engineering.

Whether a design firm or a contractor has the agreement with the owner in a design-build situation, the party who will design and construct the facility must be sure that he has the adequate licenses. In all states, professional architects and engineers must be licensed pursuant to local statutes. Thus, if a contractor has a design-build contract, he must consult with his attorney to determine whether he can make such a contract containing responsibility for design. Similarly, many states require contractors to be licensed, and if an architect or engineer agrees to supervise or manage the construction of a design-build project, he must determine whether he will need a contractor's license.

Design-build contracts basically contain a combination of the typical provisions of a professional services agreement and a construction contract. However, because of the concern that a court may place more responsibility for a project on a designer-builder than on an ordinary design professional, many design-build agreements contain a clause stating that for the design or engineering portion of the services, the designer-contractor alone will be liable if he is negligent.

The Associated of General Contractors have developed a design-build form, AGC Document No. 410, Standard Form of Design-Build Agreement and General Conditions Between Owner and Contractor.

NOTES

1. *National Housing Industries, Inc. v. E. L. Jones Development Co.*, 118 Ariz. 374, 576 P.2d 1374 (Ariz. App. 1978).
2. *Cowles v. City of Minneapolis*, 128 Minn. 452, 151 N.W. 184 (1915).
3. *Day & Zimmermann, Inc., v. Blocked Iron Corp.*, 200 F.Supp. 132 (E.D. Pa. 1961).
4. 5 Am.Jr.2d *Architects* §12 (1962), 674–675.
5. *Hubert v. Aitken*, 5 N.Y.S. 839 (CP Ct. 1889), *aff'd.*, 123 N.Y. 655 (1890), and *Roland A. Wilson & Associates v. Forty-o-Four Grand Corp.*, 246 N.W. 2d 922 (Iowa 1976).
6. 5 Am.Jur.2d*Architects* § 11 (1962), 673–674.
7. *Owen Steel Co. v. George A. Fuller Co.*, 563 F.Supp. 298 (S.D.N.Y. 1983).
8. *Phenix-Georgetown, Inc. v. Chas. H. Tompkins Co.*, 477 A.2d 215 (D.C. 1984).
9. *Davis v. Carpenter*, 247 Ga. 156, 274 S.E.2d 567 (1981).
10. *Watson Lumber Co. v. Guennewig*, 79 Ill.App.2d 377, 226 N.E.2d 270 (1967), *disagreed with Haas v. Cravatta*, 71 Ill.App.3d 325, 389 N.E.2d 226 (1979), and *Granberry v. Perlmutter*, 147 Colo. 474, 364 P.2d 211 (1961).
11. *Branna Construction Corp. v. West Allegheny Joint School Authority*, 430 Pa. 214, 242 A.2d 244 (1968) and *Air Cooling & Energy, Inc. v. Midwestern Construction Co. of Mo., Inc.* 602 S.W.2d 926 (Mo.App.1980).
12. Albert Dib, *Forms and Agreements for Architects, Engineers and Contractors*, chap. 3, §39 (New York: Clark Boardman, 1976), 3-71 to 3-72. *See also Hollerbach v. United States*, 233 U.S. 165 (1914), *United States v. Spearin*, 248 U.S. 132 (1918), and *Eastern Tunneling Corp. v. Southgate Sanitation District*, 487 F.Supp. 109 (D. Colo. 1979).
13. *Van Deloo v. Moreland*, 84 App.Div.2d 871, 444 N.Y.S. 2d 744 (1981).
14. *Independent Consolidated School District v. Carlstrom*, 277 Minn. 117, 151 N.W.2d 784 (1967).
15. *Carrols Equities Corp. v. Villnave*, 76 Misc.2d 205, 350 N.Y.S.2d 90 (1973), *Kennewick v. Hanford Piping, Inc.*, 16 Wash.App. 660, 558 P.2d 276 (1977), and *Omaha Home for Boys v. Stitt Construction Co. Inc.*, 195 Neb. 422, 238 N.W.2d 470 (1976).
16. 13 Am.Jur.2d *Building & Construction Contracts* §30, (1964), 31–33.
17. *N. E. Redlon Co. v. Franklin Square Corp.*, 89 N.H. 137, 195 A. 348 (1937), *adhered to*, 89 N.H. 148, 197 A. 329 (1938).
18. 13 Am.Jur.2d *Building & Construction Contracts* §5 (1964), 9.
19. Robert F. Cushman, Michael S. Simon, and McNeill Stokes, *Construction Industry Formbook: A Practical Guide to Reviewing and Drafting Forms for the Construction Industry* (Colorado Springs, Colo.: Shepard's/McGraw-Hill, 1979), 209.

9
Sales Contracts

A separate body of law governs contracts for the sale of products. In Chapter 7, we discussed the general law of contracts as it has developed through court decisions. In Chapter 8, we considered construction contracts. In this chapter, we shall examine the law governing contracts for the sale of goods. The legal rules applying to sales contracts are contained in Article 2 of the Uniform Commercial Code. (UCC).

An engineer working in manufacturing obviously should have some familiarity with the law governing the sale of goods, since Article 2 of the Uniform Commercial Code covers the contractual rights, obligations, and remedies of the buyer and the seller—for example, the law of warranties as it applies to product sales. In addition, the engineer working in construction needs to know the law of sales because he may become involved in specifying or purchasing materials and products to be used in a construction project.

The nine articles of the UCC set forth the law regarding commercial transactions. The first article contains general provisions. The others cover sales transactions, commercial paper (such as promissory notes), bank deposits and collections, letters of credit, bulk transfers (where an entire business is sold), documents of title (such as warehouse receipts and bills of lading), securities (stocks and bonds), and secured transactions (formerly referred to as "conditional sales" or "chattel mortgages").

Prior to the UCC, the National Conference of Commissioners on Uniform State Laws promulgated seven uniform laws or codes covering various commercial topics. These were the Uniform Negotiable Instruments Law, the Uniform Warehouse Receipts Act, the Uniform Sales Act, the Uniform Bills of Lading Act, the Uniform Stock Transfer Act, the Uniform Conditional Sales Act, and the Uniform Trust Receipts Act. The Uniform Sales Act was adopted in thirty-four states, Alaska, Hawaii, and the District of Columbia, and the Uniform Negotiable Instruments Law was adopted by every state. In addition, the other uniform laws were adopted by many states.

In the 1930s, a movement developed to write a uniform code covering commercial transactions, including those which were already covered by existing uniform laws. In 1942, the American Law Institute and the National Conference of Commissioners on Uniform State Laws joined forces to draft such a code. Lawyers and law teachers drafted various provisions of the code and consulted with respected legal scholars, including judges, lawyers, and law teachers. Each draft was reviewed by the Council of the American Law Institute and one of the sections of the Conference of Commissioners.

The first edition of the Uniform Commercial Code or UCC appeared in 1952. A draft of this edition was enacted as law in Pennsylvania in 1953 with an effective date of July 1, 1954. The UCC was then introduced as legislation in New York. However, the New York legislature did not adopt the code, but sent it to the New York Law Revision Commission for review. In 1956, the Revision Commission reported that although it accepted the concept of a uniform commercial code, it criticized certain provisions of the UCC.

Based upon the New York Law Revision Commission's comments, the UCC was redrafted and a 1957 official text was published. Revised official texts also appeared in 1958, 1962, 1964, 1966, 1972, and 1978, each containing either minor or major modifications in the language of the UCC.

The UCC has been adopted in forty-nine states. Louisiana has adopted certain sections of the UCC, but not Article 2 covering sales.

COVERAGE OF ARTICLE 2

Article 2 generally covers transactions involving "goods," including their sale. A good is defined as tangible property, such as an automobile or components for a machine. If the court concludes that a sale of or a transaction involving goods is part of the suit before it, then it should apply to the rules of Article 2 of the UCC.

Occasionally, a question arises of whether a transaction really involves goods and is covered by Article 2. There are situations where both goods and services may be part of the transaction. Under such circumstances, the courts may determine whether the transaction should be covered by the UCC or the general principles of contract law explained in Chapter 7.

Clearly, service and construction contracts are not covered by Article 2. Thus, computer service agreements are not covered by the UCC,[1] nor are construction contracts. In an Illinois case, the court held that an agreement to build a plant was not a contract of sale, but a contract for services.[2]

When there is a mixed sale of goods and services, there are at least four analyses which can be applied to determine whether the transaction is a sale of goods covered by the UCC. First, the court can look at the percentage of the assets consisting of goods.[3] In the second analysis, the court may determine that in no respect are services covered by the UCC; hence, the entire sale and the service of goods will not be covered.[4] With the third approach, the court can divide the transaction, applying the UCC provisions to the sale of the goods and the general contract law to the sale of the services.[5] Under the fourth approach, the court will look at the dominant element of the transaction. If the sale basically involves services, the court will apply the general law. If it involves basically goods, the court will apply the UCC provisions.[6]

CONTRACT FORMATION

In many respects, there is great similarity between the general law of contracts and the UCC rules applying to transactions in or sales of goods. However, there are also significant differences between them.

The basic principles of contract formation requiring both an offer and acceptance are the same under both sets of rules. Whether the parties intended to enter into a contract is determined by an objective standard under the general contract law and the UCC.

The UCC does not define an offer. Accordingly, in a UCC case, the courts frequently examine general contract cases to determine whether an offer has been made. Thus, they will probably adopt an objective standard to determine the intent of the offeror. The courts will look at the evidence and conclude whether or not the offeror reasonably led the offeree to assume that he had made an offer.[7]

Most of the cases determining whether an offer has been made under the UCC involve price quotations. Ordinarily, a price quotation is considered an invitation to negotiate, not an offer.[8] However, if it is clearly an offer, then the buyer's issuance of a purchase order amounts to acceptance of the offer.[9]

The UCC differs from general contract law in several respects. One of these involves the concept of placing greater responsibility on a "merchant" than on an ordinary buyer or seller. This is a unique concept introduced by the UCC. Under common law, there is no distinction between them. The UCC defines a merchant as a person who ordinarily deals in the goods covered by the sales agreement or who considers himself an expert or a person with special knowledge of the goods.[10]

The concept of the merchant appears in the UCC provision covering "firm offers."[11] Basically, a firm offer is merely a statement by a person that he will buy or sell goods under certain terms and conditions and that the offer will be held open for a stated period of time. Prior to the UCC, for a firm offer to be binding and not subject to cancellation, it had to be supported by some form of consideration. Thus, a buyer may have agreed to buy certain products at a certain price some time during the next two months and, in order to bind the seller, paid him a reasonable sum of money. Such transactions were often referred to as "options."

The UCC did away with the requirement for consideration to make a firm offer binding and irrevocable. However, under the UCC, only a merchant can make a firm offer, which can be for either buying or selling goods. Moreover, the offer has to be made in a written, signed document stating that it will be held open for a specific period of time. If no period of time is provided, the UCC implies that the offer becomes revocable after three months.

Under the UCC, if the offer clearly states the manner of acceptance, acceptance must meet the prescribed requirements. If there is no condition that the acceptance must be made in a certain manner, then it may be made "in any manner" and "by any medium reasonable in the circumstances."

An offer to purchase goods by prompt shipment requires that acceptance be made either by prompt shipment or by the promise to ship. As an example, if the ABC company sends the XYZ Corporation a purchase order for a carload of plywood, to be shipped promptly upon receipt of the order. The XYZ Corporation may accept the order either by promptly shipping the plywood or by sending a letter to the ABC Company promising to do so.

Acceptance by shipment can be of either conforming or non-conforming goods, unless the seller notifies the buyer that he is shipping the nonconforming goods merely as an accommodation to the buyer. If the seller ships nonconforming goods without notification, a binding contract is made, but the buyer may have the right to sue the seller for breach of contract for delivering nonconforming goods. However, if the seller notifies the buyer that he is shipping nonconforming goods, the buyer has not accepted the offer and hence there is no contract. Under such circumstances, a contract may be made when the buyer decides to accept the shipment of nonconforming goods. If the offeror has requested performance, or performance by the offeree is a reasonable method of acceptance, the offer will lapse if the offeror is not notified of acceptance after a reasonable period of time.[12] For instance, if the XYZ Corporation sends a purchase order to the ABC Company for a truck which must be manufactured, the ABC Company may accept the order, creating a contract, by starting to manufacture the truck and by so notifying the XYZ Corporation.

In its provisions concerning acceptance of offers, the UCC has done away with the distinction between unilateral and bilateral contracts. Under general contract law, a unilateral contract may be accepted only by performance, whereas a bilateral contract may be accepted only by a promise.[13]

Although the UCC still adheres to the concept of offer and acceptance in the formation of a contract, it does not recognize rigid rules for determining if a contract has been made. Under the UCC, there is no specific requirement to show when a sales agreement has been made. Article 2 provides that "a contract for sale of goods may be made in any matter sufficient to show agreement." The existence of a sales contract can be shown by the mere conduct of the parties. Further, a sales contract may exist even though the time of its making cannot be determined. Finally, even though one or more terms of a sales contract have not been agreed to, the contract may still exist if there is a reasonable basis for granting a remedy.[14]

The UCC recognizes that business people act as business people and not as lawyers. Accordingly, when making sales contracts, they often do not adhere to legal formalities and may not even resolve all contingencies in their negotiations. The UCC accepts these situations and provides a method for handling them.[15]

In a Michigan case, the court held that the seller and buyer of imported steel had made a sales contract during a series of telephone conversations, even though it could not pinpoint the exact conversation in which this occurred. Both parties had sent subsequent documents acknowledging the order. The seller was a steel broker who had several telephone conversations with the buyer. As a result, he sent the buyer a confirmation form indicating that the buyer had purchased 1,000 tons of steel. The buyer sent his own purchase order, which tracked the critical information on the seller's confirmation form. Neither the seller nor the buyer signed or acknowledged the form of the other. The steel was delivered in three shipments. The buyer refused to accept the third shipment because of allegedly late delivery, and the seller sued. The seller contended that his terms of sale were contained in his confirmation form, whereas the buyer said that the purchase order terms covered the transaction. The court rejected both arguments and concluded that sometime during the telephone conversations before either document had been sent, the parties had reached an agreement. As a result, the court apparently did not consider either form as being controlling, since both forms had been sent after the contract was made.[16]

However, because of the nature of the negotiations or the documentation used by one or both of the parties to a purported sales agreement, the court may find that certain formalities were required to make a sales contract in a specific case. In an Oklahoma case, the seller of a used printing press provided a purchase order for the prospective buyer to use in ordering the press. The purchase order stated that the order was subject to acceptance by the seller at his home office and that the seller would mail the buyer an executed duplicate copy of the purchase order, which would be the contract between them. The seller never accepted the purchase order and did not give the buyer the signed duplicate copy. Under those circumstances, the court concluded that since the formalities required for making a contract were not met, no binding sales agreement existed.[17]

One formality which may be required for a sales contract under Article 2 is compliance with the applicable statute of frauds. The UCC has its own statute of frauds for Article 2 transactions which has introduced some new twists into this area of the law. The UCC states that for contracts for the sale of goods with a price of $500 or more, there must be written documentation that a sales agreement was made and signed by the party against whom it is sought to be enforced in order for the contract to be enforceable. However, the statute of frauds makes it clear that no contract will be enforceable beyond the quantity of goods described in documentation.

For merchants, a party may send a written confirmation that a sales contract was made. This confirmation will be considered written evidence of the existence of the contract, unless the party to whom it is sent objects to its contents within 10 days after it is received. Moreover, the statute of frauds does not apply if the goods have been paid for and accepted, or the goods have been received and accepted, or, if, in the case of specially manufactured goods, the seller has made a significant move to manufacture or procure them.[18] Further, the sales contract will be enforced, even though the statute of frauds requirements have not been met, if a party admits in court that a contract was made.

When interpreting a sales contract, the courts may use other UCC provisions to provide missing terms, such as price, payment, or delivery, but they cannot provide a missing quantity. Some courts, however, have permitted the use of parole evidence to show the parties' intent regarding the quantity of goods ordered or sold.[19]

MISSING TERMS

Article 2 also contains a parole evidence rule which states the circumstances under which the parties may provide verbal testimony or documentary evidence of the contract's terms other than the contract itself. Under this rule, the UCC rule draws a distinction between two situations: first, where the parties intend the written document to contain the final agreement only on certain terms of the agreement; and second, where the parties intend the written document to contain the final statement of all the terms of the agreement.

In the first case, the written document may be supplemented by evidence on the course of dealing, usage of the trade, or course of performance. The course of dealing is the manner in which the parties have dealt with each other under other contracts. Trade usage is how the trade acts and defines certain circumstances. Course of performance is how the parties have performed under the specific contract. In addition, in the first situation, the contract may be supplemented by consistent additional terms. In the second situation, the contract may not be supplemented by either course of dealing, usage of trade, course of performance, or consistent additional terms.[20]

Under the UCC, the parties to a contract, and the courts if called upon to interpret a contract, use the UCC provisions to furnish the rules applicable to the transaction when the agreement does not cover all the terms. As an example, if the parties did not agree upon a price but did agree to a sale of the goods, Article 2 provides that the price shall be a reasonable price for the goods at the time of delivery.[21] Other rules provide answers to other questions; these rules will be discussed later.

INCONSISTENT TERMS

What if, during the negotiation or formation of the contract, the parties exchange documents containing different terms and conditions? Under the UCC, the parties and the court consider the intent of the parties and whether they actually agreed to or formed a sales contract. The UCC is not overly concerned with legal technicalities or formalities and can be readily used to enforce a contract even though the parties did not agree to all the terms.

Pursuant to the general law of contracts, as explained in Chapter 7, when the offeree responds to the offer with a proposal containing additional or different terms than those contained in the offer, the courts conclude that the offeree made a counteroffer and not an acceptance of the offer. Under the traditional legal concept, the offeree, in order to accept the offer, must accept all of its terms and conditions, and no additional or different ones. However, the drafters of the UCC have changed this rule for contracts for the sale of goods. In such contracts, an agreement may be formed or reached even though the documents of both parties contain materially different terms and conditions. The drafters of the UCC adopted this approach to recognize the realities of the business world, not the niceties of legal theory or doctrine. The UCC attempts to determine whether business people have reached or formed a sales contract. If they have, then the aim of Article 2 is to enforce the contract and not use legal technicalities to avoid enforcing it.

One result of this approach is an end to the "battles of the forms." For years, business people, guided by their lawyers, developed sophisticated sales and purchase documents containing boiler plate terms and conditions often printed on the reverse side of the document in type so small as to be nearly illegible. In interpreting such documents and deciding which one governed the transaction, the courts often went into highly technical gyrations. The aim of the UCC code is to avoid such legal arguments and recognize the realities of the business world.

The UCC provides that acceptance of a contract or written confirmation of an agreement made within a reasonable time is acceptance of the offer even though it contains additional or different terms than those offered or previously agreed to. However, if the acceptance is contingent upon inclusion of the additional or different terms, then there is no contract until those terms have been accepted by the other party. Between merchants, such terms become part of the contract unless they "materially alter it" or unless the other party objects to them within a reasonable time.[22] If there are conflicting material terms, then neither term becomes part of the agreement, and the court looks to the general UCC provisions governing the subject matter of the term to apply to its interpretation.

What if one party's document is silent about a material term and the other party's document contains an additional term covering the subject matter? For example, warranties are generally considered material terms of the sales contract under the UCC. Suppose the buyer sends a purchase order to the seller containing no warranty clause, and the seller, on receipt, sends an acknowledgment or sales order form to the buyer which contains a warranty clause favorable to the seller. In those circumstances, Article 2 provides that since the buyer's form is silent on the subject of a warranty, he has accepted the general code provisions governing warranties. Hence, the seller, by including a warranty form or clause which differs from the code of warranty provisions, has created a different or additional term which materially alters the contract and therefore does not become part of the agreement.[23]

MODIFICATION

Under common law, a contract cannot be modified unless there was new consideration. The UCC does not accept this "preexisting duty" rule of the general law of contracts. Under the UCC, an agreement may be modified without any consideration. However, if the modified contract is covered by the statute of frauds, the modification must also meet the requirements of this statute in order to be valid.[24]

DELEGATON

Under Article 2, a party may delegate his performance of a contract or his rights under the contract unless the contract documents state otherwise. However, if the delegation or assignment would have a substantial impact upon the other party, it cannot be made without consent. For example, the buyer may have an important interest in having the seller manufacture the goods, or the buyer's assignment of a contract to a third person with less capital or financial resources may increase the seller's risk of being paid. Under such circumstances, the other party would not owe the other party's rights or obligations under the contract without his consent.[25]

FREEDOM OF CONTRACT

Basically, the parties to a contract can agree to any terms they desire, subject to certain important limitations under the UCC. The right to freedom of contract is implicitly recognized by the UCC.[26] The UCC states, however, that its provisions may be varied by the parties to a sales contract, except as prescribed by the UCC and except for the "obligations of good faith, diligence, reasonableness and care" mandated by the UCC. Under the UCC, every contract must be performed and enforced in good faith.[27] This obligation of good faith exists with every contract governed by the UCC and cannot be changed or eliminated.

Five sections of Article 2 provide that they may not be modified:

1. A right to damages for breach of contract may be assigned despite an agreement to the contrary.[28]
2. Third-party beneficiary warranty rights cannot be excluded or limited.[29]
3. Any "liquidated damages" provision in a sales contract must be reasonable under the circumstances. A liquidated penalties provision in a contract provides that in the event of a breach of contract the party that breached the contract will pay the other party a stipulated sum of money.[30]
4. Consequential damages for injury to a person resulting from a consumer good may not be limited.[31]
5. The four-year statute of limitations may not be extended by contract, although it may be shortened by contract.[32]

Article 2 also provides another important limitation upon the freedom of contract. It states that a court need not enforce a contract term or a contract which it finds "unconscionable." Under such circumstances, the court need not enforce the contract or it may enforce only that part which does not contain the unconscionable provision.[33] Under this section of Article 2, the court must look at the commercial setting to determine whether any of the clauses of the contract favor one party to such an extent that they are unconscionable.

Thus, the UCC gives the parties to a sales contract great freedom in negotiating terms and conditions. Moreover, a binding sales agreement may occur even though the parties have not agreed to all of its terms and conditions. As discussed above, all the UCC requires is an objective determination that the parties intended to make a contract and did so, even though not all of the terms were negotiated. When the parties do not negotiate or agree upon all the terms, the UCC provides the missing terms.

CONTRACT TERMS

Under the UCC, the courts first look to the commercial setting to supply the open terms of the contract. Using this approach, the courts consider the course of performance of the parties, the course of conduct, and the usage of the trade. If the commercial setting or background does not furnish any of the open terms, the court will be guided by the provisions of the UCC.

The parties need not agree to the price in order for there to be an enforceable contract. Under Article 2, if they have not negotiated the price, then it will be "a reasonable price at the time for delivery.[34] However, if the parties do not intend to be bound by the contract or agreement until a price has been fixed, then there is no binding contract.[35]

As previously noted, one term which the UCC cannot and does not provide is the quantity of goods covered by the contract in the event that the parties do not reach an agreement on it. Typically, if there is no agreement on the quantity of goods, the court cannot determine it and neither can the UCC. However, the UCC will enforce output or requirements contracts.[36] Under such contracts, either the seller agrees to sell all of his product (output) to the buyer or the buyer agrees to buy all of the output he needs to fulfill his requirements from the seller.

Article 2 makes such agreements enforceable. However, the agreement must be specific and binding upon both parties. Thus, nebulous terms such as "the buyer agrees to buy all the products he may desire from the seller" are not binding and an enforceable contract will not result.[37] Under the UCC, the output or requirements must be reasonable in proportion to any estimate, or, if there is no estimate, it must be normal or related to prior output or requirements.

Article 2 also provides rules to determine the time of performance of the contract and the place of delivery of the goods if the parties have not agreed to such terms. The time for shipment or delivery of the goods is a reasonable time, and a contract may be terminated by either party only upon reasonable notification to the other party. The goods should be sent from the seller's place of business and delivered in one delivery.[38] Further, payment must be made at the time and place where the buyer receives the goods.[39]

Article 2 contains various warranty provisions in the event that the parties have not agreed upon them. First, the seller generally warrants, when selling a product, that he conveys good title and that there are no liens or encumbrances against the property.[40] The UCC recognizes that the seller may create "express warranties," which are representations as to the quality of goods.[41] However, a mere statement of opinion may not necessarily create an express warranty.[42] A description of the products to be sold, or a sample or a model, may also form the basis for an express warranty.[43]

The UCC also recognizes two implied warranties. These are warranties which become part of the contract, even though they have not been negotiated between the parties, unless the parties agree to modify or exclude them. The implied warranties are those of "merchantability" and "fitness for a particular purpose."

The implied warranty of merchantability states that the products covered by the transaction are "merchantable," that is, they are acceptable in the trade and can be used for the purposes for which such products are ordinarily used.[44] The implied warranty of fitness for a particular purpose arises when the seller knows the purpose for which the products will be used and the buyer relies upon the seller's skill in selecting products which will accomplish the task.[45]

Article 2 provides that implied warranties may be modified or disclaimed by a conspicuous writing. In order to exclude the implied warranty of merchantability, the disclaimer must use the work "merchantability." However, the use of such language as "as is" or "with all faults" will exclude all implied warranties. In determining whether the disclaimer or modification of an implied warranty has been made in conspicuous language, the courts will look at the language used and the circumstances surrounding the use of the form containing this language. Thus, the courts will determine whether the disclaimer is printed in capitals or boldface type and can be easily seen.

In a Massachusetts case, a disclaimer of implied warranties was on the reverse side of a form which the buyer had signed. The front of the form did not refer to the back, and it was difficult for the buyer to look at the reverse side before signing it. Under the circumstances, the court concluded that the disclaimer was not conspicuous because there was nothing on the front of the form referring the buyer to the reverse side.[46] In a later Kentucky case, boldface type on the front of a form referred to the reverse side of the page. The reverse side contained a boldface disclaimer of the implied warranties. The court concluded that the reference to the reverse side of the form and the use of boldface type made the disclaimer conspicuous and hence enforceable.[47]

In one respect, some of the warranty provisions of the UCC have been modified by federal law. In 1975, the Magnunson-Moss Warranty Act became law. This act applies to consumer products and contains provisions applying to written warranties on consumer products. Generally, consumer warranties must be understandable and must include certain information. Further, limitations are placed upon the language used in any disclaimer clause. Moreover, the act draws a distinction between "full" and "limited" warranties. Under a full warranty, the seller may not limit any implied warranty in any manner or exclude the buyer's right to recover consequential damages.[48]

Article 2 also defines certain commonly used mercantile terms. The term "FOB," meaning "free on board," is used in conjunction with either the place of shipment or the place of designation. Thus, if the seller is going to ship the goods he has manufactured from his plant in High Point, North Carolina, to the buyer's place of business in Detroit, Michigan, the sale may be either FOB High Point, North Carolina, or FOB Detroit, Michigan. If the sale is FOB place of shipment, then the seller must place the goods with the shipper. If the sale is FOB place of destination, then the seller bears the expense and risk of shipping the goods to the place of destination. If the FOB term also contains the language "FOB vessel" or "FOB car" the seller must actually load the goods on board. If the term is "FOB vessel," the UCC requires the buyer to name the vessel.

The term "FAS vessel," meaning "free alongside" with a named port, requires the seller to deliver the goods alongside the vessel and obtain a receipt for them.

Occasionally, the terms "CIF" and "C&F" are used. CIF means that the price includes not only the cost of the goods but also the insurance and freight charges to the destination. The term "C&F" means that the price includes only the cost and freight charges.[46]

The term "ex-ship" means that the seller bears the expense and risk of delivering the goods to a named port and is not relieved of his obligation until the goods are unloaded there.[50]

GOOD FAITH PURCHASERS

Under the UCC, when the seller transfers goods, he passes on all title to them. In the event that the seller has only a limited interest in the goods, this is all the buyer receives.[51] Thus, if a seller owns the entire interest in the goods and there are no liens or encumbrances upon them, he conveys complete ownership of or title to the goods to the buyer at the time of sale. However, if the seller has used the goods as security for a bank loan, the bank may have a security interest in the goods and their conveyance to the buyer would be subject to the bank's security interest or encumbrance. Article 9 of the UCC contains the rules for creating and enforcing security interests in goods.

The UCC also uses the concept of "voidable title." As an example, when the seller learns that the buyer received goods on credit while insolvent, the seller has the right to reclaim the goods.[52] Essentially, the buyer has received a voidable title which may be voided at the option of the seller. Another section of Article 2 provides, however, that a "person with voidable title has power to transfer good title to a good faith purchaser for value." Accordingly, if the buyer had resold the goods to another person who was unaware of the circumstances of the buyer's purchase, the buyer could transfer good title to the third person.

Similarly, the UCC provides that payment by check is conditional upon the check's being honored by the bank upon which it is drawn.[53] However, if the buyer presents a check and resells the goods to a good faith purchaser, the buyer may convey a good title even though the check is dishonored.

Under certain circumstances, a person who is "entrusted" with goods may transfer them to a good faith purchaser. Basically, "entrusting" is the delivery of goods by one party to another, such as to a pawn broker to be used as security for a loan or to a store or repair shop for repair.[54] If the goods are entrusted to a merchant who regularly deals in goods of that nature, the merchant can sell them to a good faith purchaser, who will take the goods with clear title.

Article 2 recognizes another set of circumstances under which the buyer's creditors may have a claim to the seller's goods even though technically the buyer has not purchased them. The UCC draws a distinction between "sale on approval" and "sale or return." A sale on approval occurs when the goods are delivered to the buyer who will be using them. Under normal circumstances, the buyer takes the goods on approval in order to inspect them and determine whether he will be able to use them. A sale or return occurs when goods are delivered to a buyer who intends to resell them.[55]

With a sale on approval, the goods are not subject to the claims of the buyer's creditors until the buyer actually accepts them. However, with a sale or return, the goods are subject to creditors' claims while they are in the buyer's possession. The seller may be able to preserve his ownership of the goods without being subjected to such claims if he either retains a security interest in the goods and makes the requisite public filing in accordance with Article 9 of the UCC; complies with the applicable law concerning his interest, as evidenced by a sign at his business location or other means; or establishes that the buyer is known to his creditors to be selling the goods of others.

RISK OF LOSS

The parties to a contract may allocate between themselves the risk of loss if the goods are destroyed by a casualty, such as a fire, prior to, during, or after shipment or delivery. If the parties do not do this, Article 2 provides certain rules determining who bears the risk of loss under certain situations.

If the seller is to ship the goods by a carrier, such as a railroad or trucker, risk of loss depends upon whether the seller is to deliver them to a particular destination. If the contract does not require the seller to deliver the goods to a specific location, risk of loss passes to the buyer at the time the goods are delivered to the carrier. This would be a sale FOB point of shipment. However, if the goods must be delivered to a specific place, risk of loss passes to the buyer only after the seller has tendered the goods to the buyer so that he may take delivery.[56]

If the goods are not shipped by carrier, risk of passes to the buyer when he receives the goods, if the seller is a merchant. When the seller is not a merchant, risk of loss passes when seller tenders delivery of the goods to the buyer.[57]

If the goods, when sold, are in the possession of a bailee and are to be delivered without leaving his possession, risk of loss passes from the seller to the buyer under any one of three circumstances: first, when the buyer receives a negotiable document of title second, when the bailee acknowledges the buyer's right to possession; and third, the bailee receives a nonnegotiable document of title or other written direction from the seller to deliver the goods to the buyer.[58]

However, different rules apply if either party may have breached the agreement. Under certain circumstances, if the seller has breached the agreement, the risk of loss remains with him until he either cures the breach or the buyer accepts delivery of the goods.[59] Further, when the buyer has the right to revoke his prior acceptance of the goods, the risk of loss remains with the seller, but only to "the extent of any deficiency in" the buyer's "effective insurance coverage." The buyer could revoke prior acceptance when he finds a latent defect in the goods which impairs their value and which was not noticeable upon inspection at the time of acceptance.

When the buyer breaches a contract for which goods have already been identified and the seller is not in breach, the risk of loss for a "commercially reasonable time" rests with the buyer, but only to the extent of any deficiency in the insurance coverage of the seller.

Occasionally, the buyer and seller may agree that specific goods will be sold. When those goods are identified, the contract is legally unenforceable if the goods are destroyed by no fault of either the buyer or the seller.[70] However, if the parties did not contract with the intention of selling specific identifiable goods, performance of the contract may not avoided.[61]

PERFORMANCE OF CONTRACT

The UCC also provides rules governing performance of a sales contract in the event that the parties have not agreed to all the terms. For example, tender of delivery by the seller places upon the buyer the duty to accept and pay for the goods.[62] Payment may be made by check unless the seller demands cash and gives the buyer a reasonable time to obtain it. Any payment by a check, however, is conditional, and payment has not been made if the check is dishonored by the buyer's bank.[63] If the contract requires payment before the buyer has had an opportunity to inspect the goods, he must usually pay, but payment is not considered to be acceptance of the goods and the buyer still retains the right to inspect them.[64] In all other cases, the buyer has the right to inspect the goods before payment or acceptance.[65]

REJECTION, ACCEPTANCE, AND REVOCATION

Upon delivery of the goods or tender of delivery as covered by the sales contract, the buyer has two alternatives. He can either accept the goods or reject them under certain circumstances. The basic issue under the UCC is the buyer's right to inspect the goods before acceptance. Upon inspection, he may reject any or all goods which do not conform to the contract.[66]

Under Article 2, the goods must conform in every respect to the sales contract or the buyer has the right to reject any or all of them which have been delivered or are subject to a tender of delivery.[67] This "perfect tender rule," however, has certain limitations. For example, as discussed earlier, the seller whose delivery or tender has been rejected due to nonconformity may have the opportunity to cure the defect if the time for performance had not yet expired.[68] Further, the courts have looked at the usage of the trade, the course of dealing between the parties, and the course of performance under the contract to minimize the impact of the harsh perfect tender rule. Thus, in one case where a buyer rejected steel because it did not conform to the specifications, the court found that through trade usage adjustments in price were made and the buyer's attempt to reject was denied.[69]

If the buyer rightfully rejects the goods, the other remedies he can use for breach of contract are not waived. Hence, the buyer can take whatever action is permitted under the UCC to protect himself from loss and may seek recovery from the seller for damages.[70] The buyer's rights in a case of the seller's breach of contract will be discussed later in this chapter.

Article 2 implies that the buyer will inspect the goods within a reasonable time following delivery or tender. If he fails to do so, he will be deemed to have accepted the goods.[71] However, if he does make an inspection within a reasonable time and determines that the goods do not conform to the contract, he must take certain steps to make the rejection effective. First, he must promptly notify the seller. If he has taken possession of the goods, he generally has a duty to take reasonable care of them for a period of time which should be sufficient for the seller to take them back.[72] The seller's remedies against the buyer for wrongful rejection of goods delivered or tendered will also be discussed later.

A merchant has additional duties regarding rightfully rejected goods. If the seller has no agent or place of business where the merchant buyer is located, the merchant buyer must follow reasonable instructions from the seller regarding preservation and reshipment of the goods. Further, the UCC implies that the merchant buyer must follow any instructions from the seller to resell the goods. In addition, if the goods are perishable or will rapidly decline in volume, a merchant buyer has a duty to take reasonable steps to resell them for the seller's account. In any event, the buyer is usually entitled to payment from the seller for his reasonable expenses in storing and reselling the goods if necessary.[73] The buyer may either store, return to the seller, or resell for the seller's account any goods which are rightfully rejected.[74]

The UCC also implies that the buyer must give specific grounds for rejection in notifying the seller. Article 2 states that if no specific reason is given, the buyer may not rely upon an unstated ground or defect in the goods to show that the rejection was rightful or to establish a breach of contract by the seller.[75] However, the buyer faces this limitation only under two circumstances. First, if the seller could have remedied the problem if the defect was "stated reasonably," the buyer may not rely on an unstated ground or defect in the goods. Second, between merchants, if a seller after rejection requests a written statement of the defects from the buyer, the buyer may not support his position by using defects not disclosed in the reply.

Acceptance usually occurs after the buyer decides to accept the goods after inspection. Moreover, the buyer is deemed under the UCC to have accepted the goods when he has had an opportunity to inspect them and does not make an effective rejection. Further, if the buyer does anything which interferes with the seller's ownership of the goods, Article 2 provides that he is deemed to have accepted the goods.[76]

Acceptance of the goods, however, does not mean that the buyer waives any rights he may have against the seller to recover damages or other relief if he discovers after acceptance that the goods are defective. Acceptance, though, does limit some of the buyer's remedies, especially that of returning the goods in the event that they are defective or the tender does not conform to the contract in any respect.

Acceptance places certain obligations upon the buyer. First, he must pay for the goods. Second, he can no longer reject them unless he has reasonably assumed that the nonconformity would be corrected. Third, he must notify the seller within a reasonable time after he discovers or should have discovered any breach of the contract. If he does not, his remedy will be barred. Fourth, if a claim is made against the buyer for infringement of title, the buyer must notify the seller within a reasonable time. Fifth, acceptance of the goods places upon the buyer the burden of establishing any breach regarding any of the goods. Sixth, in the event that the buyer is sued for breach of warranty for which the seller should be responsible, the buyer must give the seller reasonable notice of the suit and allow him to defend it if he so desires.

The UCC gives the buyer certain remedies to recover damages against the seller if the buyer determines after acceptance that the sales contract has been breached. Further, the UCC allows the buyer to "revoke" acceptance of the goods under certain circumstances. First, the nonconformity must substantially impair the value of the goods to the buyer. Second, the buyer must show that he was unaware of the nonconformity because of the difficulty of discovering it prior to acceptance or because he received certain assurances from the seller, such as a statement that the goods were not defective. Third, the buyer can revoke acceptance, even though he knew of the nonconformity before hand, if he reasonably assumed that it would be remedied and it was not.[77]

In determining whether there is substantial impairment, the courts have developed a subjective-objective test. The test is subjective because the UCC requires the court to look at the circumstances of the buyer himself, not the average buyer. It is objective in that the court then judges the nonconformity and whether it substantially impaired the value of the goods using an objective test.[78]

Sometimes the courts consider the repair cost to determine whether there has been substantial impairment of the value of goods. If this cost is relatively low, the courts will not sanction revocation.[79]

In order to revoke acceptance successfully, the buyer must do so within a reasonable time after he discovers, or should have discovered, the reason for the revocation. In addition, revocation must occur before there has been any "substantial change in condition of the goods which is not caused by their own defects." Further, revocation becomes effective only after the buyer has notified the seller that he has revoked acceptance.[80]

Conditions which may limit the buyer's right to revoke acceptance include depreciation of the value of the goods or continued use of the goods by the buyer after he acts or should have acted to revoked acceptance.[81]

If the buyer rightfully rejects or revokes acceptance of the goods, to whom can he return them and against whom can he seek remedy? Generally, the buyer may return the goods only to the person who sold them to him. Thus, in a breach of warranty case, the buyer must return the goods and seek remedy against the party who sold them, who frequently may not be the manufacturer.[82]

ANTICIPATORY REPUDIATION

The general law of contracts recognizes the doctrine of anticipatory repudiation. Under this doctrine, if one party indicates that he will not perform the contract, the other party may treat this action as a breach and consider the contract terminated, seeking remedies under the law. Unfortunately, the courts have treated three common situations as not necessarily being evidence of anticipatory repudiation. These cases involve the insolvency of one buyer, delayed performance by a buyer, or unsatisfactory performance of one party.[83]

The UCC recognizes the doctrine of anticipatory repudiation. It provides that when one party repudiates a sales contract, the other party may either wait for the repudiating party to perform or seek remedies for breach of contract. In either event, the party who has not repudiated may delay performance of his obligations under the contract.[84] In any case, the repudiation must substantially impair the value of the contract, and if one party desires to await performance, he can do so for only a commercially reasonable time.

The major problem with the UCC provision is that it does not resolve the question, what is repudiation? However, the UCC introduced a new concept into the law which minimizes the need for one party to run the risk that the other party may not really have repudiated the contract as determined by the courts. This is the right of the party who has not repudiated the contract to obtain adequate assurance of performance from the other party. This UCC provision does not speak about anticipatory repudiation, but states that when one party has "reasonable grounds" to suspect that the other party may not perform the contract, he may "in writing demand adequate assurance of due performance." Further, after making the demand, he may delay his performance until he receives such assurance if this is commercially reasonable. The UCC then states that if an assurance of performance is not received within a reasonable time after the demand has been made, a period not to exceed 30 days, the party making the demand may treat the contract as repudiated.[85]

IMPOSSIBILITY OF PERFORMANCE

Article 2 contains a provision similar to the doctrine of impossibility of performance which is part of the general law of contracts. Under this provision, performance of a contract is excused under certain circumstances unless the seller assumed "a greater obligation" under the agreement. If performance of the contract has been rendered "impracticable due to good faith compliance with a governmental regulation or order" or due to some failure of "a basic assumption on which the contract was made," performance is excused. If only part of the seller's obligation is affected by the impracticability of performance, the seller must allocate sales among his customers in a "fair and reasonable" manner.[86]

During the period of rapidly increasing inflation in the United States in the late 1970s and early 1980s, a question arose as to whether increased costs to the seller could excuse performance of a contract. The official comments in the UCC indicate that a mere increase in costs is an insufficient excuse. There must be some "unforeseen contingency" that has resulted in the marked increase in prices, such as material shortages due to war or strikes.[86]

SELLER'S REMEDIES

Article 2 provides the seller with certain remedies in the event that the buyer (1) wrongfully rejects acceptance of the goods covered by the contract, (2) wrongfully revokes acceptance of the goods covered by the agreement, (3) fails to make a payment when due, (4) repudiates all or part of the contract, or (5) becomes insolvent. In addition, the seller may seek remedies against the buyer if the buyer "otherwise" defaults under the contract.

Section 2-703 of the UCC outlines the remedial rights of the seller. However, if the buyer becomes insolvent only as defined by the UCC, the seller may not use these broad remedies, but must proceed in a limited manner against the insolvent buyer.[88] These limited powers allow the seller to stop delivery, unless the buyer pays cash.

Further, if the seller discovers that the buyer received goods on credit while the buyer was insolvent, he may reclaim those goods within ten days after the buyer received them. Moreover, if the buyer misrepresented his solvency to the seller within three months prior to delivery of the goods, the buyer may reclaim them at any time, without observing the ten-day limitation.[89] Further, if the buyer, while insolvent, wrongfully revokes acceptance of any of the goods, fails to make a payment when due, or repudiates the contract, the seller may also proceed against him under the general remedies provisions of the UCC.

In addition, the seller and buyer, in their contract, may substitute or name remedies for breach of contract in addition to those provided in the UCC, and the courts will generally enforce such provisions.[90] In all other cases, the general remedies under the UCC are available to the seller.

Generally, the seller has several remedies against the buyer who breaches a contract. First, the seller need not deliver the goods. If the goods are in the hands of a bailee, such as a carrier for delivery or a warehouse, he may stop delivery. Or the seller may terminate the contract and take no action whatsoever.[91] Further, he may sue the buyer for the price and "incidental damages" for goods which the buyer has already accepted or for goods which were "lost or damaged" after risk of loss has passed to the buyer. In addition, if the seller has identified items which will be delivered under the contract, he is entitled to sue for the purchase price, but only if he has been unable to resell those products in a reasonable manner. In this case the seller must hold the goods for the buyer, if they have not already been received by the buyer, and if he resells them at any time, the "net proceeds" of the resale are credited to the buyer's account.[92]

As an alternative, the seller may sue for damages for either wrongful rejection, revocation of acceptance, or wrongful repudiation of the contract. Damages are determined by calculating the "difference between the market price at the time and place for tender and the unpaid contract price together with any incidental damage . . . but less expenses saved at consequence of the buyer's breach."[93] If the damages cannot be adequately measured by this method, the seller is allowed a lost profit including reasonable overhead and incidental damages.[94]

As indicated above, one of the seller's general remedies is to identify the goods to be covered by the contract if this has not yet been done. The seller can do this even if the goods are unfinished. In the event that the goods are not finished, the seller may use his "reasonable commercial judgment" to avoid a loss. If necessary, he can either complete manufacture of the goods or stop manufacture, reselling the unfinished goods for their scrap or salvage value.[95]

As also stated above, under certain circumstances the seller may be awarded "incidental damages." These are costs that the seller would not have incurred but for the buyer's default, such as the expenses necessary to stop delivery of the goods and the care of goods identified for the contract while in the custody of the seller.[96]

If the seller decides to resell the product, he must do so in a reasonable manner. The sale may be either public or private. If it is a private sale, Article 2 requires the seller to notify the buyer of his intention to resell. If the sale is public, it must involve goods identified for the contract (unless there is an existing market for the public sale of futures of the goods that could be identified for the contract), it must take place in a recognized market, the goods must be available for inspection, and the seller himself may buy them.[97]

It is important for the seller to comply with the resale provisions of the UCC. In one case, the seller waited 14 months before reselling a used bulldozer and the court held this to be an unreasonable delay.[98] The seller of an automobile who resold it without notifying the original buyer who breached the contract was prevented from recovering damages, which were the difference between the original contract price and the resale price from the original buyer, because of the seller's failure to give proper notification of the intended sale to the original buyer.[99]

BUYER'S REMEDIES

We have discussed two of the buyer's principal remedies in the event that the seller breaches the contract. First, the buyer may reject a nonconforming tender of delivery. This occurs most commonly when the buyer, after examining the goods determines that they are either defective or not what he ordered. Further, as pointed out above, under certain circumstances the buyer may revoke acceptance of the goods and return them to the seller. As an example, revocation may occur when the buyer could not uncover a latent defect in the goods upon inspection at the time of acceptance or immediately thereafter, and the defect becomes obvious at a later date.

The UCC provides remedies in addition to rejection and revocation. In cases where the seller does not deliver the goods or repudiates the contract, or where the buyer rejects or revokes acceptance of the goods, the buyer may either "cover" or recover damages for nondelivery. Cover involves the buyer's purchasing substitute goods. Of course, Article 2 places a burden upon the buyer to act reasonably, including paying only a reasonable price for the goods. If the buyer has acted reasonably in purchasing substitute goods, he may obtain the difference between the cost of these goods and the price he was to pay the seller, along with "incidental" and "consequential" damages.[100]

If the buyer does not purchase substitute goods, he may sue the seller for damages. The damages are determined by calculating the "difference between the market price at the time when the buyer learned of the breach and the contract price together with any incidental and consequential damages . . . , but less expenses saved in consequence of the seller's breach."[101] In situations where the seller does not make delivery or repudiates the contract prior to performance, the buyer may either recover the goods if they have already been identified for the contract or, under certain circumstances, may force the seller to perform.[102] This remedy is available either when the buyer has paid for the goods before delivery and the seller becomes insolvent ten days following receipt of the price or when the goods are unique.[103]

The buyer's remedy to demand specific performance by the seller is an innovation in the law which first appeared in the Uniform Sales Act, the predecessor of Article 2. Generally, prior to this act, purchasers could not obtain specific performance for the delivery of goods. This remedy, which was an equitable action, was usually limited to the sale of real property.

The specific performance provisions of the UCC has been used by the courts in several cases. In one, the buyer had contracted to purchase cryolite, a chemical needed for aluminum production. The seller breached the contract and refused to deliver any more of the product. Because cryolite was scarce and the court concluded that the buyer probably could not obtain it elsewhere, it allowed the buyer to obtain specific performance from the seller.[104] In another case, the court enforced a long-term contract for the purchase of propane, noting that the buyer would probably be unable to find another contract of the same length.[105]

If the buyer has rejected or revoked acceptance of the goods, he must store any of the goods which are in his possession, subject to reasonable reimbursement by the seller. In addition, the buyer may resell the goods in the manner in which the seller would have to resell them in the event that the buyer breached the contract.[106]

What if the buyer decides not to reject or revoke the acceptance of nonconforming goods? Or what if the buyer has not followed the proper procedures in rejecting or revoking the goods as required by the UCC? Under certain circumstances, the buyer may sue the seller for breach of contract and recover damages. If there is a breach of warranty, the damages are determined by calculating the difference between the value of the goods as they would have been if they had not been defective and the value of the goods as they were. Further, if the court finds it appropriate, it may award incidental and consequential damages.[107] Incidental damages are expenses such as storing and reselling the goods. Consequential damages include any personal injury or property damages resulting from the breach of warranty or any other loss due to a condition known to the seller.[108]

Further, the buyer, after notifying the seller of his intent to do so, may deduct his damages due to the breach from the price due under the contract.[109]

STATUTE OF LIMITATIONS

The UCC contains a statute of limitations covering suits filed under the Code. Most of the states have adopted the UCC statute, which is four years from the time of accrual of a cause of action. The cause of action generally accrues when the breach occurs, regardless of when the aggrieved party learns of the breach. In the case of breach of warranty, the action accrues from the tender of delivery, not from the date when the buyer learned of the breach.[110] The practical effect of this UCC provision is to bar any action for breach of warranty four years after delivery of the goods. Thus, if the breach of warranty causing damage occurs after the four-year period, the buyer is barred from suing for the breach of warranty.

The parties to the contract may reduce the period to as little as one year, but they may not extend it beyond the four-year period.

NOTES

1. *Statistical Tabulating Corp. v. Bullock,* 538 S.W.2d 259 (Tex.Civ.App. 1976), *aff'd,* 549 S.W.2d 166 (Tex. 1977).
2. *Nitrin, Inc. v. Bethlehem Steel Corp.,* 35 Ill.App.3d 577, 342 N.E.2d 65 (1976).
3. *Field v. Golden Triangle Broadcasting Inc.,* 451 Pa. 410, 305 A.2d 689 (1973), *cert. denied,* 414 U.S. 1158 (1974).
4. *Meister v. Arden-Mayfair, Inc.,* 276 Or. 517, 555 P.2d 923 (1976).
5. *Foster v. Colorado Radio Corp.,* 381 F.2d 222 (10th Cir. 1976).
6. Ronald A. Anderson, *Anderson on the Uniform Commercial Code,* 2d ed., §2-105.38, (Rochester, N.Y. Lawyers Cooperative Publishing Co., 1974), 580–582.
7. *Maryland Supreme Corp. v. Blake Co.,* 279 Md. 531, 369 A.2d 1017 (1977).
8. *Farley v. Clark Equipment Co.,* 484 S.W.2d 142 (Tex.Civ.App. 1972).
9. *Wisconsin Electric Power Co. v. Zallea Bros. Inc.,* 443 F.Supp. 946 (E.D. Wis. 1978), *later app.* 454 F.Supp. 36 (E.D. Wis. 1978) *aff'd.,* 606 F.2d 697 (7th Cir. 1979).
10. U.C.C. §2-104 (1976).
11. U.C.C. §2-205 (1976).
12. U.C.C. §2-206 (1976).
13. George I. Wallach, *The Law of Sales Under the Uniform Commercial Code,* ¶1.03 (Boston: Warren, Gorham & Lamont, 1981), 1–12.
14. U.C.C. §2-204 (1976).
15. *Kleinschmidt Division of SCM Corp. v. Futuronics Corp.,* 41 N.Y.2d 972, 395 N.Y.S 2d 151, 363 N.E.2d 701 (1977).
16. *Harlow & Jones, Inc. v. Advance Steel Co.,* 424 F.Supp. 770 (E.D.Mich. 1976).
17. *Southwestern Stationery & Bank Supply, Inc. v. Harris Corp.,* 624 F.2d 168 (10th Cir. 1980).
18. U.C.C. §2-201 (1976).
19. Richard M. Alderman, *A Transactional Guide to the Uniform Commercial Code,* 2d ed., Vol. 1 (Philadelphia: American Law Institute, 1983), 36.
20. U.C.C. §2-202 (1976).
21. U.C.C. §2-305(1) (1976).
22. U.C.C. §2-207 (1976) and Wallach, *The Law of Sales,* 3-10 to 3-12.
23. *Lea Tai Textile Co. v. Manning Fabrics Inc.,* 411 F.Supp. 1404 (S.D.N.Y. 1975), *Dorton v. Collins & Aikman Corp.,* 453 F.2d 1161 (6th Cir. 1972), and *Roto-Lith, Ltd. v. F. P. Bartlett & Co.,* 297 F.2d 497 (1st Cir. 1962).
24. U.C.C. §2-209 (1976).
25. U.C.C. §2-210 (1976).
26. U.C.C. §1-102(3) (1976). See Alderman, *A Transactional Guide,* 56.
27. U.C.C. §1-203 (1976).
28. U.C.C. §2-210(2) (1976).
29. U.C.C. §2-318 (1976).
30. U.C.C. §2-718(1) (1976).

31. U.C.C. §2-719(1) (1976).
32. U.C.C. §2-725 (1976).
33. U.C.C. §2-302 (1976).
34. U.C.C. §2-305(1) (1976)
35. U.C.C. §2-305(4) (1976).
36. U.C.C. §2-306 (1976).
37. *Harvey v. Fearless Farris Wholesale, Inc.*, 589 F.2d 451 (9th Cir.1979).
38. U.C.C. §§2-307, 308, and 309 (1976).
39. U.C.C. §2-310 (1976).
40. U.C.C. §2-312 (1976).
41. U.C.C. §2-313 (1976).
42. *Interco, Inc. v. Randustrial Corp.*, 533 S.W.2d 257 (Mo. App. 1976).
43. U.C.C. §2-313 (b) and (c) (1976).
44. U.C.C. §2-314 (1976).
45. U.C.C. §2-315 (1976)
46. *Hunt v. Perkins Machinery Co.*, 352 Mass. 535, 226 N.E.2d 228 (1967).
47. *Childers & Venters, Inc. v. Sowards*, 460 S.W.2d 343 (Ky. 1970).
48. Magnunson-Moss Warranty-Federal Trade Commission Improvement Act of 1975, Title 1, §§101–112, 15 U.S.C.A. §2301 (1982).
49. U.C.C. §§2-319 and 320 (1976).
50. U.C.C. §2-322 (1976).
51. U.C.C. §2-403 (1976).
52. U.C.C. §2-702(2) (1976).
53. U.C.C. §2-511 (1976).
54. U.C.C. §2-403(3) (1976).
55. U.C.C. §2-326 (1976).
56. U.C.C. §2-509(1) (1976).
57. U.C.C. §2-509(3) (1976).
58. U.C.C. §2-509(2) (1976).
59. U.C.C. §2-510(1) (1976).
60. U.C.C. §2-613 (1976).
61. *Valley Forge Flag Co. v. New York Dowel & Moulding Import Co.*, 90 Misc.2d 414, 395 N.Y.S.2d 138 (1977).
62. U.C.C. §2-507 (1976).
63. U.C.C. §2-511 (1976).
64. U.C.C. §2-512 (1976).
65. U.C.C. §2-513 (1976).
66. U.C.C. §2-601 (1976).
67. Wallach, *The Law of Sales*, 9-12 to 9-13.
68. U.C.C. §2-508 (1976).
69. *North American Steel Corp. v. Siderius, Inc.*, 75 Mich.App. 391, 254 N.W.2d 899 (1977).
70. Comment 1, U.C.C. §2-601 (1976).
71. U.C.C. §2-606 (1976).
72. U.C.C. §2-602 (1976).
73. U.C.C. §2-603 (1976).
74. U.C.C. §2-604 (1976).
75. U.C.C. §2-605 (1976).
76. U.C.C. §2-606 (1976).
77. U.C.C. §2-608(1) (1976).

78. *Jorgensen v. Pressnall*, 274 Or. 285, 545 P.2d 1382 (1976).
79. *Freeman Oldsmobile-Mazda Co. v. Pinson*, 580 S.W.2d 112 (Tex.Civ.App. 1979).
80. U.C.C. § 2-60 (1976)8.
81. *Eckstein v. Cummins*, 41 Ohio App.2d 1, 321 N.E.2d 897 (1974), and *Gigandet v. Third National Bank*, 333 So.2d 557 (Ala. 1976).
82. *Voytovich v. Bangor Punta Operations, Inc.*, 494 F.2d 1208 (6th Cir. 1974).
83. Wallach, *The Law of Sales*, 6-3 to 6-5.
84. U.C.C. § 2-610 (1976).
85. U.C.C. § 2-609 (1976).
86. U.C.C. § 2-615 (1976).
87. *See* Official Comments, Note 4, U.C.C. § 2-615 (1976).
88. Alderman, *A Transactional Guide*, 371–372.
89. U.C.C. §2-702 (1976).
90. U.C.C. §2-719 (1976).
91. U.C.C. §2-705 (1976).
92. U.C.C. §2-709 (1976).
93. U.C.C. §2-708 (1976).
94. U.C.C. §2-708(2) (1976).
95. U.C.C. §2-704 (1976).
96. U.C.C. §2-710 (1976).
97. U.C.C. §2-706 (1976).
98. *McMillan v. Meuser Material & Equipment Co.*, 260 Ark. 422, 541 S.W.2d 911 (1976).
99. *Lee Oldsmobile, Inc. v. Kaiden*, 32 Md. App. 556, 363 A.2d 270 (Md.App. 1976).
100. U.C.C. §2-712 (1976).
101. U.C.C. §2-713 (1976).
102. U.C.C. §2-711(2) (1976).
103. U.C.C. §§2-711(2), 2-502 and 2-716 (1976).
104. *Kaiser Trading Co. v. Associated Metals & Minerals Corp.*, 321 F. Supp. 923 (N.D. Cal. 1970), *appeal dismissed*, 443 F.2d 1364 (9th Cir. 1971).
105. *Laclede Gas Co. v. Amoco Oil Co.*, 522 F.2d 33 (8th Cir. 1975).
106. U.C.C. §2-711(3) (1976).
107. U.C.C. §2-714 (1976).
108. U.C.C. §2-715 (1976).
109. U.C.C. §2-717 (1976).
110. U.C.C. §2-725 (1976).

10
Government Contracts

Federal, state, and local governments purchase billions of dollars worth of products and services each year. Because of the legal requirements of government procurement, federal, state, and many local governments have established detailed and highly technical formats for purchasing products and services. Engineers who have worked under government contracts are aware of these verbose and often confusing regulations.

A government employee cannot merely go out and procure products or services. He must have the authority to do so and must conduct the transaction in accordance with the applicable law. Both the federal and state governments have statutes granting purchasing authority and setting down the rules of the procurement process. Further, in most instances, procurement can be made only after the appropriate legislative body has passed a statute or bill appropriating the necessary funds. Finally, most, if not all, federal and state agencies engaged in procurement have developed sophisticated regulations implementing their statutory authority.

The aim of all government procurement is to obtain the best possible product or services at the lowest possible price. As a result, competitive bidding is generally encouraged, which requires openness. Attempts to prejudice the procurement process are discouraged. As an example, government regulations and court decisions discourage "sole source" procurement. Public policy usually requires that specifications for goods or services be written in such a manner that as many potential bidders as possible may submit bids for the contract. Further, attempts to influence government contracts through bribery or other more sophisticated forms of undue influence are prohibited by statute and often by government regulations. Further, some regulations forbid the use of contingent fees paid upon the successful award of a contract to a particular company.[1]

This chapter is devoted primarily to a brief overview of federal procurement law. In addition, some significant differences between court interpretations of federal and state government contract law will be mentioned.

SATUTORY FRAMEWORK

Through World War II, the federal government used a procurement system based upon laws and methods adopted during the Civil War.[2] Following the war, Congress enacted two broad statutes to govern procurement by the federal government. These were the Armed Services Procurement Act of 1947 and the Federal Property and Administration Services Act of 1948. The Armed Services Procurement Act governs purchasing, except for land, by the U.S. Departments of the Army, Air Force, and Navy, the U.S. Coast Guard, and the National Aeronautics and Space Administration (NASA). Purchasing by the General Services Administration and all other agencies is governed by the Federal Property and Administrative Services Act. Both of these acts were amended, effective April 1, 1985, by the Competition in Contracting Act, which encourages competitive bidding for all military and civilian contracts. The procedure for handling disputes arising under government contracts is governed by the Contract Disputes Act of 1978.

In 1974, the Office of Federal Procurement Policy Act was established pursuant to the Office of Federal Procurement Policy Act (41 U.S.C. 401). This office oversees all federal government procurement regulations and may issue uniform regulations to be used by the executive agencies.

There are other specialized statutes governing federal procurement. For example, the Buy American Act declares it to be public policy to purchase goods produced in the United States.[3] The Small Business Act has set up a program to encourage the participation of small businesses in federal procurement.[4] The Davis-Bacon Act has established a program of minimum wages for construction workers under federal contracts.[5]

For years, two main bodies of procurement regulations were issued under the appropriate statutes. These were the Armed Service

Procurement Regulations, often referred to as "ASPRs," issued by the Department of Defense under the Armed Services Procurement Act, and the Federal Procurement Regulations, usually referred to as "FPRs," promulgated by the General Services Administration. Further, several independent government agencies, such as NASA, issued their own procurement regulations. Many government agencies also developed supplemental regulations of directives which were subordinate to the governing regulations. Thus, in the U.S. Army, there were five different levels of regulations and instructions below the ASPRs. Moreover, other government agencies issued regulations affecting procurement, although they are not technically procurement regulations. Such agencies include the Department of Labor and the Small Business Administration.

In 1984, Federal Acquisition Regulations, referred to as "FARs," became effective. They are used for all executive agencies and were issued under the authority of the Administrator of General Services, the Secretary of Defense, and the Administrator for NASA, following policy guidelines of the Administrator for Federal Procurement Policy. The FARs replaced the FPRs, the Defense Acquisition Regulations, and the NASA Procurement Regulations.

The U.S. government publishes daily the *Federal Register,* which contains regulations promulgated by the various federal agencies. When regulations are printed *Federal Register* as final, they become valid and have the full force of law. Under federal government contract law, all clauses which are required by regulation to be included in the contract become part of the government contract, even though the contract documents do not actually contain the clauses.[6]

CONTRACTING OFFICER

The key person in the federal procurement process is the "contracting officer," a person duly designated by law with authority to enter into contracts on behalf of the United States. Only a duly designated contracting officer can make contracts which bind the United States. Generally, if a party contracts with an employee of the United States who is not an authorized contracting officer, the contract will not be enforced and the other party will not be paid.

The courts have held not only that the contracting officer must have authority to make the contract, but also that if the contract violates a government statute or regulation it is void, despite the authority granted to the contracting officer.[7] Further, even if the U.S. government agency gives its employee the apparent authority to enter into the contract, any contract made between such an employee who does not have actual contracting authority and another party is void.[8] Moreover, a binding contract cannot be created when a government agency has exceeded its statutory authority in issuing regulations under which the contract was made.[9] However, if a contract has been made on behalf of the government by one of its employees who lacks authority to do so, the action of the employee may be ratified by a contracting officer with the requisite authority, resulting in a binding contract.[10] Thus, it is extremely important for a person entering into a contract with the federal government to be sure that the contracting officer has the authority to make the agreement.

When the federal government makes a contract with a private individual, it cannot use the defense of sovereign immunity to a suit under the contract.[11] However, in some situations, the defense of sovereign immunity may still be viable. Those are instances in which the action of the federal government which allegedly caused the breach of contract was taken as a matter of public interest and general application as opposed to or directed toward a specific contract.[12]

Suits against the U.S. government for breach of contract were initially governed by the Tucker Act, which was superseded by the Contract Disputes Act of 1978.[13] The Contract Disputes Act will be discussed later.

APPROPRIATIONS

The appropriation process is the keystone of government procurement. Under the U.S. Constitution, funds may not be disbursed from the U.S. Treasury without a Congressional appropriation.[14] Further, Congress has specifically barred any officer or employee of the United States from entering into any contract without an appropriation in advance, unless otherwise authorized by law.[15]

Congress passes annual appropriation acts providing the funds necessary for government operation, including those for specific contracts. Under the law, the act must state the purpose of the appropriation and the appropriated funds may be used only for the described purpose.[16] After the appropriation act is passed, the executive branch controls the expenditures.

Appropriations may be either annual, for several years, or available for an indefinite period of time. Generally, the appropriation states when the funds may be obligated. Thus, under an annual appropriation, the contracts for the appropriation must be entered into during the fiscal year, but the funds may actually be spent in subsequent years, so long as the items purchased relate to the year of the appropriation.[17]

After an appropriation is made, the contracting process begins. Essentially, government contracts also require an offer, acceptance, and adequate consideration. However, the offer and acceptance process is extremely formal. In advertising for government procurement, an invitation for bids (IFB) is used. When contracts are to be negotiated, a request for proposals (RFP) is circulated. In an advertised bid procurement, after the lowest qualified bid is accepted, the government prepares formal contract documents. Similarly, in a negotiated contract, after the negotiations are completed, the formal contract documents are executed. A written contract is required by the Supplemental Appropriations Act of 1955. However, the act does not necessarily require a formal contract document. Other written evidence, such as a memorandum, may be used as evidence of the contract.[18]

CONTRACTOR QUALIFICATION

Generally, prequalification of bidders is not used in federal government procurement because of the fear that it may unduly restrict competition, resulting in higher prices to the government.[19] However, after accepting bids under advertised procurement or when negotiating with parties for a negotiated contract, the contracting officer must determine whether the persons or companies which may receive the contract are qualified or responsible.[20] The contracting officer must determine whether the parties will be qualified at the time the contract will be performed, not at the time the contract is agreed to by the government. In one government IFB; the bidders were required to have a certain clearance. The low bidder did not have it, but the Comptroller General ruled that he might have it at the time the work was to be performed. Hence, the Comptroller General ruled that the bidder's qualifications should not be considered as of the time of the bid opening or even at the award of the contract.[21]

The contracting officer usually looks at four major areas to determine contractor qualifications. First, he decides whether the contractor has sufficient financial resources to perform the contract. Second, he determines whether the contractor has the ability to perform. This may include a judgment on the contractor's technical and production expertise. Third, he looks at the proposed contractor's record of performance. Fourth, he weighs the contractor's integrity.

An analysis of the contractor's financial resources includes a review of his financial statements. The aim of the review is to determine whether the proposed contractor has the financial capability to perform the contract. Thus, the contracting officer considers such matters as whether the contractor has enough money to purchase the goods and services which may be needed to perform the contract.

When deciding whether the contractor has the necessary experience, the contracting officer may require him to have a certain minimum number of years of experience in manufacturing the product which is to be purchased. Such requirements are generally upheld so long as they bear some relationship to the nature of the services or products to be purchased. As an example, the U.S. Department of Justice had issued an invitation for bids to purchase radio sets. The invitation stated that the manufacturers who were bidding needed five years of experience in the design and production of the radio sets and that the sets had to have been in general public use for at least one year. A bidder protested because he lacked the second requirement. The Comptroller General upheld that requirement because it bore a reasonable relationship to reliability.[22]

In determining the question of integrity, the contracting officer determines whether the contractor has demonstrated honest in performing under other government contracts. In one situation, a proposed contractor was disqualified because one of its principal shareholders had been convicted of evading federal income taxes from other government contracts. The decision to disqualify that company was upheld by the Comptroller General.[23]

Generally, contractors for federal work need not be required to have state licenses.[24] However, invitations for bids frequently require the necessary state and local licenses.

Usually, a proposed contractor who has been disqualified by a government agency for a specific contract has no right to appeal the decision. Although he may file a suit under the Administration Procedure Act challenging the disqualification, the courts will not reverse the determination of the contracting officer or the procuring agency that a specific contractor was unqualified for a contract.[25] Moreover, the Comptroller General rarely will intervene in the decisions of contracting officers regarding contractor qualification.[26]

In addition to disqualification for a specific contract, a contractor may be listed on a barred bidders list. This list is prepared by the federal procurement agencies and identifies contractors which may not bid for or receive government contracts because of previous fraudulent or inacceptable contract performance or because they have violated certain statutes pertaining to employment or kickbacks. The debarment procedure requires the debarring agency to give the contractor a written notice indicating the reasons for the proposed debarment and granting him the right to a hearing if he so desires.[27] The usual debarment period is three years.[28] In addition, a contractor may be suspended from government contracting for a period not to exceed eighteen months pending the investigation of an alleged crime.[29]

BID PROTESTS

Parties seeking a government contract may protest irregularities in the process. There are two times when a protest may be made: first, when the bid package is circulated and before the contract is awarded, and second, after the award is made.

Protests are generally made in one of three forms. The proposed contractor may protest to the contracting agency; he may protest to the General Accounting Office, which is headed by the Comptroller General; or he may seek relief in the courts.

The protester need not file a protest with the contracting agency prior to proceeding either before the General Accounting Office (GAO) or in the courts.[30] However, award decisions are often changed or reversed after review by the contracting officer's own agency.[31] The FARs provide specific proceedings to be followed for handling protests during the bidding process. Moreover, the contracting officer usually may not award a contract until all protests have been resolved.[32]

The aggrieved party may also protest to the General Accounting Office (GAO). The GAO was established by Congress in 1921 to resolve all claims against the United States. It has established a specific procedure for handling bid protests and does so in order to prevent the unauthorized disbursement of public funds. The courts generally have upheld the GAO's policy of considering bid protests.

GAO protests must be filed in writing and within certain time limits. Although these two requirements are extremely important and rigidly enforced by the GAO, bid protests generally are handled informally.

The written protest should include the name and address of the protester, identify the procuring agency and the number of the bid or contract, state the reason for the protest, and request a ruling by the Comptroller General.[33] A copy of the protest should be sent to the contracting officer, supported by necessary documentation.

If the bid protest concerns an alleged deficiency in an invitation to bid or a request for proposals which was readily observable from the invitation documents, the protest must be submitted before the opening of the bid or before the submission of the initial proposals for a proposed negotiated contract. All other protests are due no more than ten days following the time when the protester knew or should have known of the deficiency. Generally, an award cannot be made while a protest is pending. However, it may be made under certain unusual circumstances, such as when the goods or services to be purchased are needed immediately by the government agency.

Until 1970, the aggrieved bidder's right to protest procurement irregularities before the federal courts was limited. Generally, the low bidder who had not been awarded a contract had no right to protest in the federal courts. In 1970, the Court of Appeals for the District of Columbia radically modified the law and allowed a bidder on a government contract to proceed with its protest in the federal courts.[34] In 1971, the same court backtracked and held that the right of an aggrieved bidder to proceed in the federal courts was restricted. The court stated that the federal court should not intervene and upset the decision of the procuring agency unless there was no rational basis for its decision.[35]

FORMAL ADVERTISING

There are two methods of selecting contractors in federal procurement. One is to go through a formal advertising or bidding procedure by which bids are solicited and submitted. The second method, discussed in the next section, is negotiation.

The formal advertising or bidding method of procurement is widely used in the federal government, although many purchases are made through negotiation, especially in weapons procurement programs for the Department of Defense. Generally, the contracting officer cannot use the negotiation method without adequate justification.

Public policy definitely favors the formal advertising method because it allows many contractors to bid upon government contracts, which should result in the government's paying a low competitive price. In addition, formal bidding minimizes the chances of favoritism and fraud.

When formal advertising is used, federal law requires that the bidders be allowed a reasonable period of time to prepare their bids. In addition, the specifications should be written to encourage competition. Further, the bids are opened in public and the award must be made to a responsible bidder whose bid meets the requirements of the invitation. The contracting officer, in awarding the contract, may consider other factors in addition to the price bid by the various bidders, such as quantity, quality, and delivery time.[36]

The specifications for the bids frequently follow standards laid down by various government agencies for the purpose of products which are often needed. The government publishes its specifications and standards which may be used by the contracting officer. Brand names may be specified in the invitation for bids, but only on an or-equal basis. In addition, bids submitted on this basis cannot be rejected for minor differences from the brand name product. Further, the Comptroller General has held that a determination of whether a product offered under the or-equal provision is acceptable must be based upon "performance capabilities" which are reasonably related to the design specification of the brand name product used in the invitation for bids.[37]

One aim of the formal advertising method of procurement is to solicit bids from as many sources as possible. Therefore, the contracting officer must take steps to ensure that as many potential bidders as possible are aware of the proposed contract. Thus, he may arrange to have information about the proposed contract and the bidding sent to prospective bidders. Generally, federal agencies maintain mailing lists of bidders which can be used for this purpose. Information about the proposed contract and the bidding process may also be posted in public places and summarized in the *Commerce Business Daily,* a publication of the U.S. Department of Commerce. Free publicity for the bids may also be given in other publications.

Each bidder is responsible for preparing his own bid pursuant to the invitation for bids. Each bidder must also be sure that his bid is delivered at the correct location and time. Under federal procurement regulations, late bids may be considered under two circumstances. First, if the bid is sent by registered or certified mail at least five days before the due date, it may be considered by the contracting officer. Second, if it was submitted by mail, or the invitation specified that the bid could be submitted by telegram, the contracting officer may consider the bid when the delay was due solely to mishandling by the government.[38]

The bids must be responsive to the invitation for bids. A bid which does not conform to the specifications may be found to be nonresponsive, and hence may be rejected by the contracting officer. Further, the contracting officer may not waive any of the requirements of the invitation for bids.[39] However, certain informalities may be corrected. These are details which have little or no effect upon the price, quantity, quality, or delivery date specified in the invitation for bids.[40]

Under common law, in a normal contract situation, an offeror may withdraw his offer at any time. Under procurement law, a problem arises as to the circumstances under which a bidder or offerer may withdraw his bid. The federal courts have declared that in federal procurement a bid may be withdrawn up to the time it is opened by the procuring agency.[41]

Under certain circumstances, a mistake in a bid may result in either its withdrawal or modification. However, strict standards are applied in situations where bidders attempt to correct a mistake after the bid opening and before the contract award.[42] Clerical mistakes which are apparent in the bid documents may be corrected.[43]

Generally, a contracting officer may not reject all bids, unless he has adequate justification. Otherwise, potential bidders would question the integrity of the bidding process, especially since their prices now were known to their competitors, and would be reluctant to submit bids in the future.[44]

Occasionally, two-step formal advertising is used for procurement. This method may be used when formal specifications cannot be written for practical reasons, such as for procurement of technical products or in an attempt by the government to improve the state of the art. Under this method of procurement, a contracting officer requires the bidders by a request for proposals to submit technical proposals during the first step. These proposals are then analyzed and evaluated against performance and design specifications. The bidders whose proposals are deemed to be acceptable are then invited to participate in the second step. This involves a submission of bids pursuant to regular competitive bidding procedures, although each bidder submits his own technical and pricing proposal.

NEGOTIATED PROCUREMENT

Although formal advertising may be the preferred method of procurement to ensure competitive bidding, advertising frequently is not a practical method. Thus, federal statutes and regulations authorize contracting officers to negotiate contracts.[45] Frequently, negotiation may be used in emergencies to avoid the delays inherent in the advertising method, for the purchase of professional services, for educational services to be furnished by schools and universities, for procurement outside the United States, for classified purchases, for experimental work, or for purchases of technical items, the production of which requires a substantial investment over a long period of time. However, even though the contracting officer has decided to procure products or services through negotiation, he must still conduct the negotiations in a way that ensures competition.

That is, he should negotiate with as many eligible contractors as is feasible.

Generally, the federal government procures the services of architects and engineers through negotiation. The Brooks Bill, adopted by Congress in 1972, governs the procurement of the services of design professionals.[46] Under this legislation, the various contracting officers must give notice of the requirements for professional services which are subject to negotiation. The award must be based upon the competence and qualifications of the professional, and a fair and reasonable price must be paid for his services. In addition, design professionals must submit qualifications annually, and the contracting officer must discuss the proposed contract with at least three architect or engineering firms prior to making the award. The contracting officer must then rank the firms and negotiate the price with the most qualified firm first. If a satisfactory agreement on price cannot be reached, the contracting officer negotiates with the other firms in order of priority. If no agreement is reached, the contracting officer must reinitiate the entire negotiation process.

Before other contracts are selected for negotiation, the procuring agency must justify it as one for negotiation through a formal process of determination and findings. The determination and findings should state the rationale for selecting the negotiation process for a particular contract.[46]

Negotiation usually starts with a request for proposals or request for quotations (RFQ) issued by the contracting officer. The request must state what criteria will be used in selecting the contractor, and the proposals or quotes received must be evaluated against these criteria. However, the agency's finding that a particular contractor satisfied the criteria will not be upset unless the decision was made in bad faith or there were no substantial grounds for it.[48] After the offers are received, a series of discussions occur in which the parties bargain. Generally, after the discussions, the contracting officer will set a date for the submission of "best and final" offers. This gives equal treatment to all parties with whom the government has been discussing the proposed contract and aids in preserving competition.

In 1962, Congress passed the Truth in Negotiations Act covering negotiating for procurement.[49] Under this act, a contractor may be required to submit his costs and pricing materials to the contracting officer prior to the award.

SOCIAL POLICY

Federal government procurement has been used to foster certain social and economic policies established by Congress. It has been used to encourage small business and to shift contracts to high-unemployment or labor-surplus areas. In addition, federal contracts have been used to encourage compliance with certain federal labor standards, such as payment of minimum hourly wages, conformance with standards for safe working conditions, maximum hourly limits of work per day, payment of overtime, and nondiscrimination in employment. Government contracts usually contain provisions mandated under federal legislation and regulations which require the contractor to adhere to the requirements of these federal laws.

CHANGES

Design professionals who work in construction are well aware of the changes which occur in design and specifications for a project during construction. Frequently, as discussed in Chapter 8, construction contracts provide for changes and outline a formal procedure for handling them during the construction phase. Government contracts also normally contain change provisions.

Under the FARs, the contracting officer may make changes so long as they are in writing and within the general scope of the contract. However, for the procurement of products, the contracting officer's authority is limited to making changes in plans and specifications for products specifically manufactured for the government, in the method of shipping or packing, or in the place of delivery.[50] For construction contracts, the contracting officer may make changes within the general scope of the contract, probably including changes in the plans and specifications, the method of working, the assistance to be offered by the government, and acceleration of the work.[51] Changes which are not within the scope of the contract are referred to as "cardinal changes" and may entitle the contractor to damages for breach of contract.

Over the years, the courts and government agencies have developed the doctrines of "express change" and "constructive change." An express change is one in which the contracting officer states in writing that a change is being made in the contract. A constructive change occurs when the contractor has been ordered or forced by the contracting officer to do something which is effectively a change in the contract, but not pursuant to a written order. The courts treat constructive changes as express changes. In one case, a federal employee told a contractor to redo certain welds, although they had already been passed by other government inspectors. The contractor did the work, protesting that it was extra work for which he should be compensated. The court of claims upheld the contractor's suit even though no change order had been made in writing or had come from the contracting officer.[52]

Under the typical government contract, the change clause allows the contractor an "equitable adjustment" if a change occurs under the contract. However, most clauses provide that the contractor must submit a claim for equitable adjustment within a limited number of days after he has started to incur the costs under the adjustment.

Most government construction contracts contain a provision that allows an equitable adjustment for the contractor if differing conditions are found at the job site. Usually, such differing site conditions arise during subsurface construction work. Such clauses exist for two reasons. First, the government, as owner, assumes the responsibility arising from unanticipated site conditions. Second, by eliminating from the bidding process the risk of finding unanticipated site conditions, the government encourages tighter bids from contractors.

Under the typical differing site condition clause, an equitable adjustment is allowed to the contractor only if the subsurface or other conditions are materially different from those described in the construction contract documents or if there is an unusual condition at the site which is not ordinarily encountered in that type of construction.[53]

Federal government fixed-price construction contracts also contain a provision stating that if the government is the sole or substantial cause of a delay in the performance of any part of the work for an unreasonable period of time, the contractor is entitled to an adjustment. However, this is not "equitable adjustment"; hence, the contractor may not be allowed any additional profit.[54]

TERMINATION

The government may terminate a contract either for its own convenience or for default. The federal government can terminate any contract for its convenience, ordinarily when the contracting officer determines that termination is in the best interest of the government. The right of the government to terminate a contract for its convenience is considered so fundamental that even when the relevant clause is omitted from the contract, it will be read in.[55]

The decision to terminate a contract for convenience rests solely with the contracting officer or his agency through him. There are no standards governing when a government agency may or may not so act.[56] The government may also terminate a contract for its convenience when it discovers that the specifications it has given the contractor are deficient.[57] The government's right to terminate a contract for its convenience is not unlimited. Some change in the circumstances of the bargain or in "the expectations of the parties is required."[58]

Most of the disputes which arise in termination for convenience cases involve the equitable adjustment awarded or to be awarded to the contractor. Under federal regulations, the contractor is entitled only to costs, a reasonable profit for his work, and settlement expenses.[59]

If the contractor breaches the contract, the government may terminate under the termination for default clause included in all federal contracts. When this happens, the government may purchase elsewhere the supplies or services covered by the contract. Of course, the government must follow appropriate procurement procedures in doing so. When the government purchases substitute goods or services, the contractor becomes liable for any excess costs incurred by the government. However, if the contractor's failure to perform was due to a cause beyond his reasonable control, he may not be liable for damages, since government contracts typically contain a *force majeure* clause. However, this clauses makes it clear that the cause of the delay must be unforeseen. Usually *force majeure* clauses excuse nonperformance for reasons such as acts of God, acts of a public enemy, epidemics, quarantine, strikes, and unusually severe weather.

DISPUTES

Disputes between a contractor and a government agency over a contract are generally controlled by the Contract Disputes Act of 1978.[60] This act applies to express and implied contracts between an executive agency and another party for the purchase of property, services, construction, or the sale of personal property. It does not apply to the purchase of real property. In addition, the act does not cover certain contracts of the Tennessee Valley Authority (TVA), including those related to the sale of electric power or pertaining to the TVA's operation of the electric power system. Any other contracts of the TVA are covered by the Contract Disputes Act only if they contain a clause stating that contract disputes will be handled by the agency's administrative process. Under certain circumstances, the act also does not apply to contracts with foreign governments or international organizations.

The Contract Disputes Act provides that all claims made by a contractor against the government pertaining to a contract must be in writing and must be submitted to the contracting officer for decision. Claims by the federal government against a contractor pertaining to a contract are also subject to the contracting officer's decision. The contracting officer must issue his decision in writing and send a copy of it to the contractor. Pursuant to the Contract Disputes Act, the decision must state the reasons for the contracting officer's conclusions and must advise the contractor of his right of appeal.

The contracting officer's decision is final and may only be appealed pursuant to the provisions of the Contract Disputes Act. Further, government contracts may contain a clause stating that the contractor shall continue to perform pending resolution of any appeal of the contracting officer's decision.

For claims of $50,000 or less, the contracting officer must make his decision within sixty days. For claims in excess of $50,000, he must also make his decision within sixty days or advise the contractor within this period of when the decision will be issued. If the contracting officer is dilatory in making his decision, the contractor may petition the relevant agency's board of contract appeals (BCA) for an order directing him to issue his decision within a specific time period. Surprisingly, the failure of the contracting officer to make his decision within the prescribed time period does not result in a decision in favor of the contractor. To the contrary, the contracting officer's failure to act is deemed, pursuant to the Contract Disputes Act, as a denial of the contractor's claim.

Within ninety days after the contractor has received the contracting officer's decision, the contractor may appeal to the appropriate agency BCA or, in lieu thereof, commence an action in the U.S. Claims Court. Each executive agency is permitted under the Contract Disputes Act to establish a BCA if the workload requires it. Usually board members must have five years of experience in public contract law and are appointed as hearing examiners. If the executive agency's appeal workload does not require it to have its own BCA, it may arrange to have the BCA of another agency hear the appeal.

Hearings before an agency BCA are similar to a civil trial. Members of the board are empowered to subpoena witnesses to testify and may authorize depositions or other forms of discovery.

The decision of the agency BCA is final unless the contractor appeals to the U.S. Court of Appeals for the Federal Circuit, at Washington, D.C., either within 120 days following receipt of a copy of the decision or if the agency head determines that the appeal should be taken. However, appeals by the agency may be made only with the prior approval of the U.S. Attorney General. If the agency plans to appeal the decision of its BCA, it must do so within 120 days of receipt of the board's decision.

Each agency board must establish a procedure for efficiently handling disputes involving $50,000 or less. In addition, it must establish procedures for expeditiously handling claims of $10,000 or less.

A contractor's right to appeal is not limited to an appeal of a contracting officer's decision to an agency BCA. As stated before, the contractor may elect to appeal such a decision to the U.S. Claims Court. If he so chooses, he must do so within twelve months after the date of receipt of the contracting officer's decision. Appeals from decisions of contracting officers of the TVA are made to the

U.S. District Court. Under the Contract Disputes Act, findings of fact made by the contracting officer are not necessarily binding upon the U.S. Claims Court or the U.S. District Court. However, if the contractor decides to appeal a decision of an agency BCA, the board's findings of fact are binding upon the contractor and the agency.

Either the contractor or the agency may appeal a final decision of the Court of Claims to the U.S. Court of Appeals for the Federal Circuit. The agency, however, may appeal a decision only with the approval of the U.S. Attorney General.

Government contractors must be aware of the fraudulent claims provision of the Contract Disputes Act. If a contractor files a claim which he is unable to support and his failure amounts to a misrepresentation of fact or fraud, he may be liable to the U.S. government for an amount which equals the unsupported part of his claim plus the costs incurred by the government in reviewing this part of the claim.

Federal government contracts and agency procedures generally provide a method for contractors and the agencies to use in resolving disputes informally by mutual agreement. Either a contractor or an agency may request a conference to consider settlement of a claim. The conference is usually held within thirty days after the request for it or at a later agreed-upon date. The agency head is represented by someone other than the contracting officer, who has not participated significantly in the consideration of the claim.

STATE CONTRACTS

Government contract law of the states and their subdivisions varies from one state to another. However, some threads run through all state and federal procurement. As with federal contracting, state procurement is generally based upon the concept of appropriations by state legislatures, and the public advertising method is favored. However, contracts for professional services and other matters are frequently negotiated.

In many states, each state agency and each subdivision does its own purchasing. Other states have established central purchasing agencies to handle specific types of government purchasing or as much of it as possible. For example, Illinois has established a Capital Development Board which handles contracts for the design and construction of buildings which receive state funding, such as government office buildings, university and college buildings, and local schools. In addition, some states have established specific courts which handle contract disputes between the state and private parties. As an example, Illinois has established an Illinois Court of Claims.

In 1970, the Section of Public Contract Law of the American Bar Association (ABA) began drafting a Model Procurement Code to be used by state and local governments. In 1974, the ABA established the Coordinating Committee on a Model Procurement Code for state and local governments which promulgated a final draft of the code in 1979.[61]

The code assumes that the government body adopting it will establish an independent procurement office to handle all state purchasing. It generally adopts the use of formal advertising and competitive sealed bidding. Further, it permits competitive sealed proposals under certain circumstances. In addition, contracting for architectural and engineering services is done by the consideration of proposals and qualifications submitted by design professionals.

The Model Procurement Code also contains specific requirements for construction contracts, including the right of the agency to order changes in the work, so long as it falls within a scope of the contract, or suspend the work. The code also contains a "differing site conditions" clause.

Under the Model Procurement Code, any actual or prospective bidder, offeror, or contractor may file a protest with the head of the appropriate purchasing agency or file a suit in court.

NOTES

1. 64 Am.Jur.2d *Public Works and Contracts* § 5 (1972), 847–848.
2. W. Noel Keyes, *Government Contracts in a Nutshell* (St. Paul, Minn.: West, 1979), 7.
3. 41 U.S.C.A. §§ 10a–10d (1965).
4. 15 U.S.C.A. §§ 631 (1976 and Supp. 1985).
5. 40 U.S.C.A. §§ 276a (1969).
6. *G. L. Christian & Associates v. United States*, 312 F.2d 418 (Ct. Cl. 1963), *cert. denied*, 375 U.S. 954 (1963), *opinion on reh.*, 320 F.2d 345 (1963).
7. *Federal Crop Insurance Corp. v. Merrill*, 332 U.S. 380 (1947), but see *Portmann v. United States*, 674 F.2d 1155 (7th Cir. 1982).

8. *Gordon Woodroffe Corp. v. United States,* 104 F. Supp. 984 (Ct. Cl. 1952), *cert. denied,* 344 U.S. 908 (1952).
9. *United States v. Zenith Godley Co.,* 180 F.Supp. 611 (S.D.N.Y. 1960, *aff'd.,* 295 F.2d 634 (2d Cir. 1961).
10. *Williams v. United States,* 131 Ct. Cl. 435 (1955).
11. *Cooke v. United States,* 91 U.S. 389, 398 (1875).
12. *Horowitz v. United States,* 267 U.S. 458 (1925) and *Perry v. United States,* 294 U.S. 330 (1935).
13. 41 U.S.C.A. §§ 605 (Supp. 1984).
14. U.S. Const., art. I, § 9, Cl. 7.
15. 31 U.S.C.A. § 1341 (1983).
16. 31 U.S.C.A. §1301 (1983).
17. 21 Comp. Gen. 1159 (1941).
18. 31 U.S.C.A. §1501 (1983).
19. Keyes, *Government Contracts in a Nutshell,* 92.
20. FAR 9.103.
21. 51 Comp. Gen. 168 (1971).
22. Comp. Gen. Dec. B-179793 (1974).
23. 39 Comp. Gen. 468 (1959).
24. *Leslie Miller, Inc. v. Arkansas,* 352 U.S. 187 (1956).
25. See *Scanwell Laboratories, Inc. v. Shaffer,* 424 F.2d 859 (D.C. Cir. 1970), and *M. Steinthal & Co. v. Seamans,* 455 F.2d 1289 (D.C. Cir. 1971).
26. *Central Metal Products, Inc.,* 54 Comp. Gen. 66 (1974), and *Rilcar,* Comp. Gen. Dec. B-180361 (1974).
27. Keyes, *Government Contracts in a Nutshell,* 104.
28. Glenn E. Monroe, *Government Contract Law Manual: A Summary and Comparison of Government Procurement at the State, Federal and International Level,* § 2.14 (Charlottesville, Va.: Michie, 1979), 17.
29. FAR 907.4(b).
30. 4 CFR § 21.1 (1985) and *Scanwell Laboratories, Inc. v. Shaffer,* 424 F.2d 859 (D.C. Cir. 1970).
31. Ralph C. Nash, Jr., and John Cibinic, Jr., *Federal Procurement Law,* 3d ed., Vol. 1 (Washington, D.C.: George Washington University 1977), 803. See also Comp. Gen. B-1789474, September 11, 1973.
32. FAR § 14.407-8.
33. 4 CFR § 21.1 (1985).
34. *Scanwell Laboratories, Inc. v. Shaffer,* 4211 F.2d 859 (D.C. Cir. 1970).
35. *M. Steinthal & Co. v. Seamans,* 455 F.2d 1289 (D.C. Cir. 1971).
36. 10 U.S.C.A. § 2305 (Supp. 1985).
37. 45 Comp. Gen. 462, 466 (1966).
38. FAR 4.304-1.
39. *Prestex, Inc. v. United States,* 320 F.2d 367 (Ct. Cl. 1963).
40. FAR 14.1405.
41. *Refining Associates, Inc. v. United States,* 109 F. Supp. 259 (Ct. Cl. 1953). See also 30 Op. Att'y Gen. 56 (1913) and 27 Comp. Gen. 436 (1948).
42. FAR 14.406.
43. FAR 14.406-2.
44. 36 Comp. Gen. 366 (1956).
45. See 10 U.S.C.A. §§ 2304(A) (Supp. 1985).
46. 40 U.S.C.A. §§ 541–544 (Supp. 1984).
47. 10 U.S.C.A. § 2310 (Supp. 1985).

48. 51 Comp. Gen. 431 (1972).
49. 10 U.S.C.A. § 2306 (1983 and Supp. 1985).
50. FAR 43.205 & 52.243-1.
51. FAR 43.205 & 52.243-1.
52. *Southwest Welding & Mfg. Co. v. United States*, 413 F.2d 1167 (Ct. Cl. 1969).
53. FAR 52.236-2.
54. FAR 52.212-15.
55. *G. L. Christian and Associates v. United States*, 312 F.2d 418 (Ct. Cl. 1963), *rehearing denied*, 320 F.2d 345 Ct. Cl. (1963), *cert. denied*, 375 U.S. 954 (1963).
56. *Commercial Cable Company v. United States*, 170 Ct. Cl. 813 Ct. Cl. (1965).
57. *Nolan Brothers, Inc. v. United States*, 405 F.2d Ct. 1250 (Ct. Cl. 1969).
58. *Torncello v. United States*, 681 F.2d 756 (Ct. Cl. 1982).
59. FAR 52.249-1.
60. 41 U.S.C.A. §§ 601–613 (Supp. 1984).
61. *The Model Procurement Code for State and Local Governments* (Chicago: American Bar Association, 1979).

Part IV
OTHER AREAS OF THE LAW

11
Real Property Law

The architect or engineer working in construction occasionally becomes involved in questions pertaining to real property law. For instance, construction contracts done by a design professional for the owner may contain descriptions of the property upon which a project is to be built. Questions may arise about easements, surveys, and ownership of land. The design professional may work with the owner's attorney to resolve questions involving building codes and zoning ordinances. In addition, the design professional himself may want to enforce a mechanic's lien against the real property if he has not been paid for his services.

The basis of American real property law is the English common law. Much of this law is made by court decisions. In addition, many states have adopted statutes covering various aspects of real property including the conveyance of interest in such property, zoning, condominiums, and other matters. Accordingly, certain aspects of real property law vary among the states. However, there are common threads running through the law of all the states, which we will touch upon in this chapter.

LAND

Land includes the ground or soil and everything attached to it, beneath it, and above it. Thus, land includes trees and shrubs, as well as the buildings on it. Under American law, land includes that portion of the tract which contains the surface and extends to the center of the earth in the form of an inverted pyramid. Thus, it includes the minerals beneath the surface.

In recent years, design professionals have become involved in the construction of large buildings which are actually built upon the air rights covering a portion of the earth. As an example, a major building in Chicago was constructed over the tracks of a railroad. The railroad conveyed its air rights to the developer of the building and sold him certain small lots to be used for the caissons which would hold the building.[1]

Personal property is property other than real property, such as furniture, cattle, money, automobiles, and machinery. A fixture is personal property which has become so attached to the land or a building on the land that it has become part of the real property.

The determination of whether personal property has become a fixture is important. First, if it is a fixture, it passes to the buyer upon the sale of the land. Second, liens against real property, such as mortgages and mechanics' liens, may not apply to personal property on the land which has not become a fixture.

Whether personal property becomes a fixture is determined by the intent of the party who brought it to the land. Generally, this is the objective intent of the annexer. The article need not be attached to the land. For example, a prefabricated house built on a cement foundation may be a fixture. When a fence is built around a lot, it becomes annexed to the land. Further, annexing personal property to an existing fixture on the land may make that property also a fixture.

As an example, stoves and refrigerators installed by the owner in apartment buildings to be used by tenants are often considered by the courts to be fixtures. In contrast, stoves and refrigerators used in a private house are not necessarily considered fixtures because the owner who bought them ordinarily, intends to take them when he moves.[2]

Trade fixtures have been treated differently by the courts. Fixtures installed by a tenant for his trade or business do not necessarily become fixtures under real property law. The courts traditionally treat them as personal property in order to encourage tenants to rent property and equip it for their business.

FREEHOLDS

U.S. real property law stems from the Norman conquest of England in 1066. Following the conquest, William the Conqueror instituted a new system of land tenure in England when he divided the land of the conquered lords among those who had served him in battle. By approximately 1300, during the reign of Edward I, the distinctions between free and unfree tenures in land had become part of common law.

There were two such distinctions. First, a freehold required that the services to be performed by the tenant for the lord were definite and certain. Second, the services had to be those expected of a free man. Thus, ownership of land which depended upon the tenant's performing military service or certain agricultural work for the lord were considered to have free tenure.

In medieval England, land was basically divided between those tenants who had fee tenure (or freeholds) and the lord. The persons who worked for a lord and may have occupied land were serfs and did not have free tenure. Rather, they worked the land according to the supervision of the lord. Eventually, a system of land tenure developed which gave servile tenants certain rights to convey their occupancy of the land. However, not until 1926, with the passage of the Law of Property Act by Parliament, was this ancient distinction eliminated from the English law.

During the Middle Ages, the concept of a fee simple estate developed in the real property law of England. A fee simple is maximum legal ownership of real property. It is land which the owner may hold forever and pass to his heirs. Prior to the concept of the fee simple estate, the lord could only grant an interest in land for the life of the donee; upon the donee's death, it reverted to the lord. Eventually, this limitation was removed from the common law. Even by the mid 1200s, the tenant no longer required the consent of the lord to transfer ownership of the land held in fee tenure.[3]

Today, most states have statutes governing the conveyance of real property. These statutes generally hold that when a seller conveys real property, he transfers his entire interest in it unless some words in the conveyance document indicate that he is conveying or selling a lesser estate. For example, someone may only wish to convey a life estate, which is an interest in land good only for the life of a specific person. Thus, a farmer may convey an estate to a relative such as his wife or a child, for the life of that person, with the estate reverting either to him or to another person upon the relative's death. Today, a typical example of a non-feehold estate in American real estate transactions is the lease. Under the lease, the lessee may obtain an interest in a parcel of real property for a specific number of years.

CONVEYANCING

Initially in common law, interests in feehold estates were tranferred orally in a ceremony called "feeoffment." However, certain interests in a feehold estate, such as easements, could be transferred only by a deed under seal. With the adoption of the statute of frauds, the transfer of all interest in the land was required to be in writing and signed by the person conveying the interest, although certain short-term leases did not have to be in writing.[4]

Today, the transfer of interests in land is governed by state statute. There are differences among many state statutes, but some general rules have been adopted. First, transfer of an interest in land is made by a document called a "deed." There are three basic deeds used in the United States: quit-claim deeds, warranty deeds, and deeds of bargain and sale. With a quit-claim deed, the grantor merely conveys his interest in the property. Using such a deed, the grantor does not warrant that he has any title to the land.

With a warranty deed, the grantor states that he is transferring good title to the land without any lien unless the deed states otherwise. In addition, in a warranty deed, the grantor guarantees that the grantee shall not be disturbed in his occupancy of the land. This is sometimes referred to as the "covenant of quiet enjoyment."

The deed of bargain and sale conveys the land as opposed to the grantor's interest in the land, as with a quit-claim deed. Like a quite-claim deed, a deed of bargain and sale does not contain any warranties.

Basically, a valid deed requires that the grantor be competent, that the deed describe the grantee and the consideration, that it contain the statutory words conveying the property, that it describe the land adequately, that it contain the signature of the grantor and his or her spouse (if necessary), and that it be delivered to the grantee. In describing the consideration, the deed need not state the actual price paid by the grantee. Usually, it merely states that the grantee has paid $1 or $10 to the grantor and other good and valuable consideration. In a few states, the deed must contain a seal. In many states, it must be witnessed.

Some states require that a deed be acknowledged. An acknowl-edgment is merely a executed statement usually made before a notary public by the grantor stating that the deed is a voluntary act.

Every deed must contain a legal description of the land covered by the deed. In addition, other instruments pertaining to real prop-erty, such as mortgages and leases, also contain legal descriptions. The legal description of the property states the boundaries of the land covered by the deed. A street address is insufficient. Usually, legal descriptions are prepared by a surveyor.

Originally, the American colonies followed the metes and bounds methods of describing real property. This method was also adopted by the early states. A mete is a measure of length. A bound is a boundary. With such a description, the surveyor starts at a begin-ning point and describes the boundaries of the land it meets until he returns to the starting point. Stones, fences, rivers, lakes, or roads may mark corners of the tract.

In 1796, Congress established a new land measurement system for the United States, primarily because of the need to survey the Northwest Territory. Using the metes and bounds system to de-scribe land in the wilderness would not have been suitable. Hence, Congress adopted the government survey, which provided for a rectangular system of land measurement.

The government survey required a significant landmark such as a river to be used as a starting point. From that point, a line was run north which was called the "prime" or "principal meridian." Then an east-to-west line was run which intersects the principal meridian and was called the "base line."

The surveyor then laid out additional lines parallel to the principal meridian and the base line. These lines were twenty-four miles apart. Because of the curvature of the earth, the north and south lines converge toward the North Pole. In order to keep the squares perfect, the guide meridians parallel to the principal meridian run for only twenty-four miles until they reached a correction line, which runs from east to west. At the correction line, the survey started measuring again until he reached the next correction line twenty-four miles away.

Each twenty-four-mile square was divided into tracts six miles on a side. These are called "townships." Townships, in turn, were divided into thirty-six "sections," each one mile square and containing 640 acres.

The government survey was used to survey lands in Alabama, Florida, Mississippi, and all states north of the Ohio and west of the Mississippi rivers. However, Texas was not included in the government survey.

Using the government survey, lawyers and surveyors can describe the location of a parcel of land starting with the principal meridian. In legal descriptions, townships are north and south of the principal base line and ranges are east and west of the principal meridian. Thus, a legal description may state that the property is located in a township which is the second township north of the base line and within the third range west of the principal meridian.

Ordinarily, if the deed states that the boundary of the land runs "by" or "along" a street or road, the grantee takes title to the center of the street or road. If the boundary is the center of a nonnavigable stream, it varies with the stream as the stream changes.

The land under nonnavigable streams belong to the adjoining landowners, whereas land under navigable streams belongs to the state. If a landowner owns property up to the boundary of a stream, lake, or ocean, he does not own any of the land under the water. However, this boundary may be changed due to either accretion (the addition of soil due to the water's action) or reliction (the increase in land area due to receding of the water). If a river undergoes a sudden change, referred to as an "avulsion," title to any lands involved is not altered.

Often tracts of land are subdivided into lots for building. This requires a surveyor to prepare a plat. The plat lays out the boundaries of the lots and gives each lot a number. The plat then is recorded with the appropriate county recorder or registrar of deeds. Thus, deeds and other instruments pertaining to land can refer to the appropriate lot number for ease of conveyancing.

Because buildings ordinarily are fixtures or part of the land, a deed or other instrument concerning an interest in land need not state that any buildings are conveyed. The buildings automatically pass to the grantee with the land.

If a deed or other instrument contains an incorrect description, a new deed can be prepared to resolve the problem or the grantee can file an action in court to rewrite the deed.

RECORDING

All states require that deeds and most other instruments pertaining to the title of land be recorded. A deed which is not recorded pursuant to the statue may be void for persons who may later purchase the land or take out a mortgage on it without knowledge of the unrecorded deed. Further, once a deed or other instrument is properly recorded, all persons are charged with knowledge of it.

In most states, a county official handles the recording of deeds and instruments and the maintenance of the records. This person is often referred to as the "recorder of deeds" or the "registrar of deeds."

When a person desires to record an instrument pertaining to real property, he merely gives it to the recorder. The recorder then copies the document, indexes it, and returns it to the person who left it for recording.

Usually, a person or company that purchases a piece of real property or takes out a mortgage on it will search the title to the land to be sure that the seller or mortgagor has good title. Frequently, an abstractor of title may be hired to perform this service. Alternatively, one of the parties may arrange to obtain a title insurance policy guaranteeing the legality of the title, which requires the title insurer to make a similar search.

Searches usually start with the index of the names of the grantors and grantees. They usually begin with the first conveyance from the United States to the first landowner. Then the title searcher looks through the grantor index, following the date of original conveyance to determine if and when the original owner conveyed any interest in the land. The searcher then traces all the recorded transactions involving the plot until he reaches the document conveying title to the seller or mortgagee. Finally, the searcher determines whether the seller or grantor may have conveyed any interest in the land following his purchase of it.

Under the law, every purchaser or mortgagee is under a duty to inspect the real property in order to determine whether any parties other than the seller or mortgagor may be in possession of it. Possession of the property by a third party constitutes constructive notice that this party may have an interest in the land. Thus, if I sell my land and house to you but you fail to record the deed, even though you have moved into the house, your right to the property is paramount to a subsequent purchaser, even though you did not record your deed.

SALES CONTRACTS

Ordinarily, the purchase of any land involves a contract for its sale. Purchasers and their attorneys do not merely rely upon the exchange of the deed for cash. Rather, the purchaser and seller usually sign a contract for the sale of the land, so that the purchaser may determine whether there are any defects in the seller's title and arrange for financing.

The contract states the type of title the seller must deliver and what should be done to remove any defects in it. Because this contract contains mutual promises, the seller cannot sell the property to a third person after the contract is executed, and the buyer must go through with the purchase if the conditions of the contract are met. Under the statute of fraud, contracts for the sale of land must be in writing.

The contract must contain the names of the seller and buyer, an adequate description of the land, the price, and the signature of both parties. However, even if one party does not sign the contract, he may still enforce it against the party who did sign.[5] Under the law of many states, the landowner's spouse also has certain rights in the property, such as dower or curtsey, which cannot be extinguished. Thus, the spouse's signature is often required on a sales contract.

The description of the land need not be as formal as that used in the deed. However, it must describe the land adequately. Ordinarily, the description of a street address with the city and state is sufficient. All fixtures to the land, such as buildings upon it, are also covered by the sales contract. If the contract does not state the type of deed which will be given by the seller, most states hold that the seller is only required to tender a quit-claim deed.

Most real estate contracts require the seller to convey marketable title to the real estate, which means that the title must be good and the property must be free from liens. In addition, a title is not marketable if it is subject to easements unless the buyer has agreed to take the property subject to such easements. Further, a piece of property whose title is subject to certain restrictions contained in deeds or subdivision plats is also not marketable. Also, substantial violations of zoning or building ordinances by the seller may make the title unmarketable. Finally, the title is not marketable if there are certain leases covering the land, unless the contract provides that the purchaser will take title subject to those leases.

Because of the difficulties involved in searching titles to land back many years, several states have passed marketable title laws which hold that the title searcher need only go back for a specific period. In Illinois, this period is forty years. Thus, if the title searcher can show that the title to the land has passed from one person to another for forty years, that the seller of the land holds title currently, and there are no encumbrances upon the land, the title is marketable. In addition, people who claim an interest in the land that is more than forty years sold must file an affidavit with the recorder of deeds within a certain period; otherwise their claim will be barred.

Although the seller must deliver good title, he does not have to produce any evidence that his title is good. Under the law, and generally in many real estate contracts, the burden is upon the buyer to investigate the title.

There is a conflict between the states as to whether the buyer or seller bears the risk of loss to any building on the land covered by a sales contract before the closing transaction occurs. Traditionally, the risk of loss fell upon the buyer. A number of states, however, including California, Illinois, Michigan, and New York, place the burden upon the seller. Moreover, some states hold that if the seller does not have a good marketable title when the loss occurred, he must bear the risk of loss.

Evidence of title may be furnished by one of several methods, depending upon local custom and practice. Title abstracts accompanied by a lawyer's opinion and title insurance are probably the two most prevalent methods used.

An abstract contains the history of the title. It describes the land and covers the transactions involving it. An abstractor does not guarantee the title, but in preparing the abstract, he agrees to exercise due care. He also does not give an opinion on the status of the title. That is done by a lawyer.

In a few areas, a lawyer may merely examine the public records pertaining to the title and issue a certificate stating whether it is good or has any defects.

Relying upon abstracts or certificates of title does not guarantee that there are no defects in the title. First, these documents do not guarantee against forgery. Second, they do not guarantee that a grantor or mortgagee/mortgagor in the chain of title was competent. Third, they do not guarantee the marital status of various individuals in the chain of title. Fourth, they do not guarantee that all recorded documents were examined. For example, the recorder of deeds may have misrecorded a document pertaining to the title to a particular piece of land, which may not be uncovered by the title searcher investigating the chain of title.

Title insurance is available to cover the title. Title insurance policies also usually insure against those things that cannot be covered by an abstract or title certificate, such as forgery. These policies are paid for with one premium and continue in force until the property is sold.

A few areas in the United States use the Torrens' system. Under this system, title to the property is registered in the Torrens' office. With the initial filing, an abstract of title is filed and the Torrens' office investigates the history of the title. An opportunity exists for persons to object to registration of the title to a particular person. Eventually, when the Torrens' office is satisfied that the title is good and is with the person making the application, the registrar of title issues a certificate of title.

All subsequent transactions concerning the land after it is registered must also be registered with the Torrens' office. When the land is sold, the grantee takes his deed to the registrar's office, which again investigates to determine whether it is good. If so, the Torrens' office issues a new certificate of registration.

The proponents of the Torrens' system contend that its use makes transfer of land easier after property is registered because there is no need to go back and investigate the chain of title prior to registration of the land.

MORTGAGES

Much of the land in this country is subject to a mortgage, which is often used by the purchaser of the land to finance his payment. Under the common law of the Middle Ages, mortgages were simply deeds transferring ownership of land from the *borrower* or *mortgagor* to the *lender* or *mortgagee,* but allowing the mortgagor to reacquire ownership under certain conditions, such as payment of the debt. Subsequently, to bar unjust taking of land from debtors in such situations, equity courts devised the equitable right of redemption, which would allow a mortgagor to reacquire his land, if certain conditions were met, in the event that it had been taken from him because he had not paid the debt. Due to the right of redemption, mortgagees were not sure, when they did finally take ownership and/or possession of the land from the mortgagor upon default and subsequent payment of the debt, that the mortgagee could not come back at some future date and redeem it. Accordingly, mortgagees developed the foreclosure suit, which allowed them to go into court and obtain an order stating that if the mortgagor did not pay the debt within a certain period of time, the mortgagor's equitable right of redemption would be barred. Today, most states provide for a right of redemption and a formal method of foreclosing on mortgages, which often involves public sale of the property upon foreclosure.

Today, mortgages are usually obtained after the mortgagor has filed an application with the mortgagee. After review of the application and other facts, if the mortgagee decides to make the loan, he issues a mortgage commitment, which becomes a contract of the mortgagee to make the mortgage loan to the mortgagor. Next, the mortgagor executes a promissory note and a mortgage. The mortgage is security for the note. The purpose of the note is to make the mortgagor personally liable for payment of the debt.

The mortgage must describe the land covered by the mortgage and the debt. Further, it must be executed by the mortgagor and, if necessary, his spouse.

In order for the mortgage to act as a lien which may bar subsequent purchasers or subsequent lenders to the mortgagor, the mortgage must be recorded.

MECHANICS' LIENS

All states provide a statutory framework for mechanics' liens. The purpose of a mechanics' lien is to give contractors, subcontractors, and material men who furnish labor or materials for a construction project the right to have a lien against the land and its improvements upon which they have worked in order to secure payment of sums they are owed. In many states, workers themselves and employees of contractors and subcontractors may also have a right to a mechanics' lien. Further, in many states, design professionals who design the project or render other services in connection with the construction may have a mechanics' lien.

Mechanics' lien laws vary among the states, but they do have some broad common features. First, they generally require strict compliance with the relevant statutory provisions. In order for a lien to be valid, the statutory notice and filing provisions must be followed. Deadlines for serving notices and filing liens must also be met. Further, some state statutes require that notice be given by contractors and others who may obtain mechanics' liens at the time of employment.

Usually, only work and materials which become part of the building or improvement may be subject to the lien; trade fixtures are exempt. In addition, some states provide that material which is delivered to the work site, but not yet incorporated into the structure, may become the basis for a lien.

In some states, the lien claimant must prove that he was hired by either the landowner or the landowner's agent to furnish the labor or materials. In other states, the lien claimant need only prove that the owner knew that he was doing the work and consented to it, even though the claimant may have been working for another party.

Most states require the claimant to show that he substantially performed the work covered by the lien. For example, if the construction contract states that the contractor must procure an architect's certificate prior to payment, the contractor claiming the mechanics' lien must have obtained such a certificate in order for the lien to be valid.

The advantage of a mechanics' lien is that under certain circumstances it may have priority over the claims of mortgagees. Obviously, the effect of the mechanics' lien upon mortgagees depends upon the laws of various states.

The rule governing when the lien begins or attaches to the land varies among the states. In a few states, the lien attaches at the time the contractor or vendor begins his work. In other states, all mechanics' liens start at the beginning of the project, not just the beginning of the claimant's work. In some states, the mechanics' lien is effective from the date of the contract. In other states, it attaches when notice of it is filed in the appropriate public office.

In all states, there are specific procedures to be followed by a mechanics' lien claimant. First, most states require that the claimant file a notice of the lien with the appropriate public office, usually the recorder of deeds, shortly after completion of his work. In addition, in some states, a subcontractor must serve notice of the lien upon the owner and mortgagees within a certain period after he has completed his work. The subcontractor must then wait for another period before he can file his lien of record.

In order to enforce the lien, the claimant must commence a lawsuit to foreclose, which may result in the sale of the property for satisfaction of the lien. Generally, mechanics' lien foreclosure actions must be filed within a specific period of time after the lien claim is filed. This period varies among the states but is usually one or two years.

Some construction contracts contain provisions by which the contractor or subcontractor waives any mechanics' lien rights prior to doing the work. In other construction jobs, partial waivers of liens are given by contractors and subcontractors upon payment for the work covered by the lien. When all the work is completed, the contractor and subcontractors will deliver a final lien waiver.

In many states, design professionals have right to a mechanics' lien; however, some states have limited those rights. For example, in a few states, architects and engineers have no lien rights unless construction has actually started. In other states, architects' and engineers' lien rights may be limited to the actual on-site work they have performed.

CONSTRUCTION LOANS

Financing the construction of a large project involves relatively sophisticated areas of real property law. Ordinarily, because of the large sums of money involved, the owner must obtain financing from a lender, usually a bank, insurance company, or other financial institution.

Some financial institutions do not wish to engage in construction lending, although they may be willing to take a mortgage on the project when construction is completed. Other institutions may prefer to engage in construction lending and not long-term financing. Sometimes a lender will offer a long-term mortgage upon the property with the intention of selling the mortgage to another institution after completion of construction. Whether the lender or the owner arranges for the financing of the project, it is necessary for one party to find a lender who is willing to take the long-term mortgage. When such a lender is found, he usually issues a take-out commitment obligating himself to lend the money upon completion of the project.

Usually, a construction mortgage or loan involves the disbursement of funds to the owner or contractor over a long period of time during construction. Frequently, construction loan documents contain provisions stating that before funds are disbursed, the developer must obtain upon a certificate from the architect showing that the work covered by the request has been done. The lender may also want partial lien waivers and may even retain his own architect/engineer to review the progress of construction.

For large projects, the lender usually will insist that the contractor provide performance and payment bonds. Performance bonds ensure that the building will be completed, and payment bonds ensure that the contractors/subcontractors and material men will be paid. Bonds will be discussed further in Chapter 12.

SUBDIVISIONS

Frequently, real estate developers will buy large tracts of land and subdivide them for residential purposes. The plan involves locating streets, lots, utilities, parks, and even schools. A surveyor will make a plat of the subdivision, which is signed and acknowledged by the owner. The plat is filed with the recorder of deeds and serves as the owner's dedication of the public places on the plat, such as the streets and parks. Acceptance of the public lands does not occur until the municipality has either accepted the dedication by ordinance, or paves the streets, or makes other use of the public land.

Today many communities control land and subdivision. Often a planning commission of the municipality is involved.

The developer often installs various utilities. Once installed, he has no right to remove them. Utilities become dedicated for the use of the lot owners.

In preparing subdivisions, the developer, along with his attorney and engineer, should check local zoning and building ordinances to determine lot size requirements and other restrictions. In addition, the ordinances may determine what types of buildings may be built upon the lots.

Engineers frequently check drainage on the property, as well as sewage conditions. They may also check for existing power lines, streets, and other improvements. Moreover, the developer may submit a proposed subdivision for informal review by the appropriate planning commission in order to obtain its informal suggestions.

In recent years, planned unit developments have become popular. These developments consist of various kinds of housing such as apartments, homes, and townhouses. Frequently, cluster housing design is used. A homeowners' association may be provided for as part of the development.

Plats are also used in planned unit developments similar to subdivisions. The plats usually create common areas, frequently in the form of open space, and provide for easements for utilities.

LAND USE CONTROLS

Various forms of private and public land use controls have existed for years. Building restrictions have been accomplished through both private means and public means such as municipal ordinances.

In the mid-nineteenth century, the courts accepted the creation of subdivisions by developers which contained restrictions on all lots. For example, a developer may have provided that only single-family dwellings could be constructed on the lots.

In the twentieth century, zoning ordinances became popular. Under such ordinances, municipalities are permitted to divide an area into various uses.

Private restrictions are enforced under most circumstances. The court may issue an injunction barring a violation and may even order that nonconforming structures be demolished.[6] However, general restrictions may not be enforced where the neighborhood has changed, where numerous violations of general restrictions have occurred, where there has been a delay in enforcing restrictions, where the party who seeks to enforce the restriction has committed violations, or where the restrictions may have expired because of the passage of time. In addition, several states have laws providing that such restrictions may not be enforced after a specific number of years.

In zoning ordinances, a municipality is divided into residential, commercial, and industrial or manufacturing districts. Usually, residents may be permitted to live in residential sections. Stores and residences may be permitted in commercial districts, and any use may be permitted in a manufacturing zone. In addition, residential districts may be classified according to even more specific uses. As an example, some zoning ordinances provide for single-family and multiple-family dwelling zones.

In recent years, some zoning ordinances have attempted to become even more restrictive and keep residences out of zones which are classified as commercial or industrial. Many municipalities also have ordinances determining minimum lot size requirements for particular buildings.

Building codes are enacted under the police power of either the state or the municipality. A building code provision must be reasonably connected to the purpose or objective of the police power. However, the government agency which enacts the code is given broad power in writing the provisions, and its judgment will usually not be reversed by a court unless the ordinance is clearly unreasonable.

Building codes may apply to structures built prior to the adoption of the codes. The courts have permitted retroactive application of building codes because of their safety aspect. The duty to comply with building codes is placed upon the owner of the premises.

Enforcement of building codes usually involves inspections by code officials. Generally, these officials may seek court or administrative agency orders to enforce the code provisions. Also, the building codes typically provide for fines for non-compliance. In addition, some states and municipalities permit criminal prosecution of persons who knowingly violate building codes.

Recently, innovative zoning techniques have been developed. These include clustering, density zoning, and floating zones. Clustering may be used in subdivision design when the zoning ordinance allows dwelling units to be clustered, leaving common areas for recreational and other uses. Under such ordinances, minimum lot sizes may be smaller than those required by standard zoning ordinances. The aim of clustering is to create open space.

Under a density zoning ordinance, residential districting is determined by the number of dwelling units per acre or other given area. In density zoning, the lot restrictions of standard zoning ordinances normally need not be followed. Density zoning ordinances allow developers and architects greater freedom in laying out a development.

A floating zone ordinance provides for a specific use but does not indicate any particular location on the zoning map for that use. Location is determined by the application of the property owner.

A planned development uses both zoning ordinances and subdivision regulation to develop a large tract of land for a specific use or uses. Such developments frequently use cluster or density zoning. An example of a planned development would be a large project incorporating both residential and commercial buildings.

Structures which exist at the time the zoning ordinance is adopted may remain in a zone even though they do not comply with the zoning requirement.

Most communities have adopted building codes. Some states have statewide building codes. Usually, before a building may be built, the owner must apply for a building permit. A reviewing authority will analyze the plans and specifications to determine whether the proposed building complies with the appropriate zoning ordinance and the building code. Normally, most zoning and building ordinances provide that any new building may not be occupied until a municipal official has inspected it and issued a certificate of occupancy.

EASEMENTS AND LICENSES

An easement is the right of a person to use the land of another person for a special or limited purpose. Frequently, utility companies are granted easements by developers for telephone and power lines. Or a person's land may not give him access to a highway, and he may obtain an easement to cross a neighbor's land in order to reach it.

An easement appurtenant is an easement which benefits another parcel of land. The right to use another person's land to obtain access to a highway is an easement appurtenant. Land receiving the benefit of the easement is referred to as the "dominant tenement," and the land to which the easement attaches is referred to as the "servient tenement."

An easement appurtenant runs with the land. When the land is sold, the easement passes to the purchaser, even though it may not be mentioned in the deed.

An easement which does not have a dominant tenement, such as the right of the utility company to use a portion of the land, is called an "easement in gross." An easement in gross involves only one piece of land.

A license is more limited than an easement. Some legal scholars define a license as the right given one person to enter another person's land, which may be revoked at any time. Licenses are usually temporary and may not be sold. They are generally verbal. A license occurs, for example, when an outdoor theater owner allows a person to use his property to sell goods in a flea market.

Easements develop in several ways. First, it may be created by an express grant. An easement is an interest in land and requires a grant to satisfy the technicalities of the deed. An easement may also be created by an agreement, such as a party-wall agreement. Or it may come about because of a reservation. This occurs when a person sells land, reserving an easement in the deed.

Easements may also result when a court implies a grant or reservation. Implied grants and reservations occur when there is no document creating the easement, but from the circumstances the court determines that this was intended by the parties. An implied easement comes about when, at the time of conveyance of a parcel of land, part of it is being used for another piece of land. Further, the use must be apparent, continuous, and necessary. An example of an implied easement would involve rental of an apartment or office. The tenant has an implied easement to use the stairs, elevators, and hallways.

Easements may also be obtained by a proscription. The period of time for proscription is the time required to obtain land by adverse possession. As an example, one person may obtain the right to use another person's private road or driveway if he has used it continuously, without permission, and openly for the required number of years. Further, the use must be under such circumstances that the owner's right to stop it is not recognized, and the use must be so exclusive that the owner knows of the other person's use of the property.

An easement may also be created by reference to a plat. This frequently occurs when property is conveyed and the deed describes it with reference to a plat containing a description of certain easements.

An easement is terminated when the purpose for which it was created ceases, when the owner of the easement purchases the subservient tenement, or when the owner of the easement releases or abandons his right.

NOTES

1. Bell, *Air Rights*, 23 Ill. L. Rev. 261–262 (1928).
2. Robert Kratovil and Raymond J. Werner, *Real Estate Law*, 5th ed. (Englewood Cliffs, N.J.: Prentice-Hall, 1960), 9. Kratovil's text was the primary source for this chapter.
3. Cornelius J. Moynihan, *Introduction to the Law of Real Property* (St. Paul, Minn.: West, 1962), 1–32.
4. Chester H. Smith, *Survey of the Law of Real Property* (St. Paul, Minn.: West, 1956), 55.
5. *Ullsperger v. Meyer*, 217 Ill. 262, 75 N.E. 482 (1905).
6. *Stewart v. Finkelstone*, 206 Mass. 28, 92 N.E. 37 (1910).

12
Risk Management and Insurance

Fortunately, many claims against design professionals and manufacturers may be covered by insurance. Insurance is one of the areas of risk management. The function of risk management is to identify the risks which a business faces and to develop ways to meet them. Risks may be handled by a design professional or a manufacturer through insurance, assuming the risk, loss prevention, transferral of the risk to persons or companies other than insurance companies, or self-insurance.

Many malpractice claims against architects and engineers are covered by professional liability insurance. Similarly, product liability claims against manufacturers are usually covered by a comprehensive general liability insurance policy. These policies are now called commercial liability plicies. Damage to a company's property is covered by fire insurance and other forms of property damage insurance.

Occasionally, a risk may be so minimal that a company may decide not to insure against it. Some risks may not be insurable, or the premium may be too high in relation to the risk. Thus, for various reasons, design professionals and manufacturers may decide not to insure against particular risks. As an example, a manufacturer's comprehensive general liability policy, which covers him for product liability claims, may contain an exclusion under which he will not be reimbursed for the cost of recalling defective products. The cost of recall, however, may be covered by either an endorsement to the manufacturer's insurance policy or a separate insurance policy. Nevertheless, the manufacturer may choose not to purchase such coverage because recall insurance usually requires a relatively high premium.

Loss prevention programs may also be established to minimize risks. For years, many manufacturers have had quality assurance or quality control programs to minimize the risk of defective products being placed on the market. Today, some manufacturers even have quality assurance programs which involve review of the design of new products for safety prior to manufacture. In addition, some design professional firms also have quality assurance programs which involve the review of drawings and specifications prior to release for bidding or construction.

A risk may also be transferred to a person or company other than the insurer. Frequently, equipment leases provide that the lessee will maintain insurance covering damage to the equipment. Or a design professional or manufacturer may require his client to hold him harmless under certain circumstances. In addition, it is quite common in the construction industry for owners and design professionals to require contractors to indemnify them from claims arising during construction. Indemnification will be discussed in Chapter 13.

Self-insurance is different from assumption of risk. When a company decides to assume a risk, it may not do anything about it. Alternatively, it may establish a program of risk management to assume the uninsured risk. Self-insurance requires a large number of similar risks which recur periodically and can be reliably predicted. As an example, a manufacturer may own a number of plants and offices which may be damaged due to fire or other casualties. The manufacturer may find it more reasonable to self-insure against such risks rather than purchase insurance. Or a manufacturer may have a recurring number of product liability claims and may find it more feasible to insure himself against them.

With self-insurance, some companies may set aside a separate fund as part of the program. Accounting reserves may be used, and an experienced risk manager may oversee the administration of the program.

INSURANCE COMPANIES

Four types of insurers exist in the United States: stock companies, mutual companies, interinsurance exchanges, and Lloyds of London. Stock companies are profit-making ventures. Mutual companies are owned by the policyholders. Interinsurance exchanges are groups of individuals who basically insure each other's risks by exchanging insurance contracts. Lloyds of London is composed of syndicates of individuals who underwrite various risks. The policies are issued by Lloyds in the name of the underwriters who have accepted the risk. In addition, in a few states, insurance exchanges with underwriting syndicates similar to Lloyds of London have been established.

THE INSURANCE POLICY

The insurance policy is the contract of insurance between the insured and the insurer, and contains a description of coverage along with exclusions, limitations, definitions, conditions, the amount of the premium, and other information. Usually insurance companies use printed policy forms, which frequently are standard in the industry. Generally, most insurers use the same comprehensive general liability form under which a manufacturer will obtain insurance for product liability and other risks. Professional liability insurers who cover malpractice claims against design professionals also use printed forms. There is no standard form, although there are many similarities among those of various insurers. At times, because of special risks or insurance contracts, an insurer may issue a manuscript or typewritten policy.

To many insureds, reading an insurance policy can be an exasperating experience. These policies can be confusing because of their format. In addition, precisely defined words or terms are used in the policy. Recently, a movement has developed to write policies in plain language. The incentive has come from several state legislatures which have passed laws requiring that certain legal documents, including insurance policies, be simply written.

Most insurance policies have the same basic structure: the (1) declarations section, (2) insuring agreement, (3) statement of coverages, (4) list of definitions, (5) description of exclusions, (6) statement of conditions, and (7) endorsements.

The declarations section states the name of the insurer, the name and address of the insured, and the policy period. In addition, the declarations page lists the coverages of the policy and the monetary limits of liability for each coverage. For a comprehensive general liability policy, for example, the declarations page indicates whether completed operations and product liability coverage is provided.

The insuring agreement typically is a statement that the insurer will insure the insured for certain risks in exchange for payment of the premium. The coverages section describes the coverages provided. As an example, in an automobile liability policy, there are two coverages, one for bodily injury liability and one for property damage liability. In the typical professional liability policy, the introduction states that the insurer, in consideration of the payment of the premium by the insured, will cover claims arising from a performance of professional services.

The definition section defines terms used in the policy, such as "named insured," "bodily injury," and "property damage."

The exclusions are extremely important and should be read by the insured. The exclusions eliminate from insurance coverage claims which would otherwise be covered by the insuring provision, which usually is broadly written. For example, workers' compensation claims are usually excluded from professional and general liability policies. However, for some exclusions, coverage can be obtained either by endorsement or by the purchase of an additional policy.

The conditions describe the rights and obligations of the parties under the policy. For example, the insured is usually required to give the insurer prompt notice of any claim and to send the insured copies of any suit papers.

The endorsements are used to add to or take away from the coverage of the basic policy form. For instance, most standard general liability policies do not cover host liquor liability, but this coverage can be purchased by an endorsement.

Many insurance policies also provide for a deductible. Under the deductible, the insured pays a certain amount toward the settlement of any claim or judgment covered by a liability policy. For a property damage policy, the deductible reduces the amount of payment from the insured to the insurer, but no more than the deductible amount.

Liability insurance policies are issued under either a "claims made" or "occurrence" basis. Claims-made policies are prevalent for professional liability insurance, and are becoming more used for commercial liability coverage. Occurrence policies are used for most other types of coverage.

Under a claims-made policy, the insurer becomes liable for claims made during the policy period, regardless of when the accident occurred which gave rise to the claim. An occurrence policy covers claims arising from accidents or occurrences during the policy period, regardless of when the claim is made or the suit filed.

BUYING INSURANCE

Insurance is marketed through two basic systems: the independent agency system and the direct writing system. Under the independent agency system, agents are appointed by insurance companies to represent them in given territories for certain forms of coverage. Thus, a person may be an agent for automobile and homeowners insurance and, under the insurance agency agreement, may have authority to bind the insurance company and to receive claims under the policies of the company.

The direct writing system involves the marketing of insurance directly by the insurance company to the insured, frequently by employees of the insurer. Direct writing is prevalent in the automobile and homeowners markets.

Today most independent agents are often referred to as "insurance brokers." Technically, an insurance broker is the agent of the insured in placing the insurance coverage. However, a broker may have agency agreements with one or more insurance companies.

Although some business insurance is provided on a direct writing basis, much of it is purchased through brokers. Usually, an insurance broker will meet with his customer to determine which types of risks the customer faces and to assist the customer in devising a suitable insurance program. Then the broker will contact a number of insurance companies to request quotes for specific policies covering the risks. Frequently, the insurance broker, on behalf of his customer, will negotiate with the insurance company not only on the amount of the premium, but also on specific coverages and the wording of the policy and endorsements. Brokers are usually paid by a commission on the insured's premium, even though they are the agents of the insured.

Today, there are also professional insurance consultants who act as advisors to companies. They are paid for the time they devote to specific projects.

GENERAL LIABILITY INSURANCE

Most liability risks, other than for automobile accidents and professional errors, are covered by a general liability policy. For many years, each insurance company used its own general liability form. In the 1930s, the companies, through trade organizations, drafted a standard comprehensive general liability policy. The first standard form came into use in 1940. It was revised in 1966, 1970, and 1972.[1] In addition, a new form was written in 1983. The new form with certain changes as been approved for use in many states.

General liability policies provide coverage for all sums for which the insured may be legally obligated due to either bodily injury or property damage, subject to the exclusions of the policy. Bodily injury is physical harm to the claimant's body. Property damage is physical damage to property. Moreover, damage arising from loss of use due either to property damage or to some other means is covered under the standard comprehensive general liability form. However, damage to property under the "care and custody or control" of the insured is excluded from the policy.

Coverage for personal injuries other than bodily injury may be obtained by an endorsement to the general liability policy. The endorsement covers claims arising from false imprisonment, malicious prosecution, libel, slander, defamation, invasion of privacy, and wrongful entry.

The comprehensive general liability policy has numerous exclusions. Some of the more important ones will be discussed here.

First, the policy does not cover liability arising from a contract other than an "incidental contract" as defined by the policy. An incidental contract is a lease of premises, an easement agreement, a side-track agreement, an elevator maintenance agreement, or an agreement to indemnify a municipality required by ordinance. The contractual liability exclusion, however, does not apply to warranties given by the insured. Thus, actions for breach of warranty alleging bodily injury or property damage would be covered by the general liability policy.

Contractual liability coverage may be obtained under the general liability policy through a contractual coverage part endorsement, which itself is subject to certain exclusions. Basically, this endorsement is used to insure other types of hold-harmless agreements given by the insured. It does not apply to architects, engineers, or surveyors. Such coverage must be obtained by the design professional under his professional liability policy.

Second, the general liability policy does not cover workers' compensation, employee compensation, or disability benefits claims. Workers' compensation claims may be covered under a workers' compensation policy.

Third, the policy excludes coverage for property damage or bodily injury arising from a claim due to a defect in the construction of a building, but only after the building is completed. For example, during construction, a third party may be injured due to the negligence of a contractor. Such a risk would normally be covered by the general liability policy insuring the contractor. After construction, if a third party is injured due to the negligence of the contractor during construction, the contractor would not normally be covered by the policy. However, this exclusion can usually be covered by purchasing completed operations coverage under the general liability policy.

Fourth, automobile liability is not covered. Obviously, this can be insured under an automobile liability policy.

Fifth, pollution claims are not covered by the general liability policy, although most policies issued prior to 1986 did cover certain pollution claims.

Sixth, the general liability policy does not cover claims arising from acts of war.

Seventh, the policy does not cover claims arising from the delay or failure of the insured's product or work to meet warranties or other performance obligations. These are pure business risks which the insurance industry usually does not want to insure. Of course, this exclusion does not apply to loss of the use of property due to an accident.

Eighth, the policy does not cover damage to the property or products of the insured, although it does cover damage to other property or products due to a failure of the insured's products or work.

Ninth, the standard general liability policy does not cover the claims arising from collapse, explosion, or underground work. Such a risk can be insured by an endorsement.

Tenth, the comprehensive general liability policy does not cover host liquor liability. As mentioned above, this exposure can be covered by an endorsement.

Eleventh, most comprehensive general liability policies covering design professionals usually contain an endorsement excluding coverage for professional liability claims. Professional liability policies will be discussed below.

Under a general liability policy, the named insured is the person or organization listed as the insured upon the declaration. For businesses, this may be a sole proprietorship, a partnership, or a corporation.

For sole proprietorships, the sole proprietor is insured only for acts pertaining to the business, not for personal acts. For partnerships, the partnership and the partners are the insureds. Executive officers, directors, and shareholders may also be covered for a corporation insured under a general liability policy, but other employees may not be covered. However, under some general and umbrella liability forms employees are covered for general liability claims.

General liability policies are used to cover both completed operations and products liability hazards. Completed operations hazards pertain to claims arising from bodily injury or property damage after real property has been completed or abandoned by the insured. Frequently, contractors obtain coverage for past construction projects under the completed operations hazard.

The products hazard covers claims pertaining to alleged defects in products manufactured or sold by the insured. However, coverage is provided only after the product has left the premises of the insured and is no longer under his physical control of possession.

General liability policies are usually issued on an occurrence basis. This means that the policy covers accidents occurring during the policy period. A new standard general liability form is also being introduced on a claims-made basis, covering claims made during the policy period. Also, during the last several years, some insurance companies have issued products liability coverage on a claims-made policy.

Under the standard comprehensive general liability form, the policy covers claims arising in the United States, its possessions and territories, and Canada. In addition, coverage is extended for claims arising from alleged defects in the insured's product in other countries, but only if the product was originally manufactured and sold in the United States, its possessions and territories, or Canada. Further worldwide coverage may be obtained by endorsement or an umbrella liability policy. However, some policies limit worldwide coverage to claims arising outside the United States, its territories or possessions, or Canada, so long as the suit is filed in one of these three areas.

AUTOMOBILE LIABILITY INSURANCE

Coverage for claims arising from automobile accidents are handled by an automobile liability policy, which may cover owned, non-owned, and hired automobiles. This policy usually covers not only the named insured but also any person using a covered automobile with his permission. This section of the automobile liability policy is sometimes referred to as the "omnibus clause."

UMBRELLA AND EXCESS LIABILITY INSURANCE

General liability insurance for large professional firms and corporations is usually handled in layers. For general liability insurance, the first layer is usually the comprehensive general liability policy. Since insurance companies are reluctant to insure all forms of exposure, umbrella and excess liability policies are used to guard the insured against catastrophic losses. Because most of the exposure to the insured may be covered by the first layer of insurance, the premium for the general liability policy is usually relatively high compared to the premiums for the umbrella and excess liability policies.

Umbrella liability insurance provides not only higher limits of coverage but also broader coverage. As an example, if the general liability policy does not give worldwide coverage, the umbrella policy may do so. In addition, when the limits of the comprehensive general liability policy are exhausted, the umbrella carrier becomes the primary insurer and defends the insured. Ordinarily, the general liability policy provides that when its limits are exhausted, the insurer no longer has a duty to defend the insured.

Policies above the umbrella liability limit are usually referred to as "excess policies" and ordinarily follow the form of the umbrella policy.

OWNER'S PROTECTIVE LIABILITY INSURANCE

During construction, an owner may require a contractor to purchase an owner's and contractor's protective liability policy. This policy covers both the owner and the general contractor from liability arising from independent contractor operations. This policy, however, does not provide completed operations coverage, and both the contractor and the owner have to furnish such coverage under their general liability policies.

BUILDERS' RISK INSURANCE

Builders' risk insurance covers damage to the property during construction. It can be procured by either the owner or the contractor. Such policies are usually written on an "all-risk" basis, insuring all perils unless excluded. Thus, common occurrences such as damage to construction projects resulting from fire, wind storm, explosion, and vandalism are covered. Certain electrical injuries, off-premises power interruption, and losses due to earthquakes and volcanos are not covered. Moreover, under a new standard form introduced in 1983, losses resulting from decisions of government bodies may not be covered.

The builders' risk policy usually terminates upon occupancy of the structure. Further, it does not cover damage to a construction project due to defective design or workmanship. Typically, the builders' risk policy covers the owner and the general contractor, and sometimes subcontractors and the architect/engineer.

WORKERS' COMPENSATION INSURANCE

Workers' compensation insurance policies provide two forms of coverage. First, the workers' compensation portion states that the insurer will pay all compensation and other benefits due from the insured under the workers' compensation laws of the states listed in the declarations section of the policy. Second, the employer's liability part furnishes coverage for bodily injury to employees of the insured arising from and in the course of employment not compensated under the workers' compensation statute. This part, for example, may be used to cover claims where the employee, under state law, elects not to file for workers' compensation benefits or where a third party seeks indemnification from the employer due to an injury sustained by the insured's employee.

The workers' compensation portion of the policy does not contain a monetary limit, but the employer's liability section does. Therefore, most insurance also contains, under umbrella and/or excess liability policies, coverage for employer's liability claims exceeding the limits of the underlying employer's liability coverage.

The workers' compensation laws of most states declare that if contractors or subcontractors have not provided workers' compensation insurance for their employees, the principal (owner) or contractor becomes liable for such payments. Accordingly, owners and contractors in construction ensure that the contractors and subcontractors have the required workers' compensation insurance.

PROFESSIONAL LIABILITY INSURANCE

Design professionals may be covered for malpractice claims under a professional liability policy. Such policies are commonly referred to as "errors or omissions" policies.

Ordinarily, a professional liability policy will cover all malpractice claims arising from the rendering or failure to render professional services. Typically, errors or omissions insurance is written upon a claims-made basis.

Under a professional liability policy, the insured may have a duty to notify the insurer not only of actual claims made or suits filed against the insured, but also of circumstances which may give rise to a claim. The latter duty is usually not imposed under a general liability policy. Frequently, claims-made errors or omissions policies contain a retroactive endorsement, which states that the insurer will be under no obligation for claims arising from services rendered prior to a specific date. Usually, a professional liability policy will cover the employees of the firm for professional malpractice.

As with the general liability policy, the exclusions of the professional liability policy are important. First, these policies ordinarily do not cover guarantees or warranties. Thus, if a design professional provides a guarantee which expands his traditional duty to his client, such as warranting performance of the work, the insurer is under no obligation to defend or pay any settlement or judgment. In addition, professional liability policies usually exclude coverage for automobile liability and employer liability claims. Moreover, many policies exclude coverage for electronic data processing services, although such coverage may be obtained by endorsement or by a special policy. Professional liability policies usually exclude coverage for cost guarantee estimates and for advice given by a design professional pertaining to insurance or bonds. Moreover, they exclude coverage for dishonest, fraudulent, or criminal acts.

The typical professional liability policy covering architects and engineers does not cover joint ventures. This coverage may be obtained by an endorsement. However, the endorsement ordinarily covers only the error of the insured. Thus, under the law, the insured may be responsible for a design error of his co-venturer, but he cannot obtain coverage for this error under his professional liability policy.

Some professional liability policies do not cover indemnification agreements. Others cover these agreements so long as they do not expand the design professional's liability beyond his traditional limits.

Usually a professional liability policy will not cover damages from claims arising for delay in performance and may not cover soil testing services.

A professional liability policy may be limited to claims arising from work done in the United States and/or Canada. However, some policies may be written on a worldwide basis.

FIRE INSURANCE

Insurance for damage due to fire or other perils to buildings is usually covered by a fire insurance policy. The standard policy only covers losses due to fire or lightning and losses to property temporarily taken from the building due to fire. The other perils are covered by an extended policy and cover damage due to windstorm, hail, explosions, and smoke.

The standard insurance policy will not cover loss of profits due to fire at a business location. However, business interruption insurance can be purchased to cover such a loss.

Usually a standard fire insurance policy is purchased for a period of three years.

In order for property to be covered under a standard policy, the insured must have an "insurable interest" in it. An insurable interest is frequently determined by whether the insured will receive a benefit from the property or suffer a loss due to its destruction.

Fire insurance policies generally include a co-insurance clause. These policies require the insured to maintain an insured value upon the property of either 80 to 90% of the property's cash value. If the insured does not maintain the required amount of insurance, he must pay a proportional amount of the loss. For example, if the policy has a 90% co-insurance clause and the insured has only 70% of the value insured, he must pay 2/9ths of the loss.

NUCLEAR INSURANCE

Most insurance policies exclude coverage for a nuclear accident. However, coverage for such occurrences may be obtained under a federally endorsed program of insurance and indemnification.

In 1957, the U.S. Congress passed the Price-Anderson Act, which created a government fund to indemnify companies engaging in nuclear activities against claims arising from nuclear accidents. The fund contains $500,000,000 and is in excess of the $60,000,000 worth of insurance provided by private nuclear liability insurance pools formed by insurance companies. The total of $560,000,000 is also the total limit of liability for claims arising from a nuclear incident. Thus, companies which are covered by the nuclear liability insurance pools and have an indemnification agreement with the U.S. government are not liable for claims exceeding $560,000,000.

The U.S. Nuclear Regulatory Commission determines whether an "extraordinary nuclear occurrence" has taken place. If it has, the defendants in any lawsuits waive certain defenses, but their liability is limited to $560,000,000.

The liability pool today is named the "American Nuclear Insurers." It is a group of mutual and shareholder-owned insurance companies.

Nuclear builder's risk insurance and nuclear energy property damage insurance is also available.

FIDELITY BONDS

Fidelity bonds indemnify employers for losses of money or certain property resulting from dishonest acts of employees. They may be issued to cover particular individuals or companies. Loss of money, securities, and other valuable items may also be covered. Usually, a fidelity bond will only insure against loss not exceeding a stated sum or monetary limit.

SURETY BONDS

In construction, surety or construction bonds are frequently used. With such bonds, the obligor or insurer guarantees that the principal has certain obligations to the obligee. For instance, in bonds purchased by a contractor, the principal is the contractor, the obligor is the insurance company or surety issuing the bond, and the obligee is the owner.

In the typical construction situation, two forms of surety bonds are used. First, under the performance bond, the insurer guarantees the owner that the contractor will carry out the construction contract. Under the payment bond, the insurer guarantees the owner that the general contractor will pay all subcontractors, materialmen, and laborers working upon the project. In addition, bid bonds may be used. These bonds are usually stated as a percentage of the bid price. They are paid if the contractor awarded the contract does not make an agreement with the owner.

If there is a default under either a bid or performance bond, the owner may proceed against the insurer. However, the insurer may use any defense which the contractor or principal could have used against the owner. As an example, a defense to a claim under a bid bond may be that the owner delayed in awarding the contract.

Payment bonds are used to avoid the filing of mechanics' liens against the property or to discharge such liens. Under some payment bonds, the insurer may pay subcontractors and material suppliers who have not been paid by the general contractor covered by the bond.

Some performance bonds provide not only that the insurer will guarantee completion of the project pursuant to the contract documents, but also that he will perform any warranty obligation of the contractor. Usually, the warranty period runs for one year following completion of the project.

INSURANCE CERTIFICATES

Normally, a contract states that one or both of the parties will furnish certain insurance coverage. In addition, it may state that the party providing the coverage will arrange for the other party to receive a certificate of insurance showing the existence of the coverage.

Basically, a certificate of insurance is a list of the policies purchased by the insured. It may be issued by either an insurance company or an insurance broker. In addition, many certificates state that if any of the insurance coverage is canceled, the party who received the certificate will obtain at least ten days' notice prior to cancellation.

For instance, in the construction industry, owners frequently require contractors to maintain both general liability and workers' compensation coverage. In addition, they may require that contractor to furnish builders' risk insurance. The only way the owner can verify the existence of such coverage is to obtain a copy of the insurance certificate.

Obviously, the party who received the certificate may not always want to rely upon it. He may want his attorney and/or insurance broker to review the policies underlying the certificate in order to be sure that they provide the coverage required by the contract.

In addition, one of the parties may require that the party with the insurance name him "as an additional insured" under various policies. Again, in this situation, the party who is the additional insured may request the party purchasing the insurance to provide copies of the insurance policies.

VENDOR'S ENDORSEMENTS

Manufacturers may be requested by their customers to maintain a general liability insurance policy with a vendor's endorsement. Vendor's endorsements are meant to cover product liability claims. Frequently, distributors and retailers do not think that they should be bearing the product liability risk, since they are not the manufacturers of the products they sell. Accordingly, they will request the manufacturer to have a vendor's endorsement upon his general liability policy. Basically, the vendor's endorsement extends coverage for such claims to the distributors and retailers, so long as they merely resell the product without altering its condition or making any warranties.

NOTICE OF LOSS

Insurance policies usually provide that the insured will notify the insurer of any claims made against him or suits filed against him covered by the policy. Notice provisions usually state that the insured will give the insurer prompt notice of any claim or suit. This is an important obligation, especially where the insurer has the right to defend any claim or suit filed against him covered by the policy. In the event that the insured does not give prompt notice of a claim or suit, the insurer may be prejudiced. As an example, a court may enter a default judgment against an insured in a lawsuit if the matter was not promptly reported to the insurer and the insured did not appear in the suit.

RESERVATIONS OF RIGHTS

If an insured reports to an insurer a claim which is clearly not covered under the policy, the insurer will usually deny coverage and refuse to defend any such claim. However, if there is a possibility that a claim may not be covered, usually because of an exclusion in the policy or late notice, the insurer may defend the claim under a reservation of rights.

Basically, a reservation of rights consists of a letter from the insurer to the insured advising him of the basis for the reservation and stating that the insurer will defend the claim but is preserving its rights to deny it in the future. Sometimes the insurer may file a declaratory judgment action in a court after serving a reservation of rights letter, requesting the court to determine whether the insurer is legally obligated to defend the suit.

DEFENSE OF SUITS

Under most liability policies, the insurer retains the right to defend all claims and lawsuits. In addition, the insurer usually has the right to settle a claim or suit for any amount it deems proper. However, some professional liability policies provide that the insurer will not settle any claim or suit without the consent of the insured. Such policies typically state that if the insured withholds consent, the insured becomes liable for the difference between the amount of the judgment or settlement and the amount for which it could have settled the matter.

Some insurance policies are subject to a self-insured retention. Such policies are frequently used by large manufacturers to cover general or product liability claims. Self-insured retention may run from approximately $50,000 to $1,000,000, depending upon the insurance program.

Under a self-insured retention, the insured defends all claims and suits, although the insurer usually retains the right to take over the defense of any matter if it so desires. Some of these insurance programs also provide that the insured will retain an independent claim-handling company to assist it in defending claims which are being defended by the insured.

SUBROGATION

Ordinarily, the property damage or liability insurer has a right of subrogation. This is either an equitable right or a right which is retained by the insurer in the insurance policy. Under subrogation, the insurer may recover from a third party sums that it paid to the insured, either under the policy or on behalf of the insured, if the third party is legally liable for causing the damage.

As an example, an insurance company may issue an automobile liability policy. If the insured has an accident with a third party due to the third party's negligence, the insurer may seek to recover subrogation from the third party for any damages it had to pay to the insured.

Design professionals and manufacturers frequently are targets of fire insurers under the right of subrogation. For example, a building may have been damaged by fire which was insured by the fire insurer. Through its investigation, the insurer may determine that the fire was caused either by the design error of the architect or engineer or by a defect in a piece of equipment in the building. Under such circumstances, the fire insurer may seek subrogation for the damages it paid to its insured from either the design professional or the manufacturer.

PUNITIVE DAMAGES

In recent years, there has been much discussion about whether an insurance policy covers punitive damages against an insured. Some policies specifically provide that punitive damages are not covered. Where the policy is silent upon the subject, the courts of various states have gone in two directions. Some courts hold that punitive damages may be covered. A few courts have held, however, that only punitive damages for which the insured is vicariously liable are covered. Thus, in Illinois, one court held that under an automobile liability policy covering employees of the insured, the insured was covered for punitive damages for which he was vicariously liable arising from an accident in which an employee was the driver. In another Illinois case, however, the court held that in an action against an insured for damages caused by driving while intoxicated did not cover punitive damages.[2] Other courts have held that punitive damages are not covered under any circumstances as a matter of public policy. In those cases, the courts have reasoned that punitive damages are a form of punishment for wrongdoing and that such damages arising from wrongful acts may not be covered by insurance.

EXCESS LIABILITY

Occasionally, an insured may be sued in a case in which the damages sought exceed the insured's coverage. In such instances, the insurer will usually send the insured a letter advising him of the excess exposure and informing him that if he so desires, his own attorney may associate with the counsel retained by the insurance company in defending the matter.

In such a case, the insurer must deal reasonably and in good faith regarding the uninsured exposure of the insured. If the insurance company breaches that duty, it may be liable for the amount of the judgment in excess of the limits of the insurance policy. As an example, the insurer must consider not only his interests in defending such a case, but also the interests of the insured. He must determine the plaintiff's probabilities of success and the probable judgment. If the plaintiff has a strong chance of winning and the damages would exceed the limits of the insurance policy, the court may hold that the insurer had a duty to settle the case within the limits of the policy.

NOTES

1. John Alan Appleman and Jean Appleman, *Insurance Law and Practice: With Forms* (Walter F. Berdal, rev. ed.), Vol. 7A (rev.), § 4491.3 (St. Paul, Minn.: West, 1979).
2. *Scott v. Instant Parking, Inc.,* 105 Ill.App.2d 133, 245 N.E.2d 124 (1969) and *Beaver v. Country Mutual Insurance Co.,* 95 Ill.App.3d 1122, 420 N.E.2d 1058 (1981).

13
Indemnification

Engineers working in both construction and manufacturing often hear the term "indemnification." Indemnification is simply the holding harmless of one person by another person for some harm or damage suffered by the first person.

Indemnification includes two principles. First, it may arise when one person gives security for another. For example, an insurance company may agree in a construction bond to indemnify the owner if the contractor does not honor his contract. Second, it refers to the concept of paying someone for damages. For instance, a manufacturer of a machine tool may be liable to a worker injured by the tool due to a defect in its design or manufacture. However, under certain circumstances, the manufacturer may be entitled to recover any damages he paid to the worker from the worker's employer if, for example, the employer had not adequately trained or supervised the worker.

The right to indemnification may arise by law. In such cases, the courts have held that one party is entitled to be indemnified by another even though there is no written or oral indemnification agreement. As discussed later, some states have developed a body of law referred to as "active/passive negligence." Under this doctrine, if two parties are liable for negligently causing harm to the plaintiff, but one party has been only passively negligent, this party may recover any damages he owes from the actively negligent party.

The right to indemnification may also arise from a contract. For instance, many retailers require manufacturers to indemnify them from product liability claims due to defects in the products sold by the retailer.

EXPRESSED CONTRACTS

There are no particular requirements for an indemnification agreement. Usually such agreements are in writing, but occasionally the courts have found verbal ones to be valid. The rules of contract law generally apply to the validity, effect, and construction of a written indemnification agreement.

No particular form is required for indemnification agreements. Frequently, they appear as a provision of a contract. Such a provision in a construction contract may read:

> Contractor agrees to indemnify, hold harmless, and defend owner from any and all claims, damages and liabilities arising from, or alleged to arise from, personal injury, including death, or property damage, including loss and use thereof, or otherwise, during or related to in any manner whatsoever performance of the construction contract.

An agreement to indemnify lasts for the time stated in the contract. If there is no fixed duration, it lasts for a reasonable time and may be terminated at will by either party.

Indemnification agreements are made for many reasons and generally will be upheld by the court, unless the indemnitor (the party giving indemnification) agrees to hold harmless the indemnitee (the party being indemnified) for an illegal or wrongful act or the court determines as a matter of public policy that the agreement will not be enforced. As an example, the court may not enforce an agreement to indemnify another party for his own fraud.[1]

When interpreting indemnification provisions, the courts consider not only the language used, but also the circumstances surrounding the making of the contract. If the agreement is ambiguous, the courts must give it a reasonable construction to carry out the purpose of the parties.

Frequently, an indemnification provision envisions that the indemnitor will have been the negligent party and, as a matter of fair dealing, should pay the other party for any lost occasion by his negligence. However, many indemnification agreements contain language indicating that the indemnitee will be indemnified even if he has been negligent. The courts will generally oppose such provisions, but will enforce them if the language clearly states that the indemnitee will be indemnified for his own negligence. Thus, indemnification provisions frequently state that the party being indemnified will be held harmless "whether or not his negligence contributed to the damage suffered by the third party who is making the claim or has filed the lawsuit."

Moreover, the courts are reluctant to enforce an indemnification agreement when the negligence of the indemnitee was the *sole* cause of the damage, even though the agreement provides that the indemnitee will be held harmless for his negligence. Courts frequently will go through sophisticated legal reasoning to avoid this application of a hold-harmless provision. In such situations, they will strictly construe the indemnification language in favor of the indemnitor and against the indemnitee.

INDEMNIFICATION IN CONSTRUCTION CONTRACTS

The courts generally have upheld indemnification provisions in construction contracts providing that the contractor will indemnify the owner for work-related damages or injuries caused by the owner's negligence. When determining whether the contractor intended to hold harmless the owner, the courts may weigh the contractual provisions regarding insurance, the hazardous nature of the contractor's work, the amount of the consideration, whether the contractor had exclusive control of the work, and whether the owner was doing other work in the area at the same time. In addition, the courts may consider the time or place of the injury. The courts have also upheld such provisions when the owner is being indemnified for a statutory violation, such as a violation of the Structural Work Act or Scaffolding Act.

The courts have enforced indemnification provisions stating that the owner will be indemnified even if he is negligent in cases where (1) the owner has been actively negligent, (2) the owner's negligence was unrelated to the construction contract, (3) the contractor may not have been negligent, (4) employees of the contractor or other workmen on the job were injured, and (5) injured persons had no connection with the work.[2] Not only do the courts enforce such indemnification agreements, but at least one court has viewed them favorably. In an Ohio case, the court held that the owner could be indemnified for his own negligence, as stated in a written contract with the contractor. Further, the court thought that such indemnification was desirable because it avoided the question of who was at fault.[3]

A Texas case presents an example of how far the court may go to avoid enforcing an indemnification agreement. There a partnership, acting as a contractor, needed to use transportation furnished by the railroad. The railroad obtained an indemnification agreement from the contractor stating that the contractor would be liable for all injuries or deaths to its "agents and employees" regardless of whether the railroad was negligent. One of the partners in the contracting firm was killed while riding as a passenger in a railway motor car. A suit was filed and the deceased partner's estate recovered damages. The Texas Court of Appeals interpreted the indemnification agreement narrowly and said that it applied only to agents and employees of the company, not to partners.[4]

An agreement in which the contractor holds harmless the owner for the owner's own negligence applies whether the owner is actively or passively negligent. Moreover, some courts have held that even if the agreement does not make this provision, he will still be indemnified if he was only passively negligent. In a California case, the owner sued a contractor after paying damages resulting from injuries to several of the contractor's employees who were hurt when defective roof trusses collapsed. The trusses had been installed by the contractor. The indemnification agreement did not state that the owner would be held harmless from his own negligence; however, the court concluded that any negligence of the owner was merely passive, consisting of the right to have rejected the defective trusses. Accordingly, the court determined that the owner should be indemnified by the contractor under the agreement.[5]

Some courts have refused to apply an indemnification provision for the benefit of an owner when the owner's own negligence was either the sole cause or a concurrent cause of the injuries. Courts in New York, Oklahoma, Texas, Louisiana, New Jersey, Florida, Kentucky, Maine, and Missouri have reached such conclusions. Other courts have not, and have upheld the indemnification provision even though the owner may have been the sole cause of the accident. In the past, these states included Illinois and Michigan.

Because of pressure from contractors and subcontractors, several states have passed laws making unenforceable indemnification provisions in construction contracts under which the indemnitor holds harmless the indemnitee for the indemnitee's own or sole negligence. Illinois, Indiana, and Michigan are among the states that have such statutes.

General contractors usually seek indemnification from their subcontractors. Such agreements are frequently obtained because the owner has requested the contractor to indemnify it. The same rules of law apply to these agreements. With a subcontractor, however, the indemnification provision may be contained in the purchase order issued by the contractor.[6] The indemnification agreement may also be incorporated by reference in the subcontractor's agreement with the contractor. The subcontractor's agreement may even refer specifically to the indemnification agreement in the contractor's contract, or it may incorporate all the provisions of the latter's contract.[7]

Of course, design professionals may also enter into contracts to indemnify the owner. Similarly, they themselves may be indemnified by the owner or the contractors.

A 1983 New York federal court case illustrates some of the problems facing an engineer who executes a contract providing for indemnification of the owner.[8] The engineer was retained by a county to design a sewage pipeline into the ocean. The original specifications provided that material dredged from the navigable channels should be replaced with material not containing organic silts. The first bid was too high, and as a result, the county revised its specifications, providing that material dredged from the navigable channels was acceptable as backfill. The county then began using the pipeline before it was accepted and a break occurred, requiring corrective work. The county sued the contractor and the engineer. The jury, based upon conflicting testimony, found that the cause of the break was the use of material from the navigable channels and declared the contractor not guilty. In addition, the jury found that the engineer was not guilty because the design error was due to the county's change in the specifications. However, the trial court held the engineer liable to the county under and indemnification agreement, even though he had not been negligent.

The agreement stated that the engineer would hold harmless the county from any claims "arising from the performance of the work of the engineers." The trial judge found that the indemnification language was clear, but the appellate court disagreed. The appellate court stated that indemnification agreements are usually written to cover third-party claims and that it was not clear whether the hold-harmless provision was intended to be any broader. As a result, the appellate court remanded the case to the trial court for a hearing to determine the intent of the parties pertaining to the indemnification provision.

INDEMNIFICATION IN MANUFACTURERS' CONTRACTS

Indemnification agreements may also be contained in contracts between product manufacturers and their vendors or customers. Large retailers often require suppliers of products to indemnify them from product liability claims, including not only personal injury claims but also the cost of recalls which may be required by the Consumer Product Safety Commission or some other agency, or voluntarily.

Manufacturers often require component suppliers to indemnify them. For example, a defect in a key component of a product could result in an injury to a person or damage to property, resulting in significant exposure of the manufacturer.

Often retailers and manufacturers seek separate written indemnification agreements from their suppliers. Separate agreements are made in order to impress their significance upon both parties. Moreover, these agreements may require the manufacturer or the supplier to maintain insurance.

Frequently, purchase orders from retailers and manufacturers contain a provision stating that the vendor will hold them harmless. Depending upon the circumstances regarding issuance and acceptance of the purchase order, the indemnification provision may or may not be binding. If the purchase order is executed by the vendor and both parties intend it to be the contract, then under the Uniform Commercial Code (UCC) the indemnification provision may be valid. However, if both parties do not intend the purchase order to be the sole contract, then the indemnification provision may not be valid because of the UCC's rule on the "battle of the forms" discussed in Chapter 9. Under the UCC, an indemnification agreement would probably be viewed as a conflicting material term and the courts would reject any such agreement appearing on a printed form, applying general UCC law on indemnification.

In addition, purchase orders used in manufacturing, and sometimes in construction, require the seller to hold harmless the buyer from any patent indemnification claims. Such provisions are prevalent in purchase orders used by large manufacturers. General rules of law of indemnification also apply to such hold-harmless agreements.

INDEMNIFICATION WITHOUT AGREEMENT

Indemnity without an agreement may arise either under the concept of an implied contract or under the theory that when one person has been held liable due to the actions of another person, the second person should bear the loss. Thus, an officer or director of a corporation may be entitled to indemnification by the corporation if he has used his own funds for necessary expenses of the corporation. However, in most instances where an engineer becomes involved in noncontractual indemnification, one person must pay for a wrong caused by a second person. As an example, under the Scaffolding Acts of several states, if the owner is found to be in control of the project, he may become liable for the injuries of construction workers at the site even though he has not been negligent. Frequently, the negligence causing the accident may be that of the employee or his employer. Under such circumstances, the courts may allow the owner to seek indemnification from the employer of the injured worker. Or a retailer may sell a product which is defective in design or manufacture and injures the purchaser or user. Although the retailer may be liable to the injured party under the theory of strict liability, the courts may allow him to seek indemnification from the manufacturer or the wholesaler who sold him the defective product.

Under common law, there was no right of indemnity or contribution among joint-tort feasors. Thus, if two parties were responsible for an accident which resulted in damages being assessed against one or both of them, neither party could seek indemnification or contribution from the other toward payment of the judgment. In the last several decades, however, the courts have been aware that a literal application of this rule to all negligence or strict liability cases would result in unfair treatment for certain parties. Further, the party who actually caused the injury could escape liability. Thus, the courts have developed a rule to determine the character of the negligence when two parties may be joint tort feasors. If one party is either technically or passively negligent, he may seek indemnification from the party or parties who are actively or affirmatively negligent. Thus, the retailer selling a defective product which injures the purchaser or user may be liable only in a technical sense because he has a duty not to sell defective products. However, the manufacturer of the product may be more culpable, and the courts have allowed the retailer in such situations to obtain indemnification from him. Similarly, a general contractor may be passively negligent when a subcontractor's employee has been injured at the worksite. For example, if the general contractor had done certain inspections, which he failed to do, he might have noticed the unsafe situation which eventually resulted in the worker's injury. In such a case the court may say that the jury could find that the general contractor was only passively negligent and that the real cause of the injury was the active negligence of the worker's employer (the subcontractor). Thus, the court may permit the general contractor to seek recovery from the subcontractor under the law of indemnification. As a further example, an employer may be vicariously liable to persons injured by the acts of his employee, but the employer may seek indemnification from his employee if the employee's negligence caused the injury.[9]

Under the laws of many states, actively negligent joint-tort feasors may not obtain a contribution from each other. Thus, in an Ohio case, a hot water heater manufacturer sought indemnification from his vendor for a defective valve. The valve had allegedly caused a malfunction and the court held that the manufacturer could not seek indemnification from the vendor since both were sophisticated manufacturers, each had an equal opportunity to examine the valve prior to use, the manufacturer owed a duty to his customers to inspect components, and his failure to make a simple test which could have revealed the defect all barred the indemnity claim.[10]

Similarly, in a Wisconsin case, the court reasoned that since a contractor and a real estate broker had the same duty to advise the purchaser of known latent defects in a house, neither could recover indemnification from the other due to the defects.[11]

As a further example, the driver of an automobile was found grossly negligent in the death of a passenger resulting from an accident. In the same action, the automobile manufacturer was also found liable due to defective design. The court held that the driver could not recover from the manufacturer because the driver had been found grossly negligent.[12]

In construction situations, where the owner, an engineer, or a contractor is seeking recovery from another contractor for claims made against them and for which they are seeking indemnity in the absence of a written hold-harmless agreement, the courts consider several factors to determine whether one of the contractors may be liable to indemnify the other parties. The courts examine the control of the project, who furnished certain equipment, who supervised certain work, who had safety responsibility, and whether there may have been a violation of a statute or government regulation by one of the parties.

In a Colorado case, the court held an elevator manufacturer liable to a building owner who had to pay damages to passengers who were injured when the elevator fell. The elevator company also had contracted to inspect the elevator and keep it in repair. The court noted that although the building owner may have been negligent for his failure to inspect the elevator, the elevator company could be held to indemnify him.[13]

In a New York case, a subcontractor's employee was killed by electrocution, and a suit was filed on his behalf against the developer and the general contractor. These parties filed a counterclaim against the subcontractor employer, alleging that the subcontractor's negligence was the cause of the injuries and stating that they should be entitled to indemnification from the subcontractor. The developer and the general contractor were found guilty due to their failure to provide the employee with a safe place to work. However, their claim for indemnification was allowed and upheld on appeal.[14]

In another New York case, an owner was not allowed recovery against a contractor. The owner had retained a painting contractor to do routine painting of the building. The contractor had constructed a scaffold in front of the entrance. The plaintiff had returned home from work and was told by the painter's employees that the only way he could enter the building was by using the scaffolding platform. The plaintiff did so, fell from the platform, and sustained injuries. In the trial court, the plaintiff had sued both the painting contractor and the building owner. He recovered against both, but the building owner was allowed to recover against the contractor based upon indemnification. On appeal, the judgments were affirmed. Then, on further appeal to the Court of Appeals, the highest appellate court in New York, the judgment granting the building owner indemnification from the painting contractor was reversed. The Court of Appeals noted that the owner had a "nondelegable duty" to provide a reasonably safe means for tenants to enter the building. Further, the court said that the owner had a duty, when he employed a painting contractor, to make sure that necessary precautions were taken not to endanger the tenants of the building. The court then determined that the owner's failure to comply with these duties was an act of negligence which barred his claim of indemnification against the painting contractor.[15]

Manufacturers may also be brought into a product liability lawsuit or may bring other parties into such a case when one of the parties may be liable to the defendant if the defendant is found guilty or the parties may be jointly and severally liable. Thus, a retailer may seek indemnity from a manufacturer when the manufacturer's product caused injury to one of the retailer's customers and was defective due to the fault of the manufacturer.

Section 2-607 of the UCC provides that if a seller of goods is sued for breach of warranty or for other reasons, he may give the person who sold him the product written notice of the suit. The UCC provides that if the notice states that the seller, usually the manufacturer, may enter the lawsuit and defend it and he does not do so, then he may be bound by the result in the underlying suit. The notice must be timely so that the party who is notified has an opportunity to prepare a defense.

The UCC also provides that in an infringement action, such as a suit for patent infringement, the original seller may demand that his buyer allow him to take control of the litigation. If the buyer does not permit this, the buyer's claim against the original seller is barred. Thus, in claims over patent infringement or similar forms of infringement, the notice is mandatory in order for the seller who is the defendant in the lawsuit to have a claim against the original seller. However, in a breach of warranty situation, vouching in is permissive but not mandatory.

Under the law of many states, joint tort feasors may have a right of contribution. In such situations, the jury determines what percentage of the judgment each defendant will pay based upon his degree of culpability. Many statutes provide, however, that if for some reason one defendant cannot pay his share of the judgment, the unpaid share has to made up by the other defendants. In addition, there is some confusion in a few states as to whether a right to contribution bars any action for noncontractual indemnity.

SETTLEMENTS

The person seeking indemnity is not entitled to indemnification from a third party if he pays a claim he was not legally obligated to pay. However, a person who is liable for a claim or suit may settle it and still seek indemnity from a third party if the third party is liable to the person who paid the amount in settlement. Thus, the person seeking indemnity need not have a trial on the merits of his case in order to prove his claim against the party from whom he seeks indemnity. This policy encourages settlements on a reasonable basis.

AMOUNT OF INDEMNITY

Once it is determined that the indemnitor is liable to the indemnitee, then the indemnitor is liable for the full amount of the indemnitee's loss. Most states also allow the indemnitee to recover reasonable attorneys' fees in defending the underlying action, although a few states, such as Illinois, allow recovery of such fees only if there is an indemnification agreement with this provision.

CONCLUSION

Indemnity law can be confusing in its application. As stated above, the courts will enforce indemnification agreements, but often will interpret them narrowly to avoid holding the indemnitor liable to the indemnitee. Thus, the engineer must review all documents he is requested to execute to see whether they contain an indemnification provision. If they do, he should consult with his attorney about the effect of such a provision. Moreover, he should consult with his insurance broker to determine whether the provision will or can be covered by insurance.

The party seeking indemnification should also determine whether the indemnification provision can be covered by the indemnitor's insurance. If it can, he should insist upon evidence of insurance coverage, such as a certificate of insurance. Otherwise, the indemnification provision is only as good as the collectible assets of the indemnitor if the indemnitee seeks to enforce it in court.

Frequently, design professionals in construction are requested to execute indemnification agreements which hold harmless the owner from the professional's "acts or errors" or failure to perform the contract. In certain situations, such language may be too broad, because it could obligate the design professional to hold harmless the owner for nonnegligent acts or omissions. As discussed in Chapters 2 to 5, under the law the design professional working in construction is liable only for negligent errors. These are errors which result from the design professional's failure to meet the standards of his profession. If the design professional signs a broader hold-harmless provision, he becomes liable for acts for which he is not traditionally liable. Further, most if not all professional liability policies fail to cover indemnification agreements which go beyond the traditional concept of professional liability because they are considered guarantees or warranties which are excluded from coverage.

NOTES

1. *Kansas City Operating Corp. v. Durwood,* 278 F.2d 354 (8th Cir. 1960).
2. Annotation, 27 A.L.R.3d 663 (1969).
3. *Dayton Fabricated Steel Co. v. Dayton Town & County, Inc.,* 99 Ohio App. 309, 133 N.E.23d 423 (1953).
4. *International Great Northern Railroad R. Co. v. Lucas,* 70 S.W.2d 226 (Tex. Civ. App. 1934), *reversed on other grounds,* 128 Tex. 480, 99 S.W.2d 297 (1936) modified on re-hearing on other grounds 128 Tex. 488, 100 S.W.2d 97 (1937).
5. *Safeway Stores, Inc. v. Massachusetts Bonding & Ins. Co.,* 202 Cal.App.2d 99, 20 Cal. Rptr. 820 (1962).
6. *Arthur Tickle Engineering Works, Inc. v. Oil Tank Cleaning Corp.,* 214 F.Supp. 216 (E.D.N.Y. 1963).
7. *List & Clark Construction Co. v. McGlone,* 296 S.W.2d 910 (Mo. App. 1956).
8. *Schiavone Construction Co., Inc. v. County of Nassau,* 717 F.2d 747 (2d Cir. 1983).
9. *Fireman's Fund American Ins. Cos. v. Turner,* 260 Or. 30, 488 P.2d 429 (1971).
10. *American Radiator & Standard Sanitary Corp. v. Titan Valve & Mfg. Co.,* 246 F.2d 947 (6th Cir. 1957).
11. *Kjellsen v. Stonecrest, Inc.,* 47 Wis.2d 8, 176 N.W.2d 321 (1970).

12. *Automobile Club Ins. Co. v. Toyota Motor Sales, Inc.*, 166 Mont. 221, 531 P.2d 1337 (1975).
13. *Otis Elevator Co. v. Maryland Casualty Co.*, 95 Colo. 99, 33 P.2d 974 (1934).
14. *Moses v. New York*, 15 App.Div.2d 534, 222 N.Y.S.2d 914 (1961).
15. *Bernstein v. El-Mar Painting & Decorating Co.*, 13 N.Y.2d 1053, 195 N.E.2d 456 (1963).

14
Intellectual Property Law

The four main subject areas of intellectual property law are patents, trademarks, copyrights, and trade secrets. In this chapter, we will briefly discuss each of them.

PATENTS

A patent is a form of monopoly which allows its holder to exclude others from the use of an invention.

Monopolies generally were not looked upon favorably by the common law. The English courts objected to them because they gave the monopolist power to withhold products or services from the public, resulting in higher prices. However, most countries now recognize that patents, granting the patent holder a monopoly right to an invention for a stated period of time, are necessary to encourage invention. This policy has been adopted in the U.S. Constitution. Article I, Section 8, provides in part:

> Congress shall have power . . . to promote the progress of science and useful arts, by securing for limited times to authors and inventors the exclusive right to their respective writings and discoveries.

Based upon this provision, Congress passed the first patent act in 1790. At present, patent law is governed by the Patent Act of 1952, which revised the Patent Act of 1870 and codified cases interpreting the Patent Act after 1874.

In 1802, Congress created the position of Superintendent of Patents in the U.S. Department of State; this was the start of a permanent patent bureau. In 1836, the Patent and Trademark Office was created and placed under the Commissioner of Patents and Trademarks. In 1849 the Patent and Trademark Office was transferred from the Department of State to the Department of the Interior, and in 1925 it was transferred to the Department of Commerce. Today, the Patent and Trademark Office, an agency of the Department of Commerce, administers the patent laws.

Patent Defined

A patent is a grant of specific right to an inventor by the government. In the United States, a patent runs for seventeen years. Its holder may "exclude others from making, using, or selling" the invention covered by the patent. Basically, a patent is a contract between the government and the inventor under which the inventor has a monopoly for seventeen years and the consideration is the disclosure of the invention to the public.[1] After the seventeen years, the patented invention may be used by other persons and the inventor cannot bar that use.

Processes of manufacture, machinery, products, composition of matter, improvements in any of the foregoing, and plants may be patented. The composition of matter may involve, for example, a patent for a chemical formulation.

In order for a patent to be granted, it must be novel. If the invention has been used in public or sold in the United States, the inventor must apply for a patent within one year of the first use or sale. If it has appeared in any printed publication or has been subject to public use or sale in any county before the date of the applicant's invention, a valid patent cannot be granted.

No patent may be granted if the invention would have been obvious to a person of ordinary skill in the relevant art. Thus, patents may be granted only for inventions that are both novel and nonobvious. In addition, the invention must be useful and operative.

Patent Applications

Ordinarily, patent applications are prepared by either patent attorneys or agents. The Patent and Trademark Office maintains a register of attorneys who may act as patent attorneys and nonattorneys who may act as patent agents. In order to practice before the Patent and Trademark Office, a person must have certain legal and technical qualifications and must pass an examination. A college degree in engineering or science or an equivalent degree is required. Patent agents may appear in matters before Patent and Trademark Office, but the other types of patent work they may do may be limited. For example, a patent agent may not appear in court to represent a party and in some states may not even be able to draft a patent assignment.

Under the Patent Act, the inventor himself must apply for the patent. However, if he is dead, the patent application may be made by his legal representative. If two or more persons made the invention, then they must file a patent application as joint inventors. In the United States the assignees of an invention may not file a patent application.

The patent application is a document which states the specifications of the patent and contains a drawing, if appropriate. In addition, it must be filed with the requisite filing fee, or the filing fee may be paid later with an additional penalty. The application is filed with the Patent and Trademark Office, which reviews it for completeness. If it is incomplete due to the failure to furnish a required drawing or oath, the applicant is allowed six months to complete it. The patent application must also be accompanied by a sworn affidavit or declaration of the inventor that he believes it to be original and that he is the true inventor.

After the application is filed, an examine of the Patent and Trademark Office reviews it an searches U.S. patents, available foreign patents, and other literature to determine whether the application contains a description of a new invention. If the invention is not patentable, the examiner rejects it and gives the reasons for the adverse decision, including references to other patents or publications.

If the application is rejected, the applicant may request reconsideration in writing. In the application for reconsideration, the inventor must point out the errors made out by the examiner. If the patent application is again rejected, the inventor may appeal to the Board of Appeals in the Patent and Trademark Office. The board consists of the assistant commissioners and senior patent examiners. If the Board of Appeals again rejects the patent application, the applicant may file an appeal in the U.S. Court of Appeals for the Federal Circuit (formerly the Court of Customs and Patent Appeals) or the U.S. District Court for the District of Columbia.

If two or more inventors apply at the same time for basically the same invention, an interference proceeding results. In such a proceeding, each party presents evidence regarding the date on which he made the invention. Three interference examiners then determine which party made the invention first and should be entitled to the patent. These examiners are referred to as the Board of Patent Interferences. Appeals from their decision are made to the U.S. Court of Appeals for the Federal Circuit or the U.S. District Court.

If a patent is allowed, the inventor is notified and must pay a fee to have the patent issued. During the application procedure, patent proceedings are confidential. When the patent is issued, the invention becomes public and copies of the patent are made available to the public.

Usually before a patent application is filed, the inventor will want a search to be done of existing patents to determine whether it is possible to patent his invention. Patent searches are normally conducted at the Patent and Trademark Office by patent attorneys or agents. Patents are divided into subclasses, and the patent attorney or agent chooses the appropriate subclasses which should be searched. The searcher looks for patents in those classes and subclasses which may be similar to the invention for which the patent is sought. Copies of similar patents are then sent to the inventor's patent attorney or agent, who reviews them and advises the inventor whether it is reasonable to file an application.

Patent Licenses

A patent may be sold or assigned by the owner. If it is assigned, the assignee is the owner of the patent. Partial interest in patents may also be assigned. For corporations, the patent application is made in the name of the employee who is the inventor. When the patent application is filed, the inventor usually assigns his ownership of it to the corporation.

Assignments of patents may be recorded in the Patent and Trademark Office. If a patent assignment is not recorded within three months after the date of assignment, the assignment is not good to subsequent assignees who have paid in some manner for the patent and have no knowledge of the prior assignment. Thus, recording a patent assignment has advantages similar to those of recording a deed transferring real property.

Marking Patents

When a person manufactures or sells a product which is patented, he must place upon the product the word "patent" and the patent number. If he fails to do so, he may not be allowed to recover damages from someone who infringes on the patent unless the infringer knew that the article was patented and proceeded to infringe. Occasionally, before the patent is issued, the term "patent pending" or "patent applied for" is used. Such a term is not required, but it does put potential infringers on notice that a patent application has been filed and may be granted in the future.

Infringement

An infringement occurs whenever anyone who does not own the patent or have a license to use it "makes, uses or sells" a patented invention during its term. In addition, anyone who sells a component of a patented invention knowing that it will be used to infringe a patent may be found liable as a contributory infringer.

Infringement actions are not brought in the Patent and Trademark Office, but rather in the federal courts. The party bringing the action may seek an injunction to bar continued infringement. In addition, he may seek damages in the form of an award of a reasonable royalty and actual damages suffered by the patent holder. However, damages maybe sought for only a period of six years prior to the filing of the complaint for patent infringement. During the action, the defendant may raise certain defenses, including the invalidity of the patent. The U.S. government may use any patent without the permission of the inventors or patent owner. However, the patent owner is entitled to payment form the government.

Foreign Patents

Since patents issued by the Patent and Trademark Office are good only in the United States, an inventor will frequently file patent applications in other countries to protect his invention. The Paris Convention for the Protection of Industrial Property, to which the United States and many other countries are signatories, states that citizens of the signatory countries will have the same patent and trademark rights as citizens of the country in which the application is made and the patent is granted. Further, within a prescribed period of time after an application is filed in one country, it may be filed in the other signatory countries. The date of application for the other filings is the date of the first application. If a U.S. inventor desires to file a patent application in a foreign country prior to filing the U.S. application or within six months of his filing, he must obtain a license from the Commissioner of Patents and Trademarks.

Any foreign inventor can apply for a U.S. patent. In most cases, the application must be filed no later than twelve months after any foreign application.

TRADEMARKS

Federal trademark registration is covered by the Lanham Act. This act defines trademarks, services marks, certification marks, and collective marks. A trademark is "any word, name, symbol or device or any combination thereof" used to identify a manufacturer's or merchant's products so as to distinguish them from those manufactured by others. A trade name is not necessarily a trademark. A service mark is used in connection with the sale or advertising of services. A certification mark certifies that products and services of others meet certain characteristics of origin, material, motive, quality, accuracy, and so on. A collective mark is a trademark or service mark used by a cooperative, association, or other collective group.

Registration of a trademark under the Lanham Act is not necessary to protect the right to it. However, registration does give national protection to a mark, and after the mark has been used for five years following registration, upon the filing of an appropriate affidavit, the registration becomes conclusive evidence of the right to use the trademark exclusively.

Common law trademarks still exist, and the owner may protect his right to it. However, trademarks under both the common law and the Lanham Act usually pertain only to particular uses for a specific industry or industries. Moreover, a common law trademark may be restricted to a particular geographic region.

In order for a trademark to be registered in the United States, it must be used in interstate commerce prior to registration. When the application for registration is filed with the Patent and Trademark Office, a search similar to a patent search is done. If the trademark is registered, registration is good for twenty years. However, during the sixth year of registration, the owner must file a declaration stating that the trademark is still in use or that it has not been abandoned.

Generally, trademarks must be distinctive. They cannot be geographic, confusing, or descriptive of products or services.

Frequently, trademarks are indicated by the use of the letter "R" with a circle around it. However, this designation is not required under the law.

COPYRIGHTS

Many forms of expression may be copyrighted, including books, periodicals, newspapers, lectures, dramatic scripts, music, works of art, reproductions of art, photographs, motion pictures sound recordings, and architectural drawings. A copyright refers to the manner of expression. In order for a work to be copyrightable, it must be original and creative. The information contained in a copyrighted work is not necessarily protected. Thus, a newspaper article may be copyrighted, but the information it contains may be used by others. Copyrighting protects against the actual copying of the copyrighted work.

Copyright registration is obtained from the Copyright Office of the Library of Congress. Copyrights are issued after an application for registration is filed and a fee is paid. Usually two copies of the work for which copyright is sought must be filed with the Copyright Office.

If the owner of a copyright thinks that his copyright has been infringed, he may obtain a court injunction barring the illegal use and file for damages.

Under the Copyright Statute of 1909, copyrights were issued for twenty-eight years with the right to renew for an additional twenty-eight years. Under the Copyright Act of 1976, copyrights issued in 1978 and after run for fifty years after the author's death. For certain works, such as those for which the copyright is owned by the employer, the copyright lasts for seventy-five years following publication or one hundred years following creation, whichever comes first.

Under the copyright law, there is a "fair use" exemption. This permits minor portions of a copyrighted work to be republished without permission.

At the time a work is published, the work must contain the notice prescribed by the statute and regulations of the Copyright Office.

TRADE SECRETS

Many companies have trade secrets or proprietary information for use in their business, the disclosure of which would harm them. For example, a chemical company may have a secret formula for processing a chemical, which is not patented or capable of being patented but which can be used to turn out valuable chemicals. Further, most companies have customer lists, pricing information, and cost information which is considered to be sensitive material that, if disclosed to a competitor, could be detrimental to them.

Under the law, employees owe a duty of fidelity to their employers, even though there may be no signed employment agreement. Pursuant to this duty, employees may not misuse trade secrets acquired by them during their employment.

Within a company, knowledge of trade secrets is limited to a few persons. The public is not advised of this knowledge, nor is the industry or the public. Once a trade secret becomes public knowledge, it is not longer confidential and cannot be protected by the company. However, certain publications of a trade secret do not make it public. For instance, a component manufacturer may deliver proprietary drawings to another manufacturer for review. Under such circumstances, the proprietary drawings may not necessarily become public.

If an employee or former employee misuses a trade secret, he may be sued. The plaintiff may seek an injunction barring him from disclosing or further disclosing the trade secret and may seek damages. In order for such a suit to be successful, there must be a trade secret, it must be valuable to the business seeking to protect it, the employer must have either discovered it or have ownership of it, and the employee must have learned about the trade secret in this position of trust.

In a landmark 1868 Massachusetts case, a manufacturer filed suit against a former employee. The manufacturer had developed a process which he had used successfully and kept secret. The employee had executed an agreement stating that he would protect the information from disclosure. After termination, the employee went to work for another company, intending to use the process. The court concluded that the trade secret was valuable to the former employer and that misuse of it should be prevented.[2]

Occasionally, disputes arise over who owns a trade secret. If an employee is hired specifically to invent or develop new products or manufacturing processes, the courts generally hold that the employer owns the inventions or developments. Sometimes the courts consider the employee's scope of employment to determine whether his invention or development belongs to the employer or to him. For example, if an employee is hired to develop new computer products and on his own time develops a new hybrid tulip bulb, the development of the bulb would not belong to the employer.

When an employee comes up with an invention or development which is outside the scope of this employment, under certain circumstances the employer may have a shop right to it. The employer's shop right occurs when the employee develops the invention during working hours or uses the employer's facilities. As a matter of fairness, the employer, obtains a license to use the invention and need not pay a royalty. The license is irrevocable but nonexclusive. Thus, the employee may grant licenses to other parties.

Employees may use general knowledge obtained in their former job for the benefit of a new employer. The mere fact that a person has been working for a company does not bar him from using knowledge acquired from his former employer in new employment. However, he may be barred from disclosing certain trade secret information to his new employer.

In 1979, the National Conference of Commissioners on Uniform State Laws approved and recommended for use the Uniform Trade Secrets Act. This act has been adopted in Connecticut, Delaware, Indiana, Kansas, Louisiana, Minnesota, and Washington. It was promulgated because of the lack of a trade secret law in many of the less populated states and the inconsistencies in trade laws between other states.

Copying an unpatented product or process is not a violation of the act unless unlawful misappropriation has occurred. This happens when someone acquires a trade secret knowing that it was obtained through improper means, or when a trade secret is disclosed by someone who obtained it through improper means or knew at the time of disclosure that it was acquired through improper means and under a duty of fidelity or secrecy.

Employers frequently consider customer lists to be valuable trade secrets. Generally, former employees cannot take customer lists with them to use in new employment. However, former employees may solicit customers of their former employer so long as they have not used a protected customer list, or are not barred from doing so by an employment agreement.

When deciding whether a former employee should be barred from using the customer information of his former employer, the courts usually consider how available is information about the customers, how much work the former employee used in compiling the information, whether sales in the industry depend upon customer contracts or other factors such as product quality and price, whether the former employee or the former employer put together the customer information, and the manner in which the former employee put together this information either during or after employment.

If customers can be easily located, the courts may not protect the customer list or information. If the former employer spent a good deal of time and money developing information on customers, the courts may protect this information from use by the former employee. If sales in the industry are made on the basis of product quality, price, or other factors, the courts may not prevent disclosure or further use of the customer information by the former employee. If the employee developed the customers, the courts may permit him to continue contacting them. Finally, if the employee merely recalls the names of these customers, without taking a customer list or other customer information with him, the courts will usually permit him to continue soliciting them.

NOTES

1. *Century Electric Company v. Westinghouse Electric & Mfg. Co.*, 191 F. 350 (8th Cir. 1911).
2. *Peabody v. Norfolk*, 98 Mass. 452 (1868).

15
Licensing

Professional or consulting engineers must usually be licensed in the state or states where they practice in order to engage in their profession. Generally, an architect or engineer who is an independent businessman or an employee of an architecture or engineering firm must be licensed. Of course, nonlicensed engineers may do professional work under the supervision of a licensed engineer. Many engineers who work for manufacturing companies are also professionally licensed; however, normally they need not be licensed so long as they are working exclusively for their employer.

All states have administrative procedures for licensing professionals, including architects and engineers. In many states, autonomous boards have been established to govern the licensing of specific professions. In such states, there may be separate bodies to control the licensing of architects and engineers. Some states have autonomous boards but provide for a central administrative agency to handle certain administrative functions. In a few states, the agency may also have the power to hear appeals from the decisions of the autonomous boards. In a few states, the central agency controls all licensing functions, but there are boards for particular professions which advise the agency on particular matters.

Regardless of the administrative format, licensing procedures for engineers have certain common features. First, the person seeking a license must file an application with the appropriate board. The application requires the applicant to describe his education and furnish character references. Second, most professions require certain minimal education. As an example, in architecture or engineering, the applicant may have to be a graduate of an accredited college or university with an architecture or engineering curriculum. Third, the applicant may be required to have a certain number of years of experience working under the supervision of a registered professional before he may be registered. Fourth, the applicant is usually required to take an examination or examinations given or approved by the administrative agency. Fifth, he is normally required to have his character reviewed by the agency to determine whether he is fit to practice.

Licensing of professionals is sanctioned under the police power of the state. The courts reason that the sovereign is interested in protecting the public and that one to do this is to require licensing of professionals. As an example, a challenge to the California statutes licensing professional engineers was denied. The court found that under the U.S. Constitution, the state did have the right to regulate this profession.[1] Further, the state may delegate its licensing authority to an administrative board.[2]

Many state administrative agencies pass rules to implement state licensing statutes. Sometimes the statutes delegate to the agency authority to establish the requirements for practicing a particular profession and for being licensed in it.

U.S. citizenship can no longer be required by licensing statutes. In a 1973 case arising in Connecticut, the U.S. Supreme Court struck down a requirement that in order to be admitted to practice law, the applicant had to be a citizen of the United States. The court reasoned that this requirement violated the equal protection clause of the Fourteenth Amendment to the U.S. Constitution.[3] A similar conclusion was reached in a case involving the licensing of engineers in Puerto Rico.[4] However, although resident aliens may be granted licenses to practice, they must meet the other requirements of the statute or the administrative agency.

Courts in a number of states have struck down residency requirements. For example, New York State required six months' residency in order for a person to be admitted to practice law. This requirement was held unenforceable based upon the privileges and immunities clause of the U.S. Constitution.[5]

Licensing laws requiring that applicants be of good moral character generally have been upheld. So has the requirement that the applicant have a certain educational background. Experience requirements have also been allowed by the courts.

Under state licensing laws, the administrative agency can take steps to discipline licensed professionals, including license revocation. Under the due process clause of the Fifth Amendment to the U.S. Constitution, the respondent must be given notice of the disciplinary proceeding, including the time and place of the hearing. In addition, the hearing must take place before a duly authorized board, and a statement of the charges must be given to the respondent. The respondent or his counsel must have the opportunity to cross-examine witnesses who testify against him, and he must be allowed to produce witnesses to testify on his behalf. He has the right to be represented by counsel and to obtain a record of the proceedings. The administrative board must also give reasonable or fair consideration to the evidence. Finally, some form of judicial review must be provided.[6]

Licenses may be revoked on many grounds. Conviction of a felony may be a reason, and so may alcoholism or addiction to narcotics. Professional incompetence, including repeated acts of negligence, may also be grounds for revocation. Fraud in obtaining a license or other forms of dishonesty may also be grounds for revocation.

A number of cases have involved the revocation of a license to practice architecture or engineering or other disciplinary action. In a 1978 Texas case, the court upheld the revocation of an architect's license where he had appropriated the plans of another architect, removed the first architect's seal and replaced it with his own, and submitted the plans as his own work.[7]

In a Wisconsin case, an architect's license was revoked for incompetence when the board found that due to errors in his plans the basement walls in a residence failed, he had not obtained a building permit for the residence, the building had been misplaced, on the property and that he had obtained the owner's authority for payment without telling him about certain problems with the design and construction. In addition, in another dwelling, the architect had also made errors in the plans and had failed to provide for the necessary foundations.[8]

In a New York case, the court upheld a six-month suspension of the license of an architect who had offered to arrange for payment of a bribe in order to obtain a favorable zoning ruling.[9] In another New York case, an engineer's license was suspended for six months because he had not properly tested the ventilating system for new apartment buildings and had issued erroneous certificates on the testing.[10]

In an Iowa case, an engineer's license was revoked for intentionally designing a roof that did not meet building code snow load requirements.[11] Finally, in another New York case, an engineer's license was suspended because he had made payments to a company which had done no work for him as part of a scheme to make an illegal contribution to a political party.[12]

NOTES

1. *Smith v. State of California*, 336 F.2d 530 (9th Cir. 1964).
2. *Douglas v. Noble*, 261 U.S. 165 (1923).
3. *In re Griffiths*, 413 U.S. 717 (1973).
4. *Examining Board of Engineers, Architects & Surveyors v. Flores de Otero*, 426 U.S. 572 (1976).
5. *In re Gordon*, 48 N.Y.2d 266, 422 N.Y.S.2d 641, 397 N.E.2d 1309 (1979).
6. *See Hanson v. Michigan State Board of Registration in Medicine*, 253 Mich. 601, 236 N.W. 225 (1931), *cert. denied*, 284 U.S. 637 (1931).
7. *Piland v. Texas Board of Architectural Examiners*, 562 S.W.2d 26 (Tex. Civ. App. 1978).
8. *Kuehnel v. Wisconsin Registration Board of Architects & Professional Engineers*, 243 Wis. 188, 9 N.W.2d 630 (1943).
9. *Daub v. Board of Regents*, 33 App.Div.2d 964, 306 N.Y.S.2d 869 (1970).
10. *Shapiro v. Board of Regents*, 29 App.Div.2d 801, 286 N.Y.S.2d 1001 (1968).
11. *Wright v. State Board of Engineering Examiners*, 250 N.W.2d 412 (Iowa 1977).
12. *Flack v. Commissioner of Education*, 81 App.Div.2d 976, 440 N.Y.S. 2d 161 (1981).

16
Arbitration

In recent years, arbitration has become a popular means of dispute resolution in the construction industry. In addition, many manufacturers and other businesses have adopted arbitration as a means of resolving controversies, especially where international trade is involved.

Design professionals and businessmen are attracted to arbitration because of the high costs and delays in litigation. They thing that arbitration is a way to avoid these costs and inefficiencies. In addition, many of them do not think that trials by jurors inexperienced in their professions and industries, necessarily result in reasonable or just verdicts.

Arbitration is simply a process whereby the parties voluntarily agree to place their disputes before a third impartial person or panel of persons, selected by them, who act as arbitrators and reach a decision based upon the evidence and arguments of the parties.

Arbitration may be compulsory or binding. When binding arbitration is used, the parties agree that they will be bound by the arbitrator's award. With nonbinding arbitration, the parties agree that they will not necessarily be bound by the arbitrator's award. Occasionally, nonbinding arbitration is referred to as "mediation."

Binding arbitration results from an agreement between the parties. The agreement may be made either before or after the dispute arises. Under common law, the courts were reluctant to enforce agreements to arbitrate disputes which would arise in the future. For some reason, they though that by enforcing such agreements, they would be circumventing their jurisdiction. However, in the twentieth century, the courts gradually began to enforce such arbitration provisions. Finally, in 1920, New York passed the first arbitration statute providing a structure for arbitration procedures and for enforcing arbitration awards. Today, over three dozen states have arbitration statutes. In 1955, the Uniform Arbitration Act was promulgated and has become the arbitration statute for over two dozen states. In 1925, Congress passed the United States Arbitration Act, which recognizes binding arbitration agreements in contracts involving maritime pursuits and interstate or foreign commerce.

ARBITRATION AGREEMENTS

Arbitration results essentially from an agreement between the parties to arbitrate. As mentioned above, this may involve either present or future disputes. Arbitration clauses may be separate paragraphs of formal contracts or may be part of the terms and conditions on the back of printed purchase or sales quotation forms. Frequently, an agreement to arbitrate an existing dispute is called a "submission." The general rules of contract interpretation apply to arbitration agreements.

The United States Arbitration Act and the arbitration statutes of most states require an arbitration agreement to be in writing in order to be enforced. Frequently, an arbitration agreement or provision will state that a court may enter judgment upon the award. This gives the beneficiary of the award an enforceable judgment which can be collected through ancillary proceedings, such as garnishment or execution and levy.

Generally, under the law of arbitration, disputes may arise during the term of an agreement but may be arbitrated after termination of the contract.[1] After the contract has expired, the arbitration provision in the contract is no longer effective, unless the agreement provides otherwise, and neither party has the right to demand arbitration for disputes which arose after termination.[2]

Generally, a guarantor or surety of performance is not bound by an arbitration provision of the contract.[3] In an Ohio case, a contract between a contractor and a subcontractor contained an arbitration clause. A surety issued a performance bond on behalf of the subcontractor. The court held that the surety, since it had no arbitration provision in his performance bond, could not be subject to the contractor's demand for arbitration.[4]

Disputes may not be arbitrable, as a matter of public policy, even though the parties agree to submit them to arbitration. Among those disputes which may not be subject to arbitration are controversies concerning the alleged violation of the federal antitrust laws.

DEMAND FOR ARBITRATION

Arbitration is initiated by the party who seeks it by serving a demand for arbitration upon the other party. Arbitration statutes usually require a statement of the matter in question. It should be specific rather than general. A specific statement is required so that the party who receives the demand is aware of what will be arbitrated.

Frequently, the party receiving the demand for arbitration will file an answer and may file a counterdemand. In addition, the arbitration agreement may designate the meeting place or provide that the arbitration will be conducted according to the rules of a particular agency, such as the American Arbitration Association.

THE ARBITRATOR

Selection of the arbitrator or arbitrators is crucial. At times, this will be provided for in the arbitration agreement. Frequently, both parties will appoint their own arbitrators, who in turn will select a third arbitrator.

If the rules of a trade association or professional group are to be followed, the organization will establish a method for selecting arbitrators. As an example, the American Arbitration Association maintains panels of volunteer arbitrators and will submit lists of persons from the panel to the party or parties seeking arbitration. The parties will then strike names off the list. If the parties have agreed on one or more arbitrators, the association will appoint them. If the parties cannot agree upon arbitrators, the association will appoint them.

No special qualifications are needed to be an arbitrator, although many of the professional associations which have established rules for arbitrators may prequalify arbitrators for the panels from which they are selected.

THE ARBITRATION HEARING

Technically, the arbitrators determine the time of the hearing. They must give reasonable notice of the hearing, which involves notifying the parties sufficiently in advance to allow them to prepare. As a practical matter, however, the parties and arbitrators usually agree on the time of the hearing.

The hearings are generally controlled by the arbitrators. Formal rules regarding evidence need not be observed. Hearsay evidence may be heard, and the arbitrators may accept affidavits as evidence. In addition, in many states, the arbitrator has the right to subpoena witnesses and documents.

Unless the parties agree, they have no right to discovery before the arbitration proceeding. Occasionally, they may agree to some form of limited discovery, such as the exchange of documents.

APPLYING THE LAW

Neither the United States Arbitration Act nor the state arbitration statutes give any guidance on whether arbitrators must apply substantive rules of law when reaching their decisions; nor do most arbitration provisions and contracts. Under such circumstances, arbitrators are not bound to follow rules of law. Further, even if they do or do not follow these rules, their decisions would normally not be subject to review by a court. However, a large number of arbitrators apparently attempt to follow substantive rules of law, but many do not feel they are bound to do so in order to avoid an unjust result.[5]

Although there is no requirement that arbitrators must apply rules of law, many attorneys in arbitration proceedings will argue substantive law. References to court-decided cases may have some impact upon the decision of the arbitrators.

A few states provide that an arbitrator may submit a question of law to a court in seeking guidance.[6] However, arbitrators generally must ask the parties to advise them of the pertinent legal issues and the law covering them.

CONSOLIDATION

Occasionally, consolidated arbitration proceedings may be ordered by either the arbitration tribunal or a court. As an example, the owner's contract with an architect or with the general contractor may contain a binding arbitration provision. If a problem arises during construction which requires corrective work, the owner may be unsure of whether the architect, the contractor, or both are at fault. Accordingly, he may initiate arbitration proceedings against both parties and seek to have these proceedings consolidated, since the same basic issues are involved. Under such circumstances, either the arbitration tribunal or a court may order consolidation. Generally, the courts prefer to consolidate arbitration actions.

Under certain circumstances, one or both of the parties to an arbitration action may resist consolidation. For instance, an architect may prefer to arbitrate with the owner in the absence of the contractor. In this case, a few courts have refused consolidation.[7] Of course, whether the court orders consolidation may depend upon the wording of the arbitration clause in the professional services agreement.

THE AWARD

After the arbitrators have conducted the hearing, they reach a decision and make the award. In reaching their decision, the arbitrators will review the case on its merits. Further, the award must resolve all issues raised during the proceeding. The award is usually delivered to the parties by mail. Ordinarily, monetary damages are granted in the award, although specific performance may be granted if the arbitration provision states that the arbitrator may do so.

APPEAL

The parties' right to appeal to a court for relief from an award are limited unless the arbitration provision so provides. Generally, the statutes provide that a court may act to set aside an award only if there is a showing of partiality by a supposedly neutral arbitrator, misconduct by the arbitrator (such as refusing to hear material evidence), prejudice in the conduct of the proceedings, and an award which does not resolve the issues. An award can also be set aside when the arbitrator is corrupt or fraudulent or exceeds his powers. However, in general, the reviewing court may not set aside an award merely because the arbitrator made a mistake in applying law or committed errors in making evidentiary rulings, or when some irregulatory in the proceedings occurred that was not mentioned above.

ALTERNATIVE METHODS

In recent years, methods other than binding arbitration have been used to resolve disputes. One of the simplest methods is a form of mediation or nonbinding arbitration whereby the parties meet with an impartial, respected third party to discuss the merits of the case. The mediator is used as a sounding board by both parties to determine what response an independent person has to the dispute and indicate what the result of either arbitration or a court trial may be.

Another alternative method is the "mini-trial." Usually, mini-trials are held after a lawsuit has been filed. In this proceeding, each party presents his claim to a third person. This may simply involve going through the facts and the applicable law, with each party indicating why he thinks he would be successful in the arbitration or lawsuit. The third person may or may not give his opinion on what the outcome of the trial or arbitration proceeding would be. Frequently, the principals of both parties are present at the mini-trial to determine the strengths and weaknesses of each other's case. Often, a mini-trial will encourage the parties to look more realistically at both sides of the dispute with the hope that, after a frank hearing of the evidence and discussion of the applicable law, they may reach an amicable solution.

PROS AND CONS

Over the years, there has been much discussion, especially among attorneys, on the benefits and detriments of arbitration. The proponents contend that arbitration has many advantages. First, during construction of a project or performance of a major commercial contract covering a relatively long period of time, disputes may arise. If the parties have to resort to a lawsuit, the project may not be completed or the contract may be terminated by one party. In order to avoid this result, arbitration provides a way to resolve disputes as they arise.

The proponents of arbitration also argue that many technical matters are not suitable for a jury trial. A panel of experts, the arbitrators, may be much more capable of sorting out complicated technical arguments and reaching a conclusion which may be more rational or just than that of a jury.

The proponents further argue that through the use of arbitration, the battle of the experts may be avoided. Frequently, in lawsuits involving technical matters, the plaintiff's expert takes one position and the defendant's expert takes the other, without the opportunity for the jury to reach a conclusion. With a panel of experienced people from the industry involved, such battles may be avoided.

Lawsuits can be expensive, and clients are always looking for a way to avoid such unproductive costs. The proponents of arbitration contend that this procedure may be less costly than a court trial.

The proponents also state that over the years the courts have developed rules of evidence which exclude certain facts from the jury's consideration but which may be relevant. As an example, the jury cannot consider certain documents when one party is unable to provide the proof necessary for these documents to be admitted into evidence. Arbitration may be used to get around such rules so that the arbitrators can reach a fair decision.

The opponents of arbitration have many criticisms. They contend that the parties have no right to discovery, although in certain cases limited discovery may be allowed. Without discovery of the facts prior to trial, through the use of depositions and interrogatories for example, the parties may not be able to prepare their presentations adequately.

The arbitrators are not bound by the rules of evidence. Therefore, they can listen to hearsay testimony which may not be substantiated. By considering such questionable evidence, the arbitrators may reach unjust decisions.

The opponents also point out that arbitrators are usually not controlled by any rule of law. They can reach their decision without being concerned with the law, such as statutes and court decisions which may bear upon the matter.

The opponents are concerned that the right of appeal from an arbitrator's award is limited. Further, they argue that arbitration of a complicated matter may be nearly as expensive as a lawsuit, since the proceeding could run for several days and involve much work. Finally, not all the necessary parties may be subject to arbitration. As an example, in a construction industry case, subcontractors may not be a party to the arbitration proceeding, whereas they could be made a party to a lawsuit.

NOTES

1. *River Brand Rice Mills, Inc. v. Latrobe Brewing Co.*, 305 N.Y. 36, 110 N.E.2d 545 (1953).
2. *Korody Marine Corp. v. Minerals & Chemicals Philipp Corp.*, 300 F.2d 124 (2d Cir. 1962).
3. *National Recreation Products, Inc. v. Gans*, 46 App. Div.2d 618, 359 N.Y.S.2d 803 (1974).
4. *Windowmaster Corp. v. B. G. Danis Co.*, 511 F.Supp. 157 (S.D. Ohio 1981) *disapproved, Exchange Mutual Ins. Co. v. Haskell Co.* 742 F.2d 274 (6th Cir. 1984).
5. Soia Mentschikoff, *Commercial Arbitration*, 61 Colum. L. Rev. 846 (1961).
6. Conn. Gen. Stats. Ann. § 52-415 (19) & Utah Code Ann. 78-31-13 (19).
7. *See William C. Blanchard Co. v. Beach Concrete Co.*, 121 N.J.Super 418, 297 A.2d 587 (1972) and *J. Brodie & Son, Inc. v. George A. Fuller Co.*, 16 Mich. App. 137, 167 N.W.2d 886 (1969), *disapproved, Kalman Floor Co. v. Jos. L. Mucarelle, Inc.*, 196 N.J. Super 16, 481 A.2d 553 (1984).

Index

Index